D0200854

The pocket guide to Garden Plants

Hugh Johnson
and Paul Miles

Simon and Schuster/New York

Nomenclature

The common names of garden plants vary widely and are often misleading, but the scientific (Latin) name is determined by strict international rules. Every plant has a double name, the first is the genus name, the second the species (specific) name. Thus the Peacock or Tiger flower always has the Latin name *Tigridia pavonia*. Each genus contains one or more species and several related genera are grouped into a family. A species may be divided into subspecies, and have a third name, as in *Dryas octopetala minor*. Where plants are hybrids derived from the cross breeding of two different species, names are preceded by a multiplication sign, as in the Michaelmas daisy *Aster × frikartii*. Named cultivars (cultivated varieties) of genera or species are given an additional name within quotation marks: the Lily of the valley *Convallaria majalis* 'Fortin's Giant' is a large-flowered form. Because plant names may be changed, alternatives likely to appear in books and catalogs are denoted in brackets.

Contents

Symbols, abbreviations 4
Zones of hardiness 5
Plant propagation 5
Glossary 6
Annuals and biennials 7
Herbaceous perennials 19
Alpines, rock garden plants 59
Bog, waterside and pond plants 71

Herbs 77
Ferns 82
Bulbs, corms and tubers 83
Roses 104
Climbers 112
Shrubs 120
Subtropical plants 162
Index 185

Editor Ruth Binney **Executive Editor** Susannah Read
Designer Derek St Romaine **Picture Research** Brigitte Arora
Executive Art Editor Douglas Wilson **Production** Julian Deeming
Edited and designed by Mitchell Beazley Publishers
87–89 Shaftesbury Avenue, London W1V 7AD
© Mitchell Beazley Publishers 1981
All rights reserved, including the right of reproduction in whole
or in part in any form.
Subtropicals prepared with the help of Sunset Books
Printed in Hong Kong by Mardarin Offset International Ltd.
A Fireside Book
Published by Simon and Schuster
A Division of Gulf & Western Corporation
Simon and Schuster Building
Rockefeller Center
1230 Avenue of the Americas
New York, New York 10020
Library of Congress Cataloging in Publication Data
Johnson, Hugh.
    The pocket guide to Garden Plants.
    Includes index.
    1. Plants, Ornamental. 2. Flowers. 3. Herbs.
I. Title.
SB407.J63 582'.06'1 79-19585
ISBN 0-671-24841-3

Picture credits Apart from the photographs detailed below, all the material, including the cover picture, was supplied by The Harry Smith Horticultural Photographic Collection, to whom we are indebted for their help. A–Z Collection: 111tc, 12lb, 135b, 154tc, 157t; Bernard Alfieri: 110t; William C. Alpin: 163c, 164b, 168b, 169c, 172t/c, 173tc/bc/b, 174c, 175b, 176b, 178c, 179b, 180t, 181b, 183t/b; Heather Angel: 71t/c, 72c, 74t, 154t, 155c; Pat Brindley: 7b, 8t/b, 9c/b, 10c, 11b, 12c, 14c/b, 15c/b, 16tc/bc/b, 17b, 25bc, 35bc, 53c, 55c, 59t, 61c, 78c, 81b, 106t, 110tc/bc, 122c, 125c, 158t, 159c; Derek Fell: 163t/b, 164t/c, 165t/c/b, 166t/c/b, 167t/b, 168tc/bc, 169t/b, 170t/c/b, 172b, 173t, 174t/b, 175t/c, 176c, 177t/c/b, 178b, 179t/c, 181t, 182t/bc; Valerie Finnis: 46t/b, 49tc/b, 57b, 60b, 62b, 100t, 103b, 127c, 137t; Fryers Nurseries Ltd: 111b; Brian Furner: 74b, 158b; Pamela Harper: 171t/c/b, 178t, 180c/b, 182tc/b, 183c, 184t/c/b; The Iris Hardwick Library: 10t, 113t, 142c, 146tc, 150tc, 159t; Paul Miles: 12t, 30b, 35tc, 45tc, 66b, 75t/tc, 82t, 83c, 85b, 86c, 107tc, 112t, 113bc, 127b, 134b, 139c, 152b; Bill Ross: 168t, 176t; The Royal National Rose Society: 106b, 108bc, 111t; G.S. Thomas: 111c; Michael Warren: 14t; **Artwork** by Colin Salmon. **Key** t, top; tc, top center; c, center; bc, bottom center; b, bottom

Introduction

No gardener needs telling that trying to fit the glorious richness and variety of garden plants into a truly pocketable book is a foolhardy undertaking. But how marvelous if it comes off. What a boon to be able to unpocket a mere diary-size encyclopedia and look up, there and then, whether the tempting container at the nursery or the towering specimen in a famous show place is a possibility for your own garden.

This book tries, by a combination of clear and graphic illustrations and a double-distilled text, to offer all the essential information about nearly 2,000 garden plants in a portable form. Distillation has its own virtues. The authors can vouch for the fact that, like the prospect of being hanged, it concentrates the mind wonderfully. All the dross, all the flannel, is blue-penciled away. What is left, like a fine distilled spirit, is pure, strong and (we hope) particularly tasty.

The most popular garden plants have been bred, selected and bred again until their varieties in cultivation (cultivars) are, as sand on the sea shore, without number. To list endless slightly different varieties of the same plant, however beautiful, would be tedious and, more important, would force us to leave out a great number of species that have not had the benefit of so many breeders' attentions. Where the choice has been between another variety and a different species we have come down, therefore, on the side of the species. This means that there are a good number of uncommon plants in this book. We feel very strongly that this is important. As it is, far too many gardeners grow precisely the same, unnecessarily limited, range of plants. If no one seeks out and grows the unusual it will become rare, and from rarity the next step is extinction. Every gardener can help in the conservation of the magnificent variety of plant life by looking around for something different to grow. This is an excellent place to start.

How to use this book

We have divided the world of garden plants into the conventional categories based on their management in the garden. There are many genera that have members with permanent hard wood (shrubs), members that die down to below ground every winter but come up again in spring (herbaceous perennials) and yet others with a one year life span (annuals). Where such names crop up in different sections of the book, symbols, each containing a letter (A for annuals, P for herbaceous perennials etc) refer you at a glance to the appropriate section. And for gardeners in the sub-tropical areas of the United States there is a final section containing plants most suitable for these special conditions.

The information given for each entry in the book is as comprehensive as space allows. As well as a thumbnail sketch it includes the hardiness of the plant, its average height and spread, its most usual months of flowering, its native land and, in most cases, the most convenient method of propagation. Symbols tell you about its preference for sun, soil and water, its ease of cultivation, if it has won the Award of Garden Merit, the supreme accolade of the Royal Horticultural Society, and supply cross references to other sections of the book. Although any plant that has won a place here automatically carries our recommendation (warnings about rampant growth are noted where appropriate) the accolade of an asterisk has been added to plants that we would urge you to grow. The symbols, plus the abbreviations essential for compression, are explained over the page, followed by a map of hardiness zones, notes on plant propagation and a glossary of the few botanical terms we have used.

Symbols

Plant needs	Plant type	Cross references
● Shade	🌿 Evergreen	**A** Annuals and biennials
🌓 Partial shade	🌲 Coniferous	**P** Herbaceous perennials
☀ Sun	🌊 Aquatic	**R** Alpines and rock garden plants
◒ Acid soil	🌊 Grows in bogs or at water's edge	**W** Bog, waterside and pond plants
◒ Alkaline soil		**H** Herbs
🌐 Well-drained soil	**General**	**B** Bulbs, corms and tubers
🕸 Heavy soil	🌱 Easy to grow	**C** Climbers
💧 Much water	✖ Difficult to grow	**S** Shrubs
	🏵 RHS Award of Garden Merit	**T** Subtropical plants

*Authors' personal recommendation

Abbreviations

AGM	Award of Garden Merit (RHS)	frag	fragrant	rec	recommended
		ft	feet	resp	respectively
alt	alternate	gdn	garden	RHS	Royal Horticultural Society
Apr	April	gp	group		
AM	Award of Merit (RHS)	hr(y)	hair(y)	rt	root
		hrlss	hairless	sev	several
ann	annual	Ht	height	sim	similar
aut	autumn	hyb	hybrid	smr	summer
bi	biennial	in	inch(es)	sol	solitary
bicol	bicolor	inc	include	Spd	spread
br	branch	incon-	inconspicuous	sp(p)	species (plural)
		spic		spl	sepal
c.	about	indiv	individual	spr	spring
col	color	LF	susceptible to late frost	stk(d)	stalk(ed)
con-	conspicuous			succ	succulent
spic		lf(y)	leaf(y)	unstkd	unstalked
cv	cultivar	lft	leaflet	uprt	upright
decid	deciduous	lvd	leaved	v	very
diam	diameter	lvs	leaves	var	variety
div	division	mod	moderately	varieg	variegated
esp	especially	opp	opposite	veg	vegetative
fl(d)	flower(ed)	per	perennial	vig	vigorous
Fl	flowering months	pop	popular	wtr	winter
		pr(d)	pair(ed)	Z	zone of hardiness
fol	foliage	prop	propagate		
fr	fruit	ptl	petal		

1–12	months of the year Jan–Dec	♂	male	♀	female

Plant origins

Amer	America	Is	Islands	SE	Southeast(ern)
Aust	Australia	Mar	Maritime	SW	Southwest(ern)
C	Central	Med	Mediterranean	Temp	Temperate
Cal	California	Mts	Mountains	Trop	Tropical
E	East(ern)	N	North(ern)	USA	United States
Eur	Europe	NE	Northeast(ern)	USSR	Russia
GB	Great Britain	NW	Northwest(ern)	W	West(ern)
Hem	Hemisphere	NZ	New Zealand		
Him	Himalayas	S	South(ern)		

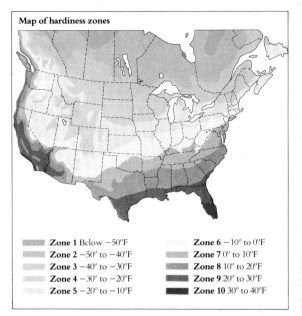

Map of hardiness zones

▨	**Zone 1** Below −50°F	▨	**Zone 6** −10° to 0°F
▨	**Zone 2** −50° to −40°F	▨	**Zone 7** 0° to 10°F
▨	**Zone 3** −40° to −30°F	▨	**Zone 8** 10° to 20°F
▨	**Zone 4** −30° to −20°F	▨	**Zone 9** 20° to 30°F
▨	**Zone 5** −20° to −10°F	▨	**Zone 10** 30° to 40°F

Except for annuals, each plant description ends with a guide to the amount of frost it will tolerate, based on the zones (**Z**) on this map which was developed by the Agricultural Research Service of the US Department of Agriculture. The United States and Canada are divided into 10 zones, ranging from zone 1 with a minimum winter temperature below −50°F to zone 10 with an average winter minimum of 30 to 40°F. On more detailed versions of this map, each zone is further divided into "a" and "b" sub-zones, the "a" sub-zone having a lower winter minimum than the "b". The zoning system is invaluable when it comes to deciding which plants will suit your garden best, and which are likely to be killed by severe frost. Special notes on gardening in subtropical areas, such as southern California, are given on p162 and as an additional guide to gardeners in temperate areas, plants susceptible to damage by late frost in early spring have been marked with the letters **LF** after the zone number.

Even on a much larger scale map it would be impossible to indicate with perfect accuracy where any one plant will grow best. The adventurous gardener will, of course, experiment and discover that plants are remarkably adaptable. Also, every garden has its own micro-climate with exposed areas in which plants are quick to succumb to frost and sheltered corners that manage to escape the worst of the weather. If all else fails you can always try a highly desirable plant in a pot, taking it indoors in winter.

Plant propagation

As a rule of thumb, species are propagated from seed, named cultivars by vegetative means. The main exceptions are shrubs, many of which are best increased vegetatively, and bulbs, corms etc which have built-in organs of vegetative reproduction. Common vegetative methods are:

Cuttings stems, roots or leaves removed from the parent plant and treated so as to produce their own roots. Take softwood cuttings from perennials and shrubs in the growing season, hardwood shrub cuttings in autumn and stem cuttings from pinks and carnations in summer.

Division the splitting of a plant into 2 or more parts. Best done in spring. Also describes the separation of groups of bulbs, corms etc.

Layers growing plants stems pegged on to the ground or covered in earth away from, but still attached to, the parent plant. The stems are cut only when roots have formed. Used for plants slow to root as cuttings.

Scales thin flaps, often modified leaves, separated from the parent plant at their base and induced to form roots.

Glossary

Aerial describes above-ground roots common on stems of climbers

Alternate (alt) leaves growing singly at intervals on alternate sides of a stem

Anther pollen-producing part of a flower (often knob-like) borne on a stalk called a filament. The top part of a stamen (see below)

Aroid member of the Arum family having a leafy cloak, the spathe, surrounding a club-like, fleshy flower head, the spadix

Axil angle between a stem and a leaf or bract

Axillary growing in an axil

Basal nearest the ground; basal leaves are often a different shape from those higher up the stem

Bicolor a flower of two distinct, often contrasting, colors

Biennial plant living 2 years, flowering in second year

Bract leaf or petal-like structure at the base of a flower

Bulb swollen underground bud used for propagation and storage

Bulblet, bulbil small bulb; may be in leaf axil or among flowers

Clone group of plants formed from one parent without sex and thus having the same genetic make up, e.g., plant propagated by cuttings

Compound in several parts, as a leaf made up of leaflets

Corm swollen underground stem, an organ of propagation and storage

Cross mating of 2 plants of different species or genera

Cultivar (cv) short for "cultivated variety". A plant chosen for garden qualities that are only faithfully reproduced by vegetative propagation. Does not come true from seed

Double, fully double, semi-double flowers with more than the normal number of petals. A semi-double has fewer petals than a double or fully double flower but more than a single

Floret small individual flower making up the head of a daisy or similar flower; may be disc-like or strap-shaped

Glaucous blue-grey in color, with a powdery or waxy covering (bloom)

Half-hardy between tender and hardy

Hardy plant capable of completing its life span without any protection in an area of marked seasons

Hybrid (hyb) plant resulting from a cross of 2 different species, true-breeding cultivars or genera. First generation hybrids are called F_1

Leaflet (lflt) several leaflets make a compound leaf

Offset young plant arising at the base of the parent e.g. Houseleek

Opposite (opp) describes leaves placed exactly opposite each other in pairs

Panicle branched flower cluster with groups of stalked flowers e.g. Lilac

Pinnate describes a leaf divided into leaflets placed opposite each other

Raceme long unbranched head of short-stalked flowers, e.g. Foxglove

Reflexed bent back

Reversion change of a plant back to its original form, e.g. a shoot of a variegated plant returning to all-green leaves

Rhizome swollen underground stem; organ of propagation and storage

Runner long prostrate shoot rooting to form a new plant at its tip or elsewhere along its length; an organ of vegetative propagation

Sepals (spls) outer ring of flower parts outside the petals. Often green but may be showy and petal-like as in *Clematis*

Serrated with a toothed edge like a saw

Single flower with the normal number of petals—not double

Spathe, spadix see aroid

Spike long unbranched head of stalkless flowers, e.g. Hollyhock

Spur in flowers, a hollow projection from the back of a petal or sepal e.g. Columbine

Stamen male flower part made up of a pollen-producing anther on a stalk or filament. Often showy and/or protruding, e.g. Bottle brush

Stigma female flower part on to which pollen is deposited. May be knob-like or feathery, usually sticky

Stolon shoot above or below ground producing a new plant at its tip

Sucker shoot growing from roots apart from the main stem or stems; may be taken off and used for vegetative propagation

Tender describes a plant likely to be damaged by frost; needs protection

Terminal at the end or top of a plant or plant part

Tuber swollen underground stem or root used for propagation and storage

Type plant typical of its species; not a hybrid or cultivar

Variety (var) for garden purposes, the equivalent of a cultivar

Variegated (varieg) with leaves marked in white, yellow or other colours

Vegetative (veg) propagation reproduction without sex (see p5). Organs of vegetative propagation include bulbs, corms, rhizomes and stolons

Annuals and biennials

Annuals are conventionally divided into "hardy" sorts that can be sown early in the open garden and will survive spring cold and "half-hardy" or "tender" ones which must be sown indoors and transplanted or sown outdoors only after the last frosts. Biennials are plants that are sown in summer to survive the winter with or without protection and flower the next year.

 Ageratum

Ageratum

A. conyzoides: C Amer. One parent of pop *A.* hybs. Lvs softly hry; fls fluffy heads 2 in wide, pale to rich blue. Try 'Blue Mink' lavender; 'Blue Bunch' mid blue; 'Fairy Pink' salmon. *Ht, Spd:* 9 in; *Fl:* 7–10

Althaea

Hollyhock

A. rosea: Orient. Per best grown as bi (rust disease spoils older plants). Lvs rounded, matte, soft green. Fls many cols, shuttlecock-shaped, 4 in wide on 8 ft stems. Double-flowered cvs inc 'Marjorette' 2 ft; 'Summer Carnival' 6 ft in white, salmon, pink or crimson. *Spd:* 2 ft; *Fl:* 6–7; *Z:* 4

A. rosea

Amaranthus

Amaranthus

A. caudatus Love-lies-bleeding: Tropics. Fls 18 in crimson tassels. Lvs large, stems succ. *A.c. viridis* pale green fls. *Ht:* 3 ft; *Spd:* 18 in; *Fl:* 7–10
A. tricolor Joseph's coat: Tropics. Lvs pink and crimson, marked green, bronze and yellow. 'Molten Fire' coppery crimson. *Ht:* 3 ft; *Spd:* 18 in; *Fl:* 7–9

A. caudatus

 Anagallis

Pimpernel

A. arvensis 'Caerulea': Eur (sp). Slight, spreading. Fls rich blue, ½ in wide, 5 ptls; lvs in whorls or pairs. *Ht:* 2 in; *Spd:* 6 in; *Fl:* 7–10

Antirrhinum

Snapdragon

A. majus*: Eur. Pers treated as anns. Lvs dark green, narrow. A huge choice from old singles to excellent rust-resistant hybs. F₁ hyb Rocket series single in tall spikes of pink, white, bronze, yellow, red, purple; also Butterfly, Coronette and double sorts. *Ht:* 3 ft; *Spd:* 18 in; *Fl:* 7–10; *Z:* 8

A. majus 'Scarlet and Gold'

Arctotis

African daisy

A. grandis★: S Africa. Per often treated as ann. Fls white, marguerite-like. Lvs grey-green, toothed. Hybs have bigger fls in warm crimsons, bronzes and yellows. Other large-fld hybs in wider col range, contrasting col bands at ptl bases. *Ht:* to 3 ft; *Spd:* 1 ft; *Fl:* 7–9

Atriplex

Orach

A. hortensis rubra Red mountain spinach, Purple orach: Eur. Fls dull but lvs and stems handsome deep crimson, edible. Highly decorative, useful for cutting. Self seeds but often ruined by birds. *Ht:* 4 ft; *Spd:* 3 ft

Brassica

Brassica

B. oleracea acephala Ornamental kale or cabbage: gdn origin. Pale green or white frilly lvs edged and/or suffused purple, red or pink. V decorative but more col than flavor. *Ht:* 15 in; *Spd:* 1 ft; *Z:* 5

Calceolaria

Calceolaria

C. hybs: C, S Amer. Fls to 2½ in, massed heads of typical pouting pouches from orange, yellow, red to cream, pink, apricot, mauve. Lvs roughly notched and veined. *C. rugosa* 'Sunshine' 10 in, fls clear yellow. *Ht, Spd:* to 2 ft; *Fl:* 6–10

C. hybrids

Calendula

Calendula

C. officinalis★ Pot marigold: S Eur. One of the oldest gdn fls. Lvs pale green, spatula-shaped. Blooms bright orange, daisy-like to 4 in wide. Many variations inc double-flowered sorts. *Ht:* to 2 ft; *Spd:* 18 in; *Fl:* 6–10

C. officinalis hybrid

Callistephus

China aster

C. chinensis: China. Single or double daisy-like fls. Lvs soft, green, toothed. Main strains inc 'Princess', soft cols, yellow centers; 'Duchesse', ptls incurved, white, blue, red, pink; 'Singles' and chrysanthemum-like 'Ostrich Feather' in sim cols; 'Master Sunray' showy selection. Also dwarfs e.g. 'Lilliput' 18 in; 'Victoria' 20 in; Pompon 18 in. *Ht:* 2 ft; *Spd:* 18 in; *Fl:* 7–10

C. chinensis

C. medium Canterbury bell: Eur.
Hry lvs in basal rosette. Fls bell-
shaped or with collar in old-
fashioned form. 'Calycanthema'
with blue, pink or white fls. Singles
are tall, pyramidal; fls rose pink,
violet blue. Doubles (offered as
mixed seed) come *c.* 65% true. *Ht:*
3 ft; *Spd:* 18 in; *Fl:* 5–6
C. pyramidalis★ Chimney
bellflower: Eur. Tall bi. Fls open
bells forming dense pyramid in icy
pale blue or crystalline white. *Ht:*
4 ft; *Spd:* 18 in; *Fl:* 7; *Z:* 9

C. medium

C. cristata Cockscomb: Trop Asia. Fls crimson crests to 5 in wide, also
mixed cols. Many vars with loose, informal plumes. *C. thompsonii magnifica*
20 in, bright red or mixed. *Ht:* 2 ft; *Spd:* 1 ft; *Fl:* 7–10

C. cyanus Cornflower, Bachelor's
button: Eur. Stems slim, lvs
narrow, fls like miniature crowns
2 in wide, intense cornflower blue.
C. × 'Blue Diadem' rich double
blue. Red, white and carmine also
available. *Ht:* 3 ft; *Spd:* 1 ft; *Fl:* 7–9
C. moschata Sweet sultan: E Med.
Effective frag full-petaled fl heads
white, pink mauve, purple or
yellow on log stems. Lvs lyre-
shaped, cleft at ends, bright green.
Ht: to 2 ft; *Spd:* 10 in; *Fl:* 6–10

C. cyanus

C. cheiri★: Eur. Per in warm, dry places but normally treated as bi. Sweet
scent epitomizes spr. Bushy; lvs narrow, fresh green. Hybs in white and
yellows to reds and rust. 'Harpur Crewe' double yellow; 'Tom Thumb'
miniatures 8 in tall. *Ht:* 1 ft; *Spd:* 10 in; *Fl:* 4–5; *Z:* 7

C. carinatum Tricolored
chrysanthemum: Morocco. Bushy
plant; lvs smooth, fleshy, almost
feathery. Fls white, yellow inner
zone, crimson center disc. New
hybs inc doubles, crimson-ptld
sorts. *Ht:* 2 ft; *Spd:* 15 in; *Fl:* 7–8
C. coronarium Crown daisy: S Eur.
Taller, lvs blunter; fls v pale yellow,
may be double. *Ht:* 3 ft; *Spd:* 4 ft;
Fl: 7–9

C. carinatum hybrids

Clarkia

C. elegans: Cal. Fls like small ruffled hollyhocks in tapering 8 in spikes. Sp has 4 ptls, most hybs generously double in soft red or pinks, deep purple or white. Fls May–June from autumn sowing. *Ht:* 2 ft; *Spd:* 1 ft; *Fl:* 6–7

C. pulchella: Cal. Elegant; fls single, with 4 clawed ptls, lavender to white, massed in sprays. *Ht:* 15 in; *Spd:* 1 ft; *Fl:* 6–7

C. elegans

Cleome

Spider flower

C. spinosa★: W Indies. Strong prickly plant with strange spidery-petaled white or pale pink fls with protruding anthers. 'Helen Campbell' white, other cvs rose or purple. *Ht:* 4 ft; *Spd:* 2 ft; *Fl:* 7–10

Coleus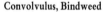

Coleus

C. blumei: Java. Bushy per grown as ann. Lvs large, oval, coarsely toothed, usually 2 or 3 cols inc purple, orange, brown, yellow, pink, silver, bright green. Pinch out white or purple fls. *Ht:* 3 ft; *Spd:* 18 in; *Z:* 9

Convolvulus

Convolvulus, Bindweed

C. tricolor Dwarf convolvulus★: SW Eur. Like a little bushy Morning glory of darker col. Fls brilliant blue funnels 1½ in wide with yellowish-white throat and center. Lvs downy. *Ht:* 15 in; *Spd:* 9 in; *Fl:* 7–9

Coreopsis

Coreopsis, Tickseed

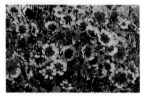

C. drummondii: Cal, Texas. Short ann version of border per. Whole plant slightly hry; daisy fls single, yellow, crimson/brown center zone. *Ht:* 1 ft; *Spd:* 18 in; *Fl:* 6–9

C. tinctoria: N Amer. Hrlss; lvs sparse, fls deep yellow or rich brown. Untidy windblown look. *Ht:* 2 ft; *Spd:* 1 ft; *Fl:* 6–9

C. tinctoria 'Dwarf Dazzler'

Cosmos

Cosmos

C. bipinnatus: Mexico. Graceful; lvs finely cut; fls big, single daisies in rose pink or purple, yellow center disc. Hybs in reds, pinks, white. *Ht:* 3 ft; *Spd:* 1 ft; *Fl:* 6–9

C. sulphureus: Mexico. Smaller sulfur-yellow sp, parent of sev orange double and semi-double cvs e.g. 'Goldcrest'. *Ht:* 2 ft; *Spd:* 1 ft; *Fl:* 6–9

C. bipinnatus

Larkspur

D. ajacis*: S Eur. One parent of gdn-bred ann hybs. 3 main sorts: Hyacinth flowered are earliest; Imperial larkspurs in white, pinks, lilac and blue; Stock flowered (form of *D. consolida**) sim cols, 'Rosamund' v good unfading rose-pink. All have dark green divided lvs. *Ht:* 3 ft; *Spd:* 1 ft; *Fl:* 6–7

D. ajacis

Dianthus

Pink, Carnation

D. barbatus Sweet William*: Eur. Best grown as bi. Jointed stems, fls in flat dome-shaped heads, white, pink, crimson often zoned and with white eye; frag. *Ht:* 2 ft; *Spd:* 1 ft; *Fl:* 6–7; *Z:* 2

D. chinensis Chinese or Indian pink*: E Asia. Compact single or double fls, fringed ptls, often darker or contrasting center. *Ht:* 1 ft; *Spd:* 6 in; *Fl:* 6–9; *Z:* 2

D. chinensis 'Juliette'

Digitalis

Foxglove

D. purpurea*: W. Eur. Bi with rosette of large sage-green basal lvs. Fls tubular, slightly pinched, purplish-pink to white, often spotted. 'Excelsior' hybs have fls all round stem. *Ht:* 4 ft; *Spd:* 18 in; *Fl:* 6–7; *Z:* 3

Dimorphotheca

Cape marigold, African daisy

D. calendulacea* Star of the Veldt: S Africa. Dark-centered glistening daisy fls open with the sun. Sp orange-yellow, hybs yellow, white, orange, salmon pink. Lvs narrow. *Ht:* 1 ft; *Spd:* 8 in; *Fl:* 6–9

Echium

Viper's bugloss

E. plantagineum hybs: Med (sp). Recent hybs have coarsely hry narrow dark green lvs and v many papery rich blue fls in dense head. Pink, lavender and white sorts available but inferior. *Ht:* 1 ft; *Spd:* 8 in; *Fl:* 6–10

E. plantagineum 'Blue Bedder'

Erysimum

Erysimum

E. perofskianum: Caucasus. Dwarf, wallflower-like. Lvs dull green; frag fls bright orange and yellow in short spikes. Can be sown in aut to fl in spr. *Ht:* 2 ft; *Spd:* 1 ft; *Fl:* 6–7; *Z:* 5

Eschscholzia

Poppy

E. californica★ California poppy: NW Amer. Brilliant yellow 4-petaled poppies. Lvs fern-like, glaucous. Hybs with *E. crocea* have orange, orange-red, crimson, scarlet, cream or white fls, some with contrasting ptl reverses. Double sorts shorter and lacking in charm. *Ht:* 18 in; *Spd:* 1 ft; *Fl:* 6–7

E. californica

Euphorbia

Spurge

E. marginata Snow on the mountain: N Amer. Spurge with white fl heads and white-margined pale green, sometimes completely white, lvs. *Ht:* to 2 ft; *Spd:* 8 in; *Fl:* 9

Glaucium

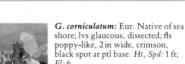

Sea poppy

G. corniculatum: Eur. Native of sea shore; lvs glaucous, dissected; fls poppy-like, 2 in wide, crimson, black spot at ptl base. *Ht, Spd:* 1 ft; *Fl:* 6

G. flavum★ Yellow horned poppy: Eur. Brilliant yellow fls 3 in wide; lvs as above. Curved seed pod to 1 ft like a horn. May survive several seasons; a thrill to grow. *Ht, Spd:* 2 ft; *Fl:* 6–8

G. flavum

Godetia

Godetia

G. amoena: W N Amer. Sp has reddish-pink fls, sev to a head on slim stems. Sev brighter hybs. *Ht:* 2 ft; *Spd:* 10 in; *Fl:* 7–8

G. grandiflora: Cal. Single hibiscus-like fls have satin sheen. Many shades from rose-red/white/crimson. Hybs double, anemone- and azalea-flowered. *Ht:* 15 in; *Spd:* 6 in; *Fl:* 6–8

G. grandiflora 'Sybil Sherwood'

Gypsophila

Gypsophila

G. elegans: Asia Minor. Ann version of per Baby's breath. Greeny-grey stems and lvs. Tiny white fls in light clouds. Pale pink, white or carmine sorts available. *Ht, Spd:* to 20 in; *Fl:* 5–9

Helianthus

Sunflower

H. annuus★ Common sunflower: USA. The monster ann to 10 ft+. Huge heavy round fls to 1 ft wide, orange or yellow pts, edible oily seeds. Hybs chestnut, yellow zoned red and brown, or double. *Spd:* 3 ft; *Fl:* 7–9

Helichrysum

Everlasting, Straw flower

H. bracteatum: Aust. Uprt, branching; fls double, daisy-like, 2 in wide, bright red, rose-pink, yellow, copper or white. Narrow lvs may have a few hrs. For drying, pick fls as they open. *Ht:* 4 ft; *Spd:* 15 in; *Fl:* 6–9

Helipterum

Everlasting

H. humboldtianum: Aust. Fls more open than sim *Helichrysum*, 3 or 4 rows of ptls round golden disc, clean yellow, sev to a head. Lvs, hry when young, clasp stem. *Ht:* 18 in; *Spd:* 6 in; *Fl:* 7–9

H. roseum: Aust. Fol slightly grey-green, freely branching. Fls as above but pink or white. *Ht:* 15 in; *Spd:* 6 in; *Fl:* 7–9

H. roseum

Iberis

Candytuft

I. amara: Eur. Low, bushy; fls white in round trusses 2 in wide. Lvs narrow, pointed tips. Also larger and dwarf forms available. *Ht, Spd:* 1 ft; *Fl:* 6–9

I. umbellata: S Eur. Taller, will grow in partial shade. Sp pink, hybs bright reds and purple to white. Dwarf forms make good edging. *Ht:* 15 in; *Spd:* 6 in; *Fl:* 5–6

I. umbellata hybrids

Impatiens

Balsam

I. balsamina: Asia. Dense, succ, tender; lvs toothed, oval, pointed; fls red, single, wide wings and spur. *L. b. camelliaeflora* double, pink, purple or red, sometimes spotted. Taller *I. biflora* (N Amer) has orange fls spotted purple-brown. *Ht:* 15 in; *Spd:* 1 ft; *Fl:* 7–9

Kochia

Kochia

K. scoparia trichophila Summer cypress, Burning bush: S Eur–Japan. Pale green thin-lvd densely bushy plant the shape of a bearskin helmet. Turns ember-hot purple/red in late smr. Fls inconspic. *Ht:* 3 ft; *Spd:* 2 ft

Lathyrus

Sweet pea

L. odoratus*: Sicily. Sweet peas have suffered many supposed "improvements" over 300 yrs and many have lost their fragrance. Cols white, reds, purples, blue; fls pea-like, 5–7 per stem. Lvs often have tendrils. 'Knee High' self supporting, bushy to 3 ft; 'Grandiflora' (smaller fls!) has sweetest smell. *Ht:* 8 ft (with support); *Spd:* 2 ft; *Fl:* 6–9

L. odoratus 'Topscore'

Lavatera

Mallow

L. trimestris (=rosea)*: Med. Shrubby; soft round lvs; fls single, open hibiscus-like, 4 in wide, rose-pink. 'Loveliness' deep rose-pink and less tall. *Ht:* 4 ft; *Spd:* 2 ft; *Fl:* 6–10

Linaria

Toadflax

L. maroccana hybrids

L. maroccana*: Morocco. Dainty, uprt. Lvs narrow; ½ in fls like massed miniature snapdragons. Sp purple, hybs from red to white and yellow eg × 'Fairy Bouquet'. *Ht:* 1 ft; *Spd:* 6 in; *Fl:* 6–9
L. reticulata: Portugal. Fls sim but larger, purple, yellow or orange in "snap". *Ht:* 3 ft; *Spd:* 1 ft; *Fl:* 5–7

Linum

Flax

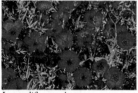

L. grandiflorum rubrum

L. grandiflorum*: N Africa. Stemmy, branching; lvs narrow, pointed. Fls rose-pink, saucer-shaped, single shiny with deeper central zone. *L. g. rubrum* rich crimson. Also a white-flowered form. *Ht:* 1 ft; *Spd:* 6 in; *Fl:* 6–7
L. usitatissimum Linseed: Eur. Fls as above but clear blue. *Ht:* 15 in; *Spd:* 6 in; *Fl:* 6–7

Lobelia

Lobelia

L. erinus 'Cambridge Blue'

L. erinus: S Africa. Per used as an ann; traditional edging plant. Lvs small, pale or v dark green; fls open tubes with violet-like 3-petaled lower lip, Cambridge or Oxford blue with white or yellow eye. Also carmine, red and white sorts and trailers for planting in hanging baskets or window boxes. *Ht, Spd:* 6 in; *Fl:* 6–10

Lobularia (=Alyssum)

Alyssum

L. maritima*: Eur. W Asia. Dwarf, bushy. Lvs tiny, fls also tiny, white, on stumpy spikes, honey scent. 'Little Dorrit' white; 'Pink Heather' bluish pink; 'Oriental Night' violet. *Ht:* 8 in; *Spd:* 1 ft; *Fl:* 6–9

Lunaria

Honesty

L. annua (=biennis)* Money plant: Eur. Bi but can fl in 1st yr. Lvs big, rough; fls bright mauve; frs like small tennis rackets, silvery sheen. *L. a. variegata* with cream/green lvs v handsome. *Ht:* 2 ft; *Spd:* 1 ft; *Fl:* 5–7; *Z:* 5

Stock

M. bicornis Night-scented stock: Greece. Wayward lilac-fld crucifer. Fls open at night, strongly frag. *Ht:* 15 in; *Spd:* 9 in; *Fl:* 6–10

M. incana and hybs: S Eur. All bi; hybs in 4 gps: Early Flowering (Mar–Apr) bushy; Brompton (May–June) v bright clear cols; Summer Bedding (June–Aug); East Lothian clean cols. *Ht:* 15 in; *Spd:* 1 ft; *Z:* 8

M. incana

Molucella

M. laevis Shell flower, Bells of Ireland: Syria. Lvs coarse, pale green. Exciting shell-shaped spl structures surrounding small white fls. Good for arranging as spls dry well. *Ht:* 2 ft; *Spd:* 15 in; *Fl:* 8

Forget-me-not

M. alpestris*: Eur. Short-lived densely bushy per grown as bi. Myriads of brilliant blue fls with tiny yellow-white eye. Rec cvs 'Royal Blue' 1 ft; 'Ultramarine' 6 in. Also pink or white hybs. *Ht, Spd:* 8 in; *Fl:* 4–6

Nemesia

N. strumosa: S Africa. Brilliantly colored fls rather like tailless nasturtiums but smaller and clustered in small dome. Fls in rich cols from red through orange and yellow to deep blue, cream and white. Hybs are dwarf strain to 8 in tall. *Ht:* to 2 ft; *Spd:* 6 in; *Fl:* 7–8

N. strumosa hybrid

Nemophila

N. menziesii* Baby blue eyes: Cal. Spreading with hrs; lvs deep lobed. Fls single, 5-petaled, clear, bright sky blue with large white eye. Also a white form. *Ht, Spd:* 8 in; *Fl:* 6–10

Tobacco plant

N. alata (= affinis)* Flowering tobacco: Brazil. Coarse plant but worthy for its scent alone. Fls tubular, frag in evening. Sp yellowish-white, modern hybs white, pink, reds. *Ht:* to 3 ft; *Spd:* 15 in; *Fl:* 7–9

N. tabacum: Trop Amer. Sim to above but fls smaller, pink, in loose clusters open in daytime. *Ht:* 5 ft; *Spd:* 2 ft; *Fl:* 7–9

N. alata 'Lime Green'

Nigella

Nigella

N. damascena* Love-in-a-mist: Med. Light blue fls in a froth of bright green feathery lvs and bracts. Seed pods green, turning fawn, bladder-like with "horns". Hybs white, pink, yellowish. *Ht, Spd:* 1 ft; *Fl:* 6–9

Papaver

Poppy

P. nudicaule

P. glaucum* Tulip poppy: Asia. Tulip-shaped buds open to brilliant crimson-scarlet fls. *Ht:* 15 in; *Spd:* 1 ft; *Fl:* 6–10

P. nudicaule* Iceland poppy: Sub-Arctic. Treat as bi. Fragile pink, orange, yellow, red or white fls. *Ht, Spd:* 1 ft; *Fl:* 5–6; *Z:* 2

P. × rhoeas: gdn origin. Bristly hyb; fls have satin sheen. *Ht, Spd:* 2 ft; *Fl:* 6–8

P. somniferum* Opium poppy: Near E. Matt blue-grey lvs; big greyish-purple fls. Also fine pink, red, white and v double forms. *Ht:* 2 ft; *Spd:* 10 in; *Fl:* 6–9

Pelargonium

Geranium

Geraniums have a unique role as *the* bedding plants with highly colored flowers in endless variety. They will withstand drought (but not freezing) and cuttings root with effortless ease.

P. peltatum 'Lyme Regis'

P. zonale 'Salmon Rings'

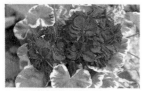

P. zonale 'Caroline Schmidt'

P. hybs* Bedding geraniums: gdn origin. Many shades and col combinations inc white, pink, reds, mauve and purple. Fls single, semi-double, double or "rosettes", eg semi-doubles 'Gustav Emich' vermilion; 'Lady Ilchester' pink; 'Vera Dillon' Tyrian purple with touch of red in center. Prop by cuttings. *Ht:* 2 ft; *Spd:* 15 in; *Fl:* 5–10

P. peltatum* Ivy-leaved geranium: S. Africa. Trailing; waxy roundish lobed lvs may have dark zone. Fls in dome-shaped heads in shades of pink or white. *Ht:* 2 ft; *Spd:* 3 ft; *Fl:* 6–10

P. zonale* Zonal or horseshoe geranium: S Africa. Bedding plants with horseshoe-shaped mark or series of marks in single or concentric bands on lvs in yellow, black or silver. Sev forms of sp have plain green lvs but 5 narrow spoon-shaped ptls, 3 forming broad lip, 2 swept back. Best cvs inc: 'Caroline Schmidt' lvs green/white, fls turkey red, double; 'Golden Oriole' lvs green/copper, fls salmon pink, single; 'Skies of Italy' lvs red/yellow/green/bronze, yellow edge, vermilion fls with central eye. *Ht:* to 6 ft; *Spd:* 1 ft; *Fl:* 5–10

Petunia

P. × hybrida*: S Amer. One of the best anns for dry soil and hot sun. Range of superb dwarf to double bedding plants. All have clammy lvs and big funnel-shaped velvety-throated fls with cloying scent in all cols inc striped and frilly-edged (picotee) sorts in white, pink, yellow, pale and navy blue. *Ht, Spd:* 1 ft; *Fl:* 6–10

P. × hybrida 'Satellite'

Phacelia

P. campanularia*: Cal. One of the truest-blue anns—strident as a gentian. Bushy, softly hry with oval lvs. Fls clustered, individually bell-shaped, 1 in wide. *Ht:* 9 in; *Spd:* 6 in; *Fl:* 6–9

Phlox

P. drummondii* Annual phlox: Texas, New Mexico. Bright-eyed bushy plants with large fl heads v like border pers. Rich cols—fls pink, red, scarlet, crimson, mauve, blue or white. *Ht, Spd:* 18 in; *Fl:* 6–9

Mignonette

R. odorata: N Africa. Sub-shrubby; can be per in frost-free gdn. Lvs blunt, oval; fls yellowish, open, star-like in loose spike, v strongly frag. Try 'Crimson Giant'; 'Golden Goliath'. *Ht, Spd:* 2 ft; *Fl:* 6–10

Coneflower

R. bicolor Annual rudbeckia: S USA. Hybs of sp as restrained as Indian war-paint. Lvs dark green, bristly; fls daisy-like, large central disc or cone, in reddish brown/ yellow bicol, disc purple-brown. Also double, 1-col and dwarf forms. 'Hurst's Marmalade' has fls to 5 in wide. *Ht, Spd:* 15 in; *Fl:* 6–10

R. bicolor 'Hurst's Marmalade'

Salpiglossis

S. sinuata*: Chile. Exotically striped and veined hyb; petunia-like, trumpet-shaped sticky fls to 2 in. in gold, rose, red, blue, violet, cream and bicols. Lvs wavy-edged. *Ht:* 2 ft; *Spd:* 1 ft; *Fl:* 7–9

Sage

S. splendens* Scarlet sage: Brazil. Guardsman-scarlet tubular fls in slim spikes on stocky bush. Lvs bright green, dark in hybs. *S. patens* taller with fls of glorious singing blue. *Ht:* 1 ft; *Spd:* 10 in; *Fl:* 7–10

Scabiosa

Scabious, Pincushion flower

S. atropurpurea Sweet scabious: SW Eur. Pale stemmy plant with jaggedly cut lvs. Fls pretty maroon pincushions of stamens among ptls. Also brighter forms from scarlet to powder blue. *Ht:* 3 ft; *Spd:* 1 ft; *Fl:* 7–9

Senecio

Ragwort

S. (=Cineraria) maritima Cineraria, Sea ragwort: Eur. Grown for its deep-lobed almost white lvs which have silver effect. Fls inconspic. 'Silver Dust' and 'Diamond' fern-like and v pale resp. *Ht, Spd:* 2 ft

Tagetes

Marigold

T. erecta* African marigold: Mexico. Dissected lvs and distinctive smell. Pompons of full-ptld double fls to 5 in wide. Hybs pale to deep yellow or orange. *Ht:* 3 ft; *Spd:* 1 ft; *Fl:* 7–10
T. patula French marigold: Mexico. Hybs in all shades of yellow-orange, plain or bicol, single, double, crested, brocaded. *Ht:* 1 ft; *Spd:* 10 in; *Fl:* 7–10

T. erecta 'Diamond Jubilee'

Tropaeolum

Nasturtium

T. majus*: Peru. Bushy, trailing, sometimes climbing. Pale, round, tasty lvs. Fls tubular, long-spurred; singles in primary shades or pale green. Doubles decorative, less elegant. Lvs of *T. alaska* hybs beautifully marbled and striped cream. *Ht, Spd:* 4 ft; *Fl:* 6–10

Verbena

Verbena

V. × hybrida: gdn origin. Per grown as ann. Small lvs; tiny primula-like fls in circular heads 3 in wide in white, blue, red, often with lighter eye; v frag. Tender *V. rigida* good for bedding. *Ht, Spd:* 1 ft; *Fl:* 7–11

Zea

Maize, Indian corn

Z. mays: gdn origin. Ornamental sweet corn, subtropical in looks. Long lvs enclose broad shining ears ripening yellow, brown, red or varieg in Aug–Sept. Cvs have varieg or multicolored fol. *Ht:* 4 ft; *Spd:* 2 ft

Zinnia

Zinnia

Z. elegans: Mexico. Sev strains under this name, all uprt with coarse oval pointed lvs. Fls double or single rosettes of closely packed ptls notched at tip in poster-paint cols— pink, red, white, yellow, orange. 'Envy' is superb Chartreuse green. *Ht:* 3 ft; *Spd:* 8 in; *Fl:* 7–9

Z. elegans 'White Giant'

Herbaceous perennials

Most "border" plants are classed as herbaceous perennials, i.e. permanent plants that die back to ground level in winter. In practice some are evergreen and a few (notably *Helleborus*) actually flower in winter. The demands of herbaceous perennials vary from dust-dry to swampy soil where they merge with bog plants. Most flower best in full sun but those of woodland origin—which are usually early-flowering—need some shade.

  Acanthus

Bear's breeches

 A. spinosus★: S Eur. Statuesque with lustrous deeply divided evergreen hry lvs to 3 ft and stiff 18 in fl spikes of squat white and purple tubes interspersed with spiny bracts. *Ht:* to 4 ft; *Spd:* 30 in; *Fl:* 7–8; *Z:* 6

Achillea

Yarrow, Milfoil

Flat, generally yellow or white composite flower heads over rough-textured feathery foliage. Robust and wiry, long lasting and drying well. More useful than glamorous as garden plants.

A. filipendulina: Caucasus. Stout plant with hry greyish-green aromatic lvs. Fls golden yellow in densely packed heads. 'Gold Plate'★ is one of the best cvs. Prop by div. *Ht:* 4 ft; *Spd:* 18 in; *Fl:* 7–8; *Z:* 2

 A. 'Moonshine'★: gdn origin. Shorter cv with silvery-green lvs and bright yellow fls. *Ht:* 2 ft; *Spd:* 18 in; *Fl:* 6–8; *Z:* 2

A. filipendulina 'Gold Plate'

Aconitum

Monkshood

A. napellus: Eur, Asia. Poisonous tuberous-rooted plant with stiff stems bearing dark green deeply divided lvs and spikes of helmet-shaped 1½ in fls from July–Aug; × 'Bicolor' is one of sev good gdn hybs with bright blue and white fls. Other sorts are indigo, e.g. 'Spark's Variety', or white. Prop by div. *Ht:* 3 ft; *Spd:* 8 in; *Z:* 2

Agapanthus

Blue African lily

Tall swaying stems supporting bunches of blue or white lily-like flowers over smooth leaves. One of the best late summer flowers.

A. campanulatus★: S Africa. Smaller in all its parts and hardier than *A. umbellatus* with sky-blue 2 in fls. There are also white and deep blue forms. Prop by div in spring, seedlings variable. *Ht:* 30 in; *Spd:* 18 in; *Fl:* 7–8; *Z:* 9

A. umbellatus (= africanus, orientalis, praecox): S Africa. Strap-shaped glossy deep green lvs 2 ft × 2 in; green unbranched stems and terminal heads of deep blue funnel-shaped 3 in fls. Free-flowering dwarf evergreen 'Peter Pan' to 18 in v pop. Prop by div. *Ht:* 4 ft; *Spd:* 30 in; *Fl:* 7–9; *Z:* 9

A. campanulatus

Agave

Century plant

A. americana: Mexico. Sub-tropical succ, spectacular in foliage and fl with thick, fleshy, glaucous, spiny 4 ft lvs. Produces stems to 20 ft with yellowish fls after many yrs then dies. Tender. *Ht:* 4 ft; *Spd:* 9 ft; *Fl:* 8; *Z:* 7

Ajuga

Bugle

A useful low leafy carpeter, creeping with stoloniferous roots; a native of clay soils. In early spring spikes of bluish flowers arise. Admirable cover for short-stemmed spring bulbs.

A. pyramidalis: Eur. Dark green, rounded lvs and blue-purple fls in pyramidal 6 in spikes. *Ht:* 4 in; *Spd:* 18 in; *Fl:* 5–7; *Z:* 2
A. reptans: Eur. Fls blue, white or pink. Cvs 'Multicolor', 'Variegata' and 'Burgundy Delight' have darker, variegated and metallic lvs respectively. Prop by div. *Ht:* 3½ in; *Spd:* 15 in; *Fl:* 6–7; *Z:* 2

A. reptans 'Burgundy Delight'

Alchemilla

Lady's mantle

A. mollis*: Asia Minor. Forms dense clumps of rounded, downy, pale greyish-green lvs on long single stalks. Much praised when spangled with dew or raindrops. Branched fl stems bear myriads of yellow-green star-like ¼ in fls. Prop by div or seed. *Ht:* 18 in; *Spd:* 2 ft; *Fl:* 6–8; *Z:* 3

A. mollis

Aloe

Aloe

A. aristata: S Africa. A succ, sprawling rosette of alt narrow fleshy-toothed lvs and flared tubular orange fls on branched 1 ft spikes in late June. Fairly hardy in a v dry place. *Ht:* 2 ft; *Spd:* 3 ft; *Z:* 9

Alstroemeria

Peruvian lily

Little lily-like flowers in generous bunches on tall pliant stems. Needs deep planting, slow to establish, but long-lasting.

A. aurantiaca*: Chile. Smooth-stemmed slightly fleshy-leaved clumps; terminal clusters of open fierce orange 2 in tubes. Also a yellow form. Rts inclined to run, stems need support. Prop by seed. *Ht:* 3 ft; *Spd:* 1 ft+; *Fl:* 6–8; *Z:* 8
A. ligtu*: Chile. Chiefly seen as 'Ligtu Hybrids' ranging in col from bright pink to yellow, orange and salmon pink. Prized as cut fls. Prop by seed, plant from pots. *Ht:* to 4 ft; *Spd:* 18 in; *Fl:* 6–8; *Z:* 8

A. aurantiaca

Pearl everlasting

A. cinnamomea: Asia. Stems uprt, lvs rich green on top, woolly white beneath. Fls long-lasting branches flat heads of yellow-centered white. Tolerates more moisture than sim spp. *Ht:* 18 in; *Spd:* 2 ft; *Fl:* 8; *Z:* 3

Anchusa

A. azurea: Caucasus. Top-heavy middle-of-the-border plant with v branched hairy lvs and stems; $\frac{1}{3}$ in fls are open funnels in a rare, valuable shade of intense blue. 'Loddon Royalist' (AGM) is one of the best. Short lived; renew by seed or root cuttings. *Ht:* to 4 ft; *Spd:* 2 ft; *Fl:* 5–8; *Z:* 4

A. azurea 'Loddon Royalist'

Anemone, windflower

A. hupehensis* Japanese anemone: China. Among the most useful, graceful and long-lasting late smr fls. *A. hybrida (=japonica)* sim. Lvs rough, vine-like, 2 in fls dusky pink, purplish or white. 'Luise Uhink' (AGM) is semi-double white. *Ht:* to 4 ft; *Spd:* 2 ft; *Fl:* 8–10; *Z:* 6

Columbine

A. hybrid strains: gdn origin. Pretty but short-lived plants with tap roots and fern-like, sometimes glaucous lvs. Fls to 3 in across have spurs at the back and come in a wide range of plain and mixed cols. Casual crossing often produces muddy cols; purchase guaranteed seed. 'McKana Hybrids' are large-flowered, yellow and crimson. *Ht:* 3 ft; *Spd:* 1 ft; *Fl:* 5–6; *Z:* 3

A. 'McKana Hybrids'

Arctotis

A. decurrens: S Africa. Woolly divided evergreen lvs and open single white purplish-centered daisy fls *c.* 2 in wide. Several spp have been crossed with venidiums to produce × *Venidio-arctotis* (p 56), half-hardy perennials and bedding plants. *Ht:* to 30 in; *Spd:* 30 in; *Fl:* 7–8; *Z:* 3

Thrift, Sea pink

A. plantaginea Giant thrift: Eur. Large sp with long green lvs and rounded heads of pink fls on stiff stems. 'Bees Ruby' (AGM) has deep reddish-pink fls. *Ht:* 18 in; *Spd:* 1 ft; *Fl:* 6–8; *Z:* 4

Artemisia

Wormwood

Members of the daisy family on the borderline between perennials and shrubs. All but *A. lactiflora* are grown for their foliage.

A. ludoviciana 'Silver Queen'

A. absinthium: Eur. Woody with finely-dissected shining silvery-grey lvs. 'Lambrook Silver'★ is best selection. Prop by cuttings. *Ht:* 2 ft; *Spd:* 3 ft; *Z:* 2

A. lactiflora: Asia. Uprt plant with terminal 8 in spikes of creamy white fls on stiff stems of coarse-lobed green lvs. Prop by div. *Ht:* to 5 ft; *Spd:* 2 ft; *Fl:* 7–8; *Z:* 3

A. ludoviciana: N Amer. Sprawling, white-stemmed with narrow grey-green lvs. 'Silver Queen' is smaller with divided lvs. May run. *Ht:* 3 ft; *Spd:* 2 ft; *Z:* 3

Aruncus

Goat's beard

A. dioicus (= sylvester)★: N Hem. Makes handsome pale green ferny clumps with plumes of creamy-white ⅛ in fls in June–July. Lvs have 1–3 corrugated leaflets. Tough rootstock to divide. *Ht, Spd:* 4 ft; *Z:* 2

Asclepias

Milkweed

A. tuberosa Butterfly weed, Pleurisy root: N Amer. Tap-rooted plant best in poor soil. Pointed lvs and stems hry. Orange ¼ in fls from late June–Aug form bun-shaped heads. Prop by seed. *Ht:* to 30 in; *Spd:* 18 in; *Z:* 4

Aster

Aster, Michaelmas daisy

Chiefly late and long-flowering and all with blooms on the white-purple side of the spectrum. Varied in size, vigor and proneness to disease but all best propagated vegetatively.

A. novi-belgii

A. novae-angliae

A. amellus: Italy. Useful late-flowering sp with coarse lvs and stems. Fls 1½ in wide, pink, mauve or violet in late July or Oct depending on cv. *Ht:* 14 in; *Spd:* 2 ft; *Z:* 6

A. × frikartii: gdn origin. Taller and larger in fl than *A. amellus* which is one of its parents. 'Mönch'★ with bright blue fls and pronounced yellow center disc is best form. *Ht:* 30 in; *Spd:* 18 in; *Fl:* 7–9; *Z:* 6

A. novae-angliae: N Amer. Tough back-of-the-border sp with rough stems and lvs. 'Harrington's Pink' a familiar favorite, also mauve, crimson and purple-blue sorts. *Ht:* 4½ ft; *Spd:* 2 ft; *Fl:* 8–9; *Z:* 4

A. novi-belgii: E USA. Shorter than above but a wider selection of white, pink, red, blue and purple-flowered sorts, e.g. 'Winston Churchill' ruby red. *Ht:* to 4 ft; *Spd:* 28 in; *Fl:* 9–10; *Z:* 5

Astilbe

Handsome long-lasting plume flowers; some straight and single, others multiple or drooping. Happy in boggy ground.

A. × arendsii*: gdn origin. Dense lfy clumps and tapering fluffy 1 ft plumes in the white-red col range dying to a handsome dark brown. A race of hybs, e.g. 'Rheinland' rose-pink. Prop by div. *Ht:* to 3 ft; *Spd:* to 2 ft; *Fl:* 7–8; *Z:* 4

A. chinensis 'Pumila': China. One of sev dwarf sorts. Needs dampness and partial shade. Fl spikes mauve. *Ht, Spd:* 1 ft; *Fl:* 7–8; *Z:* 4

A. taquetii*: China. Distinct tall sp. Fls rich reddish mauve esp in the selection 'Superba'. *Ht:* to 4 ft; *Spd:* 2 ft; *Fl:* 8; *Z:* 4

A. × arendsii

Masterwort

A. major*: Eur. Quietly attractive plant with bold divided lvs and wiry green stems. Tiny purplish-white fls arranged in a dome on a saucer of larger ptl-like bracts, sev on a stem. *A. maxima* is light pink and shorter, *A. carniolica* 'Rubra' reddish. Prop by div or seed. *Ht:* 2 ft; *Spd:* 18 in; *Fl:* 7–8; *Z:* 7

A. major

Blue or false indigo

B. australis*: E USA. Uprt member of the pea family with glaucous leaflets and paler stems. Indigo-blue fls ¾ in wide in June followed by decorative seed pods. Prop by seed. *Ht:* to 4 ft; *Spd:* 2 ft; *Z:* 5

Bergenia

Valuable low evergreen with bold rounded upright or flopping fleshy leaves of shining green. Pink flowers in spikes in spring.

B. cordifolia (= Saxifraga megasea)* Pig squeak: Siberia. Toothed rounded lvs turning bronze in winter and 1 in fls in sprays on thick stems. Prop by div. *Ht:* 15 in; *Spd:* 2 ft; *Fl:* 3–4; *Z:* 5

B. crassifolia: Siberia. Has woody rootstock and oval lvs becoming reddish in wtr. Fls of the sp 1 in long, light pink; gdn forms can be pink or rosy red. Prop by div. *Ht:* 2 ft; *Spd:* 18 in; *Fl:* 3–4; *Z:* 5

B. 'Silberlicht' (= 'Silver Light')*: gdn origin. A white-flowered form with spoon-shaped lvs a shade lighter green. Prop by div. *Ht:* 1 ft; *Spd:* 18 in; *Fl:* 4–5; *Z:* 5

B. cordifolia

Bromeliad

B. agavifolia: Cayenne. Tender rosette-former with spiny near-stemless lvs. Fls pale red in collar of short lvs. *Ht:* 4 ft; *Spd:* 5 ft+; *Fl:* 3; *Z:* 10

Brunnera

Brunnera

B. macrophylla (= Anchusa myosotidiflora)*: Caucasus-Iran. Big heart-shaped soft green lvs and sprays of ¼ in bright forget-me-not-blue fls. There is a less vig variegated form*. *Ht:* 18 in; *Spd:* 2 ft; *Fl:* 4–6; *Z:* 4

Campanula **A R T**

Bellflower

Varying from tall border plants to tiny alpines but all with clear-cut flowers on the grey or purple side of blue (or white).

C. latiloba

C. lactiflora*: Caucasus. Fls palest blue, bell-shaped, 1½ in wide, many per stem. Good cvs inc 'Loddon Anna' pale pink; 'Prichard's Variety' violet blue. Prop by div. *Ht:* 5 ft; *Spd:* 2 ft; *Fl:* 7–9; *Z:* 6
C. latifolia Great bellflower: Kashmir-Eur. Reliable per. Fls blue, funnel-shaped, 2 in. Rts inclined to run. 'Brantwood' is a deeper col. *C. latiloba* equally good but smaller. *Ht:* 5 ft; *Spd:* 20 in; *Fl:* 7; *Z:* 4
C. persicifolia Peach-leaved bell-flower: Eur, N Africa, W Asia. Clumps of narrow-lvd rosettes. Hrlss stems to 3 ft, fls large, open, blue. *Spd:* to 3 ft; *Fl:* 7–8; *Z:* 4

Canna **B**

Canna

C. iridiflora

C. iridiflora: Peru. V tall elegant plant with exciting long pendulous, rose-pink, tube-like 3 in fls and ptls curved back at the mouth. Lvs wide, glaucous, to 2 ft long. Prop by div. Related *C. indica* grown as a bulb. *Ht:* 4 ft; *Spd:* 3 ft; *Fl:* 7–8; *Z:* 3

Catananche

Cupid's dart

C. caerulea: Med. Forms a clump of short, narrow, hoary lvs. Papery blue fls 1½ in wide are cornflower-like on 2 ft stems. 'Major' is deep lavender blue. 'Perry's White' less tall. Prop cvs by div, spp by seed. *Spd:* 18 in; *Fl:* 6–8; *Z:* 3

Knapweed

Flowers in intricate thistle-like design, easy to grow in sunny, well-drained preferably limy soil.

C. hypoleuca 'John Coutts'

C. hypoleuca: Iran. Deeply lobed green lvs are whitish on their underside. Fls rose-pink, 2 in wide. Forms dense clumps but inclined to run: 'John Coutts' is the best form. Prop by div. *Ht:* 2 ft; *Spd:* 18 in; *Fl:* 6–7; *Z:* 5

C. macrocephala: Caucasus. Taller and with coarser lvs and hollow stems. Fls to 4 in wide, bright yellow, borne on rounded, scaly heads. Prop by div. *Ht:* to 4 ft; *Spd:* 30 in; *Fl:* 7; *Z:* 3

C. montana Mountain knapweed: Eur. Rather floppy plant with narrow green lvs and wide cornflower-like heads of fls from late April–June. Blue, but purplish, white and reddish sorts available. Prop by div. *Ht:* 18 in; *Spd:* 2 ft; *Z:* 5

C. macrocephala

Valerian

C. (= Kentranthus) ruber: Eur. Almost woody; glaucous lvs and bold heads of clustered ⅓ in fls pink in the type but in best forms, 'Albus' and 'Atrococcineus', white and reddish resp. *Ht:* 30 in; *Spd:* 18 in; *Fl:* 6; *Z:* 4

Cephalaria

C. gigantea (= tartarica) Giant or Tartarian scabious: Siberia. Has pale creamy-yellow scabious-like fls on tall stems above basal clumps of dark green lvs. Prop by div in spr. *Ht:* 7 ft; *Spd:* 4 ft; *Fl:* 6–7; *Z:* 2

C. gigantea

Turtle head

C. obliqua Rose turtle head: USA. Dark green plant with shiny lvs in pairs on 2½ ft stems. Fls 1 in, mop-like, turtle-head-shaped, deep rose-pink. Prop by div, seed, soft cuttings. *Spd:* 1 ft; *Fl:* 8–9; *Z:* 4

C. obliqua

Chrysanthemum

⊕ ⊛ **A** **T**

Chrysanthemum

Indispensable daisy flowers in infinite variety from spring to autumn, lacking only in shades of blue.

C. maximum

C. coccineum Pyrethrum: W Asia. Simple fls on slim stems over fern-like lvs. Cvs in various cols. *Ht:* 30 in; *Spd:* 18 in; *Fl:* 5–6; *Z:* 3
C. maximum Shasta daisy: Eur. Invaluable white full-petaled fls. *Ht:* 3 ft; *Spd:* 2 ft; *Fl:* 7–8; *Z:* 4
C. morifolium Florists' chrysanthemum: China. Parent of v useful pers in many forms and cols from white through bronze to red. *Ht:* to 4 ft; *Spd:* 2 ft; *Fl:* 9–11; *Z:* 3

Cimicifuga

⊛ ⊛

Snakeroot, Bugbane

Slender, graceful white or whitish flower spikes in late summer over distinctly stylish leaves. Needs moisture but not support.

C. racemosa

C. racemosa★: E N Amer. Clumps of deeply cut rounded lvs give rise to tall branching slender stems with 1 ft pokers of white fls. Prop by div or fresh seed. *Ht:* to 8 ft; *Spd:* to 2 ft; *Fl:* 6–8; *Z:* 3
C. simplex (= foetida intermedia): USSR-Japan. Toothed lvs and branched stems of greenish-yellow $\frac{1}{4}$ in fls. Prop as above. *Ht:* to 5 ft; *Spd:* 2 ft; *Fl:* 8–10; *Z:* 3

Cineraria

⊛ ⊛ ⊛ **A**

Cineraria

C. stellata

C. stellata: singles: gdn origin. Hybs derived from *Senecio cruentus*, a Canary Is sp. Useful as pot plants and in gdns in warm countries. Lvs big, light green, fls daisy-like, 3 in wide in round heads and clean cols from red-pink to white and blue. Best from seed and may be treated as biennials. *Ht, Spd:* 18 in; *Fl:* 12–3, 6; *Z:* 9

Clematis

⊛ ⊛ **C**

Clematis

C. integrifolia

C. integrifolia: S Eur. Woody sp, needs support. Lvs dark green, oval, pointed, clasping. Fls deep blue, bell-shaped, 1½ in diam. Slow from seed, difficult by div. *Ht:* to 4 ft; *Spd:* 2 ft; *Fl:* 6–8; *Z:* 3
C. recta: Eur. Free-flowering, frag, straggling bush. Lvs divided, the best sorts are purplish. Fls ¾ in diam, seed heads fluffy. *Ht:* to 4 ft; *Spd:* 3 ft; *Fl:* 6–7; *Z:* 3

Coreopsis, Tickseed

G. grandiflora: S USA. Lfy branching per. Lvs smooth, green, fls bright yellow, daisy-like to 1½ in wide. 'Mayfield Giant' and 'Sunburst' are among the best cvs. *Ht:* 3 ft; *Spd:* 30 in; *Fl:* 6–8; *Z:* 6

C. verticillata★: E USA. Neat and bushy; bedecked with yellow stars. 'Grandiflora' is larger and better. *Ht:* 30 in; *Spd:* 20 in; *Fl:* 6–9; *Z:* 7

C. verticillata 'Grandiflora'

Pampas grass

C. selloana (= argentea): Temp S Amer. Giant grass with narrow glaucous lvs and immense silky white fl plumes. 'Sunningdale' is shorter but excellent. Burn off dead lvs in wtr. *Ht:* to 10 ft; *Spd:* 6 ft; *Fl:* 10; *Z:* 8

Crambe

C. cordifolia★: Caucasus. Spectacular with huge limp dark green lvs below much-branched stems bearing clouds of tiny frag white fls. Stems whiten when dead and are handsome in wtr. *Ht, Spd:* 6½ ft; *Fl:* 6–7; *Z:* 7

C. maritima Seakale: Eur. Pale grey elaborately lobed lvs; frag white cabbage fls. Often grown for its edible stems. *Ht:* 2 ft; *Spd:* 30 in; *Fl:* 6; *Z:* 7

C. cordifolia

Orchid

D. (= Orchis) elata★ Algerian orchid: Algeria. An easy garden orchid with long spikes of rich violet-purple fls and plain green lvs. Propagate by dividing tubers. *Ht:* 2 ft; *Spd:* 8 in; *Fl:* 6; *Z:* 7

Delphinium

The true-blue aristocrats of the summer border: magnificent flower spikes above pale, fingery leaves.

D. hybs, Large-flowered★: Eur–W Asia. Mainly hybs of *D. elatum*, to 7 ft according to cv. Cols white through all shades of blue to rose-pink, red and yellow. Most have pronounced eye. Double-flowered cvs inc 'Alice Artindale'. *Spd:* 30 in; *Fl:* 6–7; *Z:* 2

D. belladonna hybs★: gdn origin. Shorter, bushier, longer flowering; often fl twice. Fls single, blue, white or rose-pink. 'Connecticut Yankee' to 3½ ft v pop. *Ht:* to 5 ft; *Spd:* 20 in; *Fl:* 6–7; *Z:* 2

D. hybrid 'Blue Jade'

Dianthus

Pink, carnation

Short-lived, little plants including carnations, pinks and Sweet Williams. Most are evergreen with more or less narrow grey or greyish leaves. Many have an intensely sweet scent. All like limy, well-drained soil.

D. Garden pink 'Mrs Sinkins'

D. Border carnations: gdn origin. Range of dependable hardy carnations with wider glaucous lvs and more uprt habit than gdn pinks. Fls frag, white, pale yellow, pink, red or crimson, 1½ in wide, ptls may be flecked. Prop by layers or cuttings. *Ht:* 1 ft; *Spd:* to 18 in; *Fl:* 6–9; *Z:* 2

D. Garden pink 'Doris'

D. Garden pinks: gdn origin. Richly frag edge-of-the-border plants derived from sev spp. Evergreen, narrow, glaucous, pointed lvs; fls carnation-like and usually with split sepal ring. Cols white, pink, red or purplish sometimes ringed with a white/crimson center or flecked. 'Sam Barlow' is a ringed cv. Prop by cuttings in July. *Ht:* 1 ft; *Spd:* 2 ft; *Fl:* 6–7; *Z:* 2

Dicentra

Dicentra

D. spectabilis

D. formosa: W N Amer. Tufty; lvs smooth, pale green, ferny. Mauve fls heart-shaped, pendulous, sev per stem. 'Bountiful' has blue-green lvs and plum-red fls. Prop by div. *Ht, Spd:* to 18 in; *Fl:* 4–6; *Z:* 2
D. spectabilis* Dutchman's breeches, Bleeding heart: Siberia, Japan. V pretty: lvs v cut; locket-shaped rosy-red fls on arched stems. *Ht, Spd:* 18 in; *Fl:* 5–6; *Z:* 2

Dictamnus

Gas plant, Fraxinella, Dittany

D. albus: Eur, Asia. Robust with glossy aromatic lvs and v frag white open tubular fls. Poisonous. *Ht:* 30 in; *Spd:* 2 ft; *Fl:* 6–7; *Z:* 5

Digitalis

Foxglove

D. purpurea 'Excelsior'

D. grandiflora (= ambigua): Eur. Creamy-yellow 2 in fls and sage-green lvs. Not long-lived but easily renewed by seed or div. *Ht:* to 30 in; *Spd:* 1 ft; *Fl:* 7–8; *Z:* 3
D. purpurea hybs: Eur. The common purple or white-flowered sp is biennial but some hybs, e.g. 'Excelsior Strain' are longer lived with wider col range. Fls tubular 2 in long on lfy spikes. *Ht:* to 5 ft; *Spd:* 30 in; *Fl:* 6–8; *Z:* 3

Leopard's bane

A cheerful yellow daisy most notable for being much the earliest of its character—similar plants are more common later on.

D. 'Miss Mason'*: gdn origin. Yellow daisy-flowered plant with heart-shaped toothed light green lvs. Fls 2½ in diam. Prop by div. *Ht:* 18 in; *Spd:* 2 ft; *Fl:* 4–6; *Z:* 4

D. plantagineum: W. Eur. In flower early then gets tall and lfy. Lvs smooth, coarsely toothed. *Ht:* 30 in; *Spd:* 2 ft; *Fl:* 4–6; *Z:* 4

D. 'Spring Beauty': gdn origin. Full-petaled yellow fls make solid early splashes of col. Lvs toothed. *Ht:* 18 in; *Spd:* 2 ft; *Fl:* 4–6; *Z:* 4

D. 'Spring Beauty'

 Echinacea

Purple or hedgehog coneflower

E. (= Rudbeckia) purpurea: USA. Lvs dark green, stems stout, branched. Large daisy-like burnished burgundy fls 4 in wide like old wicker beehives with central cone. 'White Lustre' good. *Ht:* 4 ft; *Spd:* 20 in; *Fl:* 8–9; *Z:* 4

Echinops

Globe thistle

The name globe thistle perfectly describes these easy, tenacious plants with prickly leaves and drumstick flower heads.

E. ritro*: E Eur, W Asia. Sturdy plant with jagged lvs and round steely-blue heads of fl 2 in wide which are prickly to touch. For the back of the border. 'Taplow Blue' is lighter blue and taller, reaching 5 ft. Prop by div. *Ht:* to 4 ft; *Spd:* 2 ft; *Fl:* 7–8; *Z:* 4

E. ritro

 Epimedium

Barrenwort

In the department of tasteful understatement. Pretty little smooth green leaves on tall stems with unshowy flowers.

E. grandiflorum: Japan, Manchuria. Slowly spreading; 1 ft lvs have heart-shaped lflts on wiry stems; 1 in fls pale yellow but rose and white forms known. Remove lvs in Jan to show off fls. Prop by div. *Ht, Spd:* 1 ft; *Fl:* 5–6; *Z:* 4

E. perralderianum*: Algeria. Has evergreen lvs and small yellow fls, sev per stem. Prop by div. *Ht:* 1 ft; *Spd:* 18 in; *Fl:* 5–6; *Z:* 4

E. × versicolor: gdn origin. Young lvs reddish, turning green then bronze. Fls yellow, spls and lvs, spurs reddish. Sev selected sorts. *Ht, Spd:* 1 ft; *Fl:* 5; *Z:* 4

E. × versicolor

Erigeron

Fleabane

Fleabanes have been bred in all colors from pink to purple, single and double. The effect is of early Michaelmas daisies.

E. hybrid 'Mrs F.H. Beale'

E. aurantiacus: Turkestan. Velvety-leaved short-lived per. Fls v full-petaled, bright orange. *Ht, Spd:* 1 ft; *Fl:* 6–7; *Z:* 6

E. hybrids: gdn origin. Daisy-like fls range in col from mauve, rose-pink to blue-violet or white. Best inc 'Darkest of All' violet-blue; 'Prosperity' mauve-blue. *Ht:* to 30 in; *Spd:* 20 in; *Fl:* 6–8/9; *Z:* 6

Eryngium

Eryngium

E. tripartitum*: origin unknown. Splendid tall thistle with dark green basal lvs and spiky steel-blue fls. *Ht:* 4 ft; *Spd:* 3 ft; *Fl:* 8–9; *Z:* 6

Eupatorium

Eupatorium

E. purpureum* Joe-pye weed: N Amer. Striking tall late-flowering per; enjoys moist soil. Purplish fls on darker stks in flat heads 5 in wide. Stems lfy, stiff and pointed long into wtr. *Ht:* to 7 ft; *Spd:* 3 ft; *Fl:* 8–9; *Z:* 4

Euphorbia

Spurge

Unlikely relations of some fierce cactus-like subtropicals; fashionably low-key in shades of green and (in one case) orange.

E. griffithii 'Fire Glow'

E. characias wulfenii

E. characias*: Eur. Shrubby evergreen, lvs narrow, grey-green finely hry. Sp has green, brown-centered fls unlike *E. c. wulfenii* with yellow-green fls and yellow centers. *Ht, Spd:* 4 ft; *Fl:* 4–5; *Z:* 4

E. griffithii 'Fire Glow'*: W Asia. Outstanding for its heads of flame-red fls 4 in wide effective over a long period. V densely bushy, lvs thin. Runs. *Ht:* 30 in; *Spd:* 2 ft; *Fl:* 4–6; *Z:* 3

E. polychroma (= epithymoides)*: Eur. Closely packed stems grow into dense mound of dark green lvs. Fls brilliant chrome yellow. *Ht:* 18 in; *Spd:* 2 ft; *Fl:* 4–5; *Z:* 3

E. robbiae*: Asia Minor. Rosettes of dark evergreen lvs and narrow plumes of light green fls. Invaluable ground cover. Stoloniferous. *Ht, Spd:* 2 ft; *Fl:* 4–5; *Z:* 3

Fascicularia

Fascicularia

F. bicolor: Chile. A nearly-hardy bromeliad suitable for warm ledges. Lvs narrow, v toothed in rosettes. Fls pale blue in conspicuous flesh-pink bracts. Prop by div. *Ht:* 20 in; *Spd:* 2 ft; *Fl:* 8–9; *Z:* 9

Fescue

F. ovina Sheep's fescue: Temp zones. Fine-lvd tuft-forming grass. *F. glauca* is blue-green leaved and best for garden purposes. Good edging plant. Prop by div or seed. *Ht, Spd:* 10 in; *Fl:* 7–8; *Z:* 3

Filipendula

F. hexapetala Dropwort: Eur, Asia. Neat, clump-forming; lvs finely cut, rich green. Fls creamy-white in flat fluffy heads. 'Flore Pleno' double flowered more effective. *Ht:* to 3 ft; *Spd:* 18 in; *Fl:* 6–7; *Z:* 4
F. ulmaria Meadowsweet: Eur, Asia. As above but fls v frag. Young lvs of 'Aurea' golden-green. *Ht:* to 3 ft; *Spd:* 18 in; *Fl:* 6–8; *Z:* 2

F. ulmaria 'Aurea'

Maiden's wreath

F. sonchifolia*: Chile. Outstandingly graceful plant bearing long stems of delicate pale pink fls over substantial rosettes of fiddle-shaped deeply lobed lvs. Prop by div, seed. *Ht:* 30 in; *Spd:* 18 in; *Fl:* 7; *Z:* 6

Gaillardia

G. × grandiflora: gdn origin. Short-lived but valuable, producing large daisy-like fls, 3 in wide, of yellow, orange or mahogany col over a long period. Lvs oblong, softly hry. 'Ipswich Beauty' orange-red, tipped yellow and 'Wirral Flame' mahogany red, tipped yellow, are good cvs. Prop by root or basal cuttings. *Ht:* to 30 in; *Spd:* 18 in; *Fl:* 6–9; *Z:* 3

G. × grandiflora

Galax

G. urceolata (= aphylla): E N Amer. Has rounded shiny lvs that become a reddish-bronze in autumn. Fls white in slender spikes. Prop by div. *Ht:* 18 in; *Spd:* 1 ft; *Fl:* 6–7; *Z:* 7

Goat's rue

G. × hartlandii: gdn origin. Bushy per "sweet pea". Fls small, lilac or white in 1½ in spikes. Lvs grey-green. Prop by div. *Ht:* to 5 ft; *Spd:* 3 ft; *Fl:* 6–7; *Z:* 4
G. orientalis: Caucasus. A little shorter but otherwise v like above. Fls bluish-white in 1 in spikes. Invasive. Prop by div. *Ht:* 4 ft; *Spd:* 3 ft; *Fl:* 6–7; *Z:* 4

G. × hartlandii

Gazania

G. × splendens: gdn origin. Lvs narrow, evergreen, rich green above, silvery-white beneath. Daisy-like fls 3 in wide in brilliant yellow, orange and dark red open in sun. *Ht, Spd:* 1 ft; *Fl:* 6–10; *Z:* 5

Gentiana

Gentian

G. asclepiadea

G. asclepiadea Willow gentian: Eur. Arching lfy stems with paired willow-like lvs and rich gentian-blue fls. Prop by seed. *Ht:* 30 in; *Spd:* 18 in; *Fl:* 8–9; *Z:* 4

G. lutea Gentian root: Eur. Robust and v unlike other spp in looks with glaucous, puckered lvs and star-shaped yellow 1 in fls followed by attractive seed heads. Prop by seed. *Ht:* 3 ft; *Spd:* 2 ft; *Fl:* 7–8; *Z:* 6

Geranium

Cranesbill

The cranesbills, not to be confused with the tender South African geraniums (p 16) are hearty, reliable ground-smotherers with dense leafage of great character and a long season of blue, pink or white flowers.

G. 'Johnson's Blue'

G. endressii 'Wargrave Pink'

G. endressii 'Wargrave Pink': Pyrenees. Lfy sprawler. Fls bright pink, open, 1 in wide, lvs small, veined, lobed. Prop by div. *Ht, Spd:* 2 ft; *Fl:* 6–7; *Z:* 7

G. 'Johnson's Blue': Gdn origin. Vig, lfy hyb producing generous quantities of luminescent blue fls to 2 in wide. Prop by div. *Ht:* 18 in; *Spd:* 2 ft; *Fl:* 6–9; *Z:* 5

G. macrorrhizum*: S Eur. Excellent almost evergreen ground cover plant with pale green aromatic lvs that redden in aut. Fls mauve-pink, 1 in wide. 'Walter Ingwersen' is clear pink; there is also a white form. Prop by div. *Ht:* 1 ft; *Spd:* 18 in; *Fl:* 5–7; *Z:* 4

G. × magnificum (= ibericum, platypetalum)*: Caucasus–Iran. Clump-forming hyb with rounded crinkly nettle-green lvs and sticky fl stalks. Fls violet-blue, 1 in diam. Good aut col. Prop by div. *Ht, Spd:* 2 ft; *Fl:* 6–8; *Z:* 5

G. pratense Meadow cranesbill: N Eur. A clump of deeply divided lvs coloring well in aut. Fls bright blue to 2 in wide. White and blue double-flowered forms available, e.g. 'Caeruleum Plenum'. Prop spp by seed or all by div. *Ht, Spd:* 2 ft; *Fl:* 6–9; *Z:* 5

G. × magnificum

Gerbera

G. jamesonii Barbeton daisy: S Africa. Brilliantly colored daisy, fls 5 in and more across on a plant hry in all its parts. Sp fls bright orange. *G.* × *jamesonii*, the Transvaal daisy, varies from pink to red, yellow and orange shades. Prop from side shoots or seed. *Ht:* 18 in; *Spd:* 15 in; *Fl:* 5–6; *Z:* 8

G. jamesonii

Geum

G. 'Borisii': Bulgaria. Good front-of-the-border hyb. Lvs rounded and hry, 1 in fls like open buttercups but glowing orange. Prop by div. *Ht, Spd:* 1 ft; *Fl:* 6–9; *Z:* 4
G. chiloense: Chile. Parent of 2 or 3 more useful hybs inc × 'Mrs Bradshaw' bright red; × 'Fire Opal' orange-red; × 'Lady Stratheden' golden yellow. Prop by div, seed. *Ht, Spd:* 2 ft; *Fl:* 5–6; *Z:* 5

G. chiloense × 'Mrs Bradshaw'

Gypsophila

G. paniculata Baby's breath: Eur, Siberia. A tangle of pale green stems and a froth of white ¾ in fls. 'Bristol Fairy' has double fls; 'Rosy Veil' (18 in) pale pink; likes lime. *Ht:* 3 ft; *Spd:* 4 ft; *Fl:* 6–8; *Z:* 3

Ginger lily

H. densiflorum: Him. Rhizomatous plant with aspidistra-like soft green lvs clasping the stems. Fls orange-red *c.* 2 in wide in a broad terminal spike. Easy to grow, harder to find. Prop by div, seed. *Ht:* 3 ft; *Spd:* 18 in; *Fl:* 5–7; *Z:* 9

H. densiflorum

Helenium

H. autumnale Sneezeweed: Canada, E USA. Valuable spp and cvs for late smr. Single daisy-type fls with pronounced center disc. 'Moerheim Beauty' mahogany; 'The Bishop' rich yellow. *Ht:* 4 ft; *Spd:* 20 in; *Fl:* 7–9; *Z:* 3

Sunflower

H. decapetalus: C USA, Canada. Perennial sunflower with coarse lvs and stiff stems. The selection 'Loddon Gold' has deep yellow semi-double fls 3 in wide. Prop by div. *Ht:* to 5 ft; *Spd:* 2 ft; *Fl:* 8–10; *Z:* 4

Helichrysum

Everlasting flower

H. × 'Sulphur Light' (= × 'Schwefellicht'): gdn origin. Flat heads of sulfur-colored 1½in fls over woolly grey-white lvs. One of the few hardy pers of the genus and well worth growing. *Ht, Spd:* 18 in; *Fl:* 6–8; *Z:* 8

Helictotrichon

Helictotrichon

H. sempervirens (= Avena candida): Eur. Splendid blue-grey grass forming neat clumps with graceful arching fl stems effective over a long period. Prop by seed, div in March. *Ht:* 3 ft; *Spd:* 15 in; *Fl:* 6–9; *Z:* 3

Heliopsis

Heliopsis

H. scabra: N Amer. Lusty coarse-lvd plant. Stiff stems and common yellow daisy-fls 3 in wide. 'Golden Plume' has double fls acceptable to gardening "gentry". Prop by div. *Ht:* 4 ft; *Spd:* 2 ft; *Fl:* 7–9; *Z:* 3

Heliotropium

Heliotrope, Cherry pie

H. peruvianum★: Peru. The common heliotrope has flat heads, 3 in or more wide, of deliciously fragrant violet or mauve fls. 'Marina' is deeper in color. Planted out annually where it is not hardy. Prop by cuttings. *Ht:* to 3 ft; *Spd:* 3 ft; *Fl:* 5–9; *Z:* 10

H. peruvianum

Helleborus

Hellebore

Stands up to the winter and announces spring with long-lasting flowers of incomparable texture and quality. Most are evergreen.

H. corsicus (= argutifolius, lividus corsicus)★: Corsica, Sardinia, Balearics. Has cup-shaped apple-green fls 2 in wide and leathery glaucous lvs. Inclined to sprawl; prop by seed. *Ht:* 2 ft; *Spd:* 3 ft; *Fl:* 4–5; *Z:* 7

H. foetidus★ Stinking hellebore: Eur. Lvs cut into long thin lflts on almost shrubby stems; 1 in fls cup-shaped, green, edged soft maroon. *Ht, Spd:* 20 in; *Fl:* 2–5; *Z:* 6

H. corsicus

H. niger★ Christmas rose: Eur, W Asia. Saucer-shaped sol white fls to 2 in wide on short stems. Ptls often pink on their backs, lvs divided, dark. Protect fls to keep them clean; can fl by Christmas. *Ht:* 1 ft; *Spd:* 18 in; *Fl:* 12–2; *Z:* 5

H. orientalis★ Lenten rose: Greece, Asia Minor. True white-fld sp rare but many excellent hybs with up to 4 fls, each 2½ in wide, on a stem; some fls spotted within. *Ht:* 18 in; *Spd:* 2 ft; *Fl:* 2–4; *Z:* 6

H. orientalis

Day lily

Each day lily lasts only a day but the supply is endless in all colors from lemon to mahogany over brilliantly green leaves.

H. flava★ Lemon lily: China. Smaller than *H. fulva* with sweet-scented pale yellow lily-fls and narrow lvs. Fls early. Spreads by runners but not invasive; prop by div. *Ht, Spd:* 2 ft; *Fl:* 5–7; *Z:* 4

H. fulva 'Kwanso Flore Pleno' Double day lily: Japan. Clumps of smooth bulb-like strap-shaped lvs with green stems each bearing sev burnt orange funnel-shaped semi-double fls 4 in across; indiv fls last only 1 day. Rts a mass of small rhizomes. Prop by div. *Ht:* to 4 ft; *Spd:* 3 ft; *Fl:* 6–8; *Z:* 3

H. gdn hybs★: gdn origin. The existence of the Hemerocallis Society indicates the no of hybs. Mainly to 4 ft × 3 ft but sev dwarf cvs. Fls in all shades of yellow and orange, also pink, maroon and greenish yellow. *Fl:* 6–8; *Z:* 3

H. fulva 'Kwanso Flore Pleno'

H. flava

Hesperis

H. matronalis Sweet rocket: S Eur–Siberia. Sweetly frag short-lived per; enjoys lime. Narrow 4 in lvs and small white, mauve or purple fls in loose 18 in clusters. Some doubles. *Ht:* 3 ft; *Spd:* 18 in; *Fl:* 6–7; *Z:* 3

Coral flower

Clumps of strong low leaves are the base for airy spikes of bell flowers of various sizes and many colors.

H. × brizoides: gdn origin. Matted clumps of heart-shaped mottled dark green lvs are the foil for dainty stems liberally adorned with little bell-shaped fls brilliantly colored in shades of pink and red, e.g. 'Coral Plume' coral-red. Prop by div. *Ht:* 2 ft; *Spd:* 1 ft; *Fl:* 6–10; *Z:* 5

H. cylindrica 'Greenfinch': N Amer. Cv interesting to flower arrangers. Lvs roughly heart-shaped, dull green; fl stems stiff and erect bearing 1 ft spikes of greenish fls. Prop by division. *Ht:* 3 ft; *Spd:* 15 in; *Fl:* 6–10; *Z:* 5

H. sanguinea Coral bells: SW USA, Mexico. Lvs more mottled than *H. × brizoides* and fl spikes shorter, otherwise sim. Good hybs inc × 'Shere Variety' bright scarlet; × 'Pearl Drops' pearly white. Prop by div after flowering. *Ht:* 18 in; *Spd:* 1 ft; *Fl:* 6; *Z:* 5

H. sanguinea × 'Sunset'

H. sanguinea 'Red Spangles'

Hibiscus

H. moscheutos Swamp mallow: E USA. Hry-stemmed with soft, toothed lvs hry on the underside. Fls to 11 in across, rose-pink, hollyhock-like with a satin sheen. Hybs range through pink to crimson in color. Prop from seed. *Ht:* 3 ft; *Spd:* 2 ft+; *Fl:* 6–8; *Z:* 5

Hosta (= Funkia)

Plantain lily

H. fortunei 'Aureomarginata'

H. fortunei 'Albopicta'

H. fortunei*: Japan. Grey-green lvs and pale lilac 1½ in fls. Good cvs inc 'Albopicta' lvs yellow, green edges, fls lavender; 'Marginata-Alba' lvs green, broad white margins, fls lavender. Prop by div, seed. *Ht:* 20 in; *Spd:* 2 ft; *Fl:* 7–8; *Z:* 5

H. plantaginea: China. One of the few good in full sun. Lvs shiny, lettuce green; white fls sweetly frag. 'Grandiflora'* has narrower lvs, larger fls and rarely sets seed. *Ht,* *Spd:* 2 ft; *Fl:* 8–9; *Z:* 5

H. sieboldiana (= glauca)*: Japan. V large-lvd sp also good in sun. Glaucous lvs to 1 ft wide; fls a faded lavender. Good buff aut col. *Ht:* 30 in; *Spd:* 2 ft; *Fl:* 7–8; *Z:* 5

H. 'Thomas Hogg'*: gdn origin. One of the best cvs: dark green lvs with narrow white edges, fls lilac (unlike *H. crispula* with undulating lvs and white fls in July–Aug). Prop by div. *Ht, Spd:* 18 in; *Fl:* 6–7; *Z:* 5

Incarvillea

Incarvillea

I. delavayi

I. delavayi: W China, Tibet. Lvs deep shining green divided into several lfts. Fls to 3 in, wide-mouthed trumpets of bright rose-red, several on a stem. *I. mairei* 'Bees Ruby' is pale pink and only 7 in tall. Prop by div or seed. *Ht:* 18 in; *Spd:* 1 ft; *Fl:* 5–6; *Z:* 6

Inula

Inula

I. ensifolia

I. ensifolia: Caucasus. Dwarf daisy-flowered front-of-the-border plant. Narrow lvs, yellow 2 in fls, 1 or more per stem. Prop by seed, div. *Ht, Spd:* 1 ft; *Fl:* 8; *Z:* 3

I. magnifica*: Caucasus. Straggling great lfy plant. Stout chocolate-colored hry stems and flat heads of golden yellow fls. Taller and coarser than *I. helenium* (Elecampane). Prop by div, seed. *Ht:* to 6 ft; *Spd:* 3 ft; *Fl:* 6–8; *Z:* 3

Iris

Very consistent in design, irises are most diverse in life style, between them flowering all year in conditions from dust to mud.

I. Bearded German iris: gdn origin. Typical border irises. Lvs glaucous, sword-shaped, stems branched, may bear sev large fls each with 3 inner incurved ptls (standards) and 3 larger reflexed ptls (falls). Fleshy rhizomes must not be buried. Select from huge var of cols and combinations. Prop by div. *Ht:* 3 ft; *Spd:* 10 in; *Fl:* 6; *Z:* 3

I. foetidissima Gladwyn iris: Eur. Evergreen lvs arching, fls inconspicuous but pods bear bright orange seeds. Giant, white varieg and yellow/mauve 'Citrina' forms grown. *Ht, Spd:* 2 ft; *Fl:* 5–6; *Z:* 7

I. germanica German iris: Eur. Has glaucous lvs and frag purple fls to 5 in wide in gdn form. Sev brown cvs inc 'Brazilia'. Needs lime. *Ht:* to 3 ft; *Spd:* 10 in; *Fl:* 5–6; *Z:* 3

I. germanica 'Brazilia'

I. unguicularis (= stylosa)★ Winter-flowering iris: Algeria, Med. Bright blue fls to 3 in wide nestle among a dense clump of thin green lvs in mild periods in wtr. Selected forms cherished. Prop by div. *Ht:* 1 ft; *Spd:* 2 ft; *Fl:* 11–3; *Z:* 7

I. unguicularis

Kirengeshoma

K. palmata★*:* Japan. Late-flowering Japanese woodlander enjoying moist soil. Lvs opposite, strikingly vine-like on arching stems. Long, waxy creamy-yellow buds open to shuttlecock-shaped fls up to 1½ in across. Prop by div or seed. *Ht:* 3 ft; *Spd:* 2 ft; *Fl:* 9–10; *Z:* 6

Red hot poker, Tritoma

South African plants not guaranteed hardy. They make the most telling exclamation marks in a brimming late summer garden.

K. caulescens★*:* S Africa. Distinct sp. Lvs in rosettes, evergreen, succ, sword-shaped. Fl spikes to 1 ft, opening soft rose-red, turning pale greenish-yellow. Prop by div or offsets. *Ht:* to 5 ft; *Spd:* 3 ft; *Fl:* 7–10; *Z:* 7

K. dwarf hybs: gdn origin. Many unusual cols inc 'Maid of Orleans'★ ivory; 'Jenny Bloom' salmon-peach; 'Dainty Maid' cream and white. Dwarf sp *K. galpinii* has orange fls. *Ht:* 30 in; *Spd:* 2 ft; *Fl:* 7–9; *Z:* 5

K. tall hybs: gdn origin. Sev tall hybs stand out splendidly. 'Bees Lemon' is pale yellow; 'Royal Standard' lemon and scarlet; 'Samuel's Sensation' coral red. *Ht:* 4 ft; *Spd:* 30 in; *Fl:* 7–9; *Z:* 5

K. tall hybrid 'Royal Standard'

Lamium

Deadnettle

L. maculatum Dwarf deadnettle: Eur, N Africa, W Asia. Neat ground-covering plant with small nettle-like opposite evergreen lvs each with central white stripe. Fls tubular, 2-lipped, usually purple and *c*. 1 in long. 'Album' white and 'Roseum' pink are good, so are 'Beacon Silver' silvery-white lvs and 'Aureum' golden-yellow but may scorch in sun. Prop by div. *Ht, Spd:* 1 ft; *Fl:* 5–7; *Z:* 3

L. maculatum

Lamiastrum

Lamiastrum, Archangel

L. luteum 'Variegatum' (= Lamium galeobdolon, Galeobdolon luteum): Eur. Vig deadnettle spreading widely by stolons. Silver variegated lvs and clustered light yellow fls in axils. *Ht:* to 18 in; *Spd:* 5 ft; *Fl:* 5–7; *Z:* 3

Lathyrus

Sweet pea

L. (= Orobus) vernus: Eur. Forms a shining clump of vetch or pea-like lfy stems with $\frac{1}{2}$ in purple and blue fls. There are also white and pink-flowered forms. Prop by div or seed. *Ht, Spd:* 1 ft; *Fl:* 5–6; *Z:* 6

L. vernus

Leonitis

Lion's tail

L. leonurus: S Africa. Technically a shrub but cut down annually in most countries and thus included as an herbaceous per. Lvs narrow, sage green, hry. Fls tubular in lf axils, bright orange. Prop by cuttings. *Ht:* to 7$\frac{1}{2}$ ft; *Spd:* 30 in; *Fl:* 10–12; *Z:* 10

L. leonorus

Liatris

Gayfeather

L. spicata Spiked gayfeather: USA. Grassy-lvd, clump forming, producing stout 1 ft spikes of feathery purple fls. *Ht:* 2 ft; *Spd:* 1 ft; *Fl:* 9; *Z:* 3

Libertia

Libertia

L. formosa: Chile. Narrow grassy lvs and thin stems bearing small pure white saucer-fls in dense clusters. Prop by div or seed. *Ht:* 30 in; *Spd:* 2 ft; *Fl:* 5; *Z:* 8

Ligularia

L. (= Senecio) przewalskii: N China. Striking chocolate-stemmed plant with deeply lobed lvs and terminal 2 ft spikes of little yellow fls. 'The Rocket' is a robust form worth growing. Prop by div. *Ht:* 5 ft; *Spd:* 30 in; *Fl:* 7–9; *Z:* 6

L. przewalskii

Limonium

Sea lavender, Statice

L. latifolium: Bulgaria, S USSR. Has rosettes of wide green leathery lvs and wiry stems carrying a froth of papery lavender-blue fls in groups to 9 in long. 'Blue Cloud' is especially good. Dries well. Prop by div, root cuttings. *Ht:* 18 in; *Spd:* 2 ft; *Fl:* 5–7; *Z:* 5

L. latifolium 'Blue Cloud'

Linum

Flax

L. narbonnense: S Eur. An erect sp with fine glaucous lvs and glorious shining blue funnel-shaped fls 1 in wide produced for many weeks. Sev named sorts available. Needs frequent renewing by cuttings or seed. *Ht, Spd:* 18 in; *Fl:* 6–9; *Z:* 5
L. perenne: Eur. Fls a paler blue and lvs equally fine but greener. Pink and white flowered sorts known, also 'Tetra Red'. *Ht:* to 18 in; *Spd:* 1 ft; *Fl:* 6–8; *Z:* 5

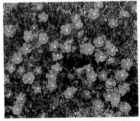

L. narbonnense

Liriope

Lily turf

L. (= Ophiopogon) muscari Blue lily turf: E Asia. Dark green grassy lvs in dense clumps sometimes used for edging. Fls tiny, rich violet-blue bells crowded on 4 in spikes. Named sorts, also white-flowered and yellow-variegated forms are available. Prop by div. *Ht:* 1 ft; *Spd:* 15 in; *Fl:* 9–11; *Z:* 6

L. muscari

Lunaria

Honesty

L. rediviva* Perennial honesty: Eur. Perennial form of the biennial honesty with sim big basal lvs and paler lavender fls. Produces attractive flat, papery seed pods after flowering. *Ht:* 30 in; *Spd:* 2 ft; *Fl:* 4–6; *Z:* 5

Lupinus

Lupine

L. hybrid Russell lupines

L. garden hybrids: gdn origin. Best known are the Russell lupines developed from sev spp using *L. polyphyllus* from N Amer as the dominant parent. Prefer a not too rich acid or neutral soil. Fl range includes all cols except green, including bicolors. Lvs are silky, round, divided or pleated. Prop by seed, basal cuttings. *Ht:* to 4 ft; *Spd:* 30 in; *Fl:* 5–6; *Z:* 3

Lychnis

Campion, Catchfly

L. chalcedonica

L. flos-jovis

L. chalcedonica: E USSR. Tall hry plant with small more or less oval lvs and brilliant orange-red fls in roughly cross-shaped heads 4 in long. Prop by div, seed. *Ht:* to 3 ft; *Spd:* 18 in; *Fl:* 6–8; *Z:* 2

L. coronaria (= tomentosa, Agrostemma coronaria) Rose campion: Eur. Ever-grey woolly-stemmed plant with grey-white basal lvs and single bright cerise or white fls 1½ in across. Seeds itself freely. *Ht:* 30 in; *Spd:* 20 in; *Fl:* 7–8; *Z:* 4

L. flos-jovis Flower of Jove: C Alps. Whiter than above and just as woolly. Fls are purple, white or scarlet and ½ in wide. 'Hort's Variety' is shorter and has pink fls. Prop by seed. *Ht:* to 2 ft; *Spd:* 1 ft; *Fl:* 6–7; *Z:* 5

Lysimachia

Loosestrife

Upright spikes of yellow or white: primula relations not to be confused with the purple loosestrife (*Lythrum*).

L. clethroides

L. clethroides: China, Japan. The white fls are buddleia-like, arched over and turned up at the tips. Lvs undistinguished but col well in aut. Inclined to run; prop by div. *Ht:* to 3 ft; *Spd:* 2 ft; *Fl:* 7–9; *Z:* 5

L. punctata: Asia Minor. Uprt plant with green pointed oval lvs and whorls of yellow star-like fls in 8 in spikes. Can be invasive. Prop by div or seed. *Ht:* to 3 ft; *Spd:* 2 ft; *Fl:* 6–8; *Z:* 4

Loosestrife

L. salicaria Purple loosestrife: N temp zones, Aust. Bushy; lvs narrow on slim stems. Long spikes of red/purple fls effective for weeks. 'Robert' rose-carmine a good cv. *Ht:* 3 ft; *Spd:* 20 in; *Fl:* 6–9; *Z:* 3
L. virgatum: Asia Minor. Smaller and less vig; fls purple. 'The Rocket' is rose-pink; 'Firecandle' rosy red. *Ht:* 2 ft; *Spd:* 15 in; *Fl:* 7–9; *Z:* 4

L. virgatum

Plume poppy

M. cordata★: China, Japan. Invasive architectural plant with magnificent lobed glaucous lvs, milky white beneath with bright orange sap in their veins. Terminal plumes of off-white tubular fls. Prop by div. *Ht:* to 8 ft; *Spd:* 30 in; *Fl:* 8–9; *Z:* 3
M. microcarpa (= Bocconia cordata): China. Tall plumes of pinky-buff fls. 'Coral Plume' is deeper in col. *Ht:* 8 ft; *Spd:* 3 ft; *Fl:* 7–9; *Z:* 6

M. microcarpa

Mallow

M. alcea: Eur. Bushy sp with bright green lobed downy lvs and purplish-rose shuttlecock fls to 2 in wide. 'Fastigiata' is more uprt with reddish fls. *Ht:* to 4 ft; *Spd:* 30 in; *Fl:* 7–10; *Z:* 5
M. moschata Musk mallow: Eur. Finely dissected dark green lvs and long-lasting pink fls 2 in wide. 'Alba' is white. *Ht:* to 30 in; *Spd:* 20 in; *Fl:* 5–10; *Z:* 4

M. moschata

Meconopsis

The genus of the fabulous Himalayan blue poppy has members of many colors—all outstandingly beautiful in flower and leaf.

M. grandis★: Nepal, Tibet, Sikkim. Easier and longer lived than *M. betonicifolia* (Himalayan blue poppy). Lvs oblong, toothed, slightly bristly in a handsome clump. Fls to 5 in wide, nodding, purple-blue, poppy-shaped. Prop by seed. *Ht:* 3 ft; *Spd:* 2 ft; *Fl:* 5–6; *Z:* 3
M. regia: Nepal. Tall yellow-flowered and usually bi. Lvs hry, silvery or golden, fls sev on a branching stem. Prop by seed. *Ht:* to 5 ft; *Spd:* 6 ft; *Fl:* 6–7; *Z:* 3

M. grandis

Melissa

Balm

M. officinalis Lemon balm: Eur. Deadnettle-like softly hry lvs strongly lemon-scented when crushed. Fls small, white. 'Aurea' has lvs splashed with butter-yellow variegation. *Ht:* 2 ft; *Spd:* 20 in; *Fl:* 6–10; *Z:* 3

Mertensia

Mertensia

M. virginica

M. virginica Virginia bluebell: Virginia. Purple/blue tubular 1 in fls in drooping heads over smooth blue-grey spatula-shaped lvs in spring. Needs moisture and cool conditions. Prop by div, seed. *Ht:* 18 in; *Spd:* 1 ft; *Fl:* 5–6; *Z:* 5

Mimulus

Monkey flower

Vivid yellow, orange and red snapdragon-like flowers in profusion, commonly associated with bog gardens.

M. aurantiacus

***M. aurantiacus* (= *Diplacus glutinosus*):** Cal. Shrubby; lvs sticky, fls bright orange funnel-shaped. Prop by cuttings, seed. *Ht:* to 5 ft; *Spd:* 20 in; *Fl:* 6–10; *Z:* 5
M. cardinalis: Oregon–Mexico. Colorful, uprt plant with typical snapdragon or "monkey" fls in red or red and yellow. Lvs downy and tacky. 'Rose Queen' has pink fls. *Ht:* to 3 ft; *Spd:* 2 ft; *Fl:* 6–9; *Z:* 5

Mirabilis

Mirabilis

M. jalapa Marvel of Peru, Four o'clock: Trop Amer. Has composite lvs and heads of tubular frag fls 1½ in wide opening in afternoon. Fls white, pink or crimson, may be striped or blotched. *Ht, Spd:* 2 ft; *Fl:* 6–9; *Z:* 10

Miscanthus

Miscanthus

M. sinensis 'Variegatus'

***M. sacchariflorus**:** Asia, Siberia. Giant grey-green-leaved grass forming bamboo-like clumps. Fls terminal, feathery, brownish. Dies to pale buff; stands up well in wtr. *Ht:* 8 ft; *Spd:* 3 ft; *Fl:* 8–9; *Z:* 4
***M. sinensis* (= *Eulalia japonica*):** China, Japan. Clump-forming with terminal plumes of silver-white pink-tinged fls. Lvs glaucous. 'Variegatus'* has white-striped lvs; 'Zebrinus'* wider lvs, horizontal yellow bands; 'Gracillimus' thin green lvs. *Ht:* to 5 ft; *Spd:* 30 in; *Fl:* 8–9; *Z:* 4

Moor grass

M. caerulea Purple moor grass: Eur, Asia Minor, N Asia. The sp is a dainty clump-forming grass found on wet soils. 'Variegata'*★ is valued for its yellowish-white striped lvs. Fls bluish. *Ht:* 15 in; *Spd:* 10 in; *Fl:* 7–9; *Z:* 6

M. caerulea

Bergamot

M. didyma★ Oswego tea, Bee balm: N Amer. Paired lvs and hooded nettle-like scarlet fls in whorls. 'Cambridge Scarlet' a brighter shade and 'Croftway Pink' rose-pink good cvs. Also grown as a herb. *Ht:* 3 ft; *Spd:* 18 in; *Fl:* 6–9; *Z:* 3
M. fistulosa★: Virginia. Similar to above. Sp has purple fls; 'Prairie Night' is deeper in col. Prefers dry soil. Prop by div. *Ht:* to 5 ft; *Spd:* 20 in; *Fl:* 6–8; *Z:* 4

M. didyma

Morina

M. longifolia★ Whorl flower: Nepal. Thistle-like in growth. Shining spiny lvs in whorls. Long-lasting 1 in fls are tubular, initially white, becoming pink then crimson. Prop by div or seed. *Ht:* to 3 ft; *Spd:* 1 ft; *Fl:* 6–8; *Z:* 5

M. longifolia

Catmint

Colored like lavender and prefers the same sunny well-drained position. Ideal ground cover for old pink and red roses.

N. × faasenii (= mussinii)★: gdn origin. Common sage-green-leaved aromatic; lavender-blue fls in whorls all smr. Excellent edging, carpeting. Prop by div, cuttings. *Ht, Spd:* 18 in; *Fl:* 5–9; *Z:* 4
N. × gigantea: gdn origin. Hyb with lavender-blue fls. Like the blue-fld 'Souvenir d'André Chaudron' nearly twice above in height. *Spd:* 2 ft; *Fl:* 6–9; *Z:* 4

N. × faasenii

Nicotiana

Tobacco plant

N. sylvestris: Argentina. Robust heads of narrow pendulous sweetly frag white 3½ in fls, best in late evening. Can last 2 or 3 years in a warm dry place. Prop by seed. *Ht:* 4 ft; *Spd:* 2 ft; *Fl:* 8–9; *Z:* 8

Oenothera

Evening primrose

O. missouriensis (= macrocarpa)*: SC USA. Sprawling; narrow dark lvs and wide open funnel-shaped lemon fls to 4 in wide. Prop by seed. *Ht:* 10 in; *Spd:* 2 ft; *Fl:* 6–8; *Z:* 4
O. tetragona (= fruticosa): E N Amer. Dark basal lvs in rosettes; reddish slim stems and buds. Fls bright yellow, 1½ in wide. 'Fireworks' has bronze-red lvs. *Ht:* 18 in; *Spd:* 9 in; *Fl:* 6–8; *Z:* 4

O. missouriensis

Omphalodes

Navelwort

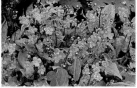

O. cappadocica (= cornifolia): Lazistan, Cappadocia. Creeping plant with long-stalked, heart-shaped pointed lvs and taller loose sprays of pale blue 5-petaled flowers each ¾ in wide. Prop by div of rhizomatous rts. *Ht:* 9 in; *Spd:* 15 in; *Fl:* 5–7; *Z:* 6

O. cappadocica

Onopordon

Onopordon

O. acanthium* Common cotton thistle, Scotch thistle: Eur, Siberia. Huge, sculptural branched white-woolly plant with fierce prickles. Large fls 2 in across are soft purple and thistle-shaped. Prop by seed. *Ht:* to 7 ft; *Spd:* 3 ft; *Fl:* 7; *Z:* 6

O. acanthium

Osteospermum (= Dimorphotheca)

Cape marigold, African daisy

O. ecklonis: S Africa. Evergreen with shiny lvs and daisy fls 3 in wide on tall slim stems. Fls gleaming white with blue eye and silvery reverse to ptls. Prop by cuttings. *Ht, Spd:* 2 ft; *Fl:* 6–10; *Z:* 8
O. juncundum: S Africa. Paler lvs and smaller fls usually pale pink but sometimes white. Prop by cuttings. *Ht:* 15 in; *Spd:* 18 in; *Fl:* 6–10; *Z:* 8

O. ecklonis

Oxalis

O. lasiandra (= floribunda) Pink shamrock: Mexico. Blue-green lvs and bright pink fls ¾ in wide, which open in sunshine. Consider before cultivating; once established cannot be eradicated. *Ht, Spd: 9 in; Fl: 6–10; Z: 9*

Peony

The aristocrats of the buttercup family with some of the most sumptuous flowers of spring and early summer. They are not hard to grow but like to be left undisturbed. Double forms last longest in bloom.

P. arietina: S Eur, Asia Minor. A less common sp with grey-green lvs and 5 in fls. Try 'Mother of Pearl' dusky pink and 'Northern Glory' a deeper pink. *Ht: 2 ft; Spd: 2 ft; Fl: 5; Z: 3*

P. lactiflora★ Chinese peony: Siberia, Mongolia. V beautiful with shining lvs and red-tinged stems. Single white frag fls 4 in wide. *Ht: 30 in; Spd: 2 ft; Fl: 6; Z: 3*

P. officinalis★: S Eur. Common deep red single sp of old gdns. 'Rubra Pleno' double red, and double pink and white forms good. *Ht, Spd: 28 in; Fl: 5; Z: 3*

P. gdn hybs★: Robust plants spectacular in fl. Rec are 'Albert Crousse' double, pink, frag; 'The Moor' single, deep crimson; 'Lemon Queen' anemone-flowered, white, yellow center. *Ht: 30 in; Spd: 2 ft; Fl: 6; Z: 3*

P. 'Saunders Hybs'★: Range created by Dr A. P. Saunders in the USA. Some, e.g. 'Chalice' single, white; 'Constance Spry' rich rosy-red, are v elegant with 4 in fls and fine lvs. *Ht: 22 in; Spd: 2 ft; Fl: 6; Z: 3*

P. wittmanniana: NW Caucasus. An excellent taller sp. Lvs vig, puckered and shining, fls 5 in wide, single and light yellowish-green. 'Avant Garde' has soft warm pink fls. *P. mlokosewitschii* equally good with lemon-yellow fls. *Ht: 3 ft; Spd: 2 ft; Fl: 4–5; Z: 3*

P. hybrid 'Chief Justice'

P. mlokosewitschii

P. officinalis 'Rosea-plena'

Poppy

P. orientale★ Oriental poppy: Armenia. Tall hairy-leaved per; dies away in mid- to late summer. Huge single or double brilliantly colored fls 4 in or more across are borne on hry stems to 3 ft high. Spp fiery orange; select cvs inc 'Perry's White' single, white, maroon blotch; 'Stormtorch' single, intense bright red; 'Salmon Glow' double, orange-salmon. Prop by div. *Ht: to 3 ft; Spd: 2 ft; Fl: 5–6; Z: 3*

P. orientale

Pennisetum

P. alopecuroides*: E Asia, E Aust. A soft grass with fluffy spikes of fl to 8 in long which give a purplish-grey effect over grey-white lvs. Prop by seed. *Ht:* 30 in; *Spd:* 2 ft; *Fl:* 8–10; *Z:* 4

Penstemon

Penstemon

An American genus with bright, tubular foxglove-like flowers. On the borderline of hardiness (and in many cases shrubbiness).

P. campanulatus

P. × gloxinioides

P. campanulatus: C Amer. Narrow-leaved bushy sp with pink to deep purple bell-shaped fls 1 in long. 'Garnet', an old cv, fls until first frosts, glowing wine red and virtually evergreen. *Ht:* 20 in; *Spd:* 20 in; *Fl:* 6–7; *Z:* 6

P. gentianoides: C Amer. Softly hry uprt plant; sturdy spikes of 1 in mauve-pink fls. Prop by cuttings. *Ht:* 3 ft; *Spd:* 2 ft; *Fl:* 5–6; *Z:* 6

P. × gloxinioides: gdn origin. A makeshift name covering a race of tender large-flowered hybs best planted out annually except in warm areas. Wide lvs with open trumpet-shaped fls 1½ in long in rich cols. *Ht:* 2 ft; *Spd:* 18 in; *Fl:* 6–10; *Z:* 6

Perovskia

Perovskia

P. atriplicifolia

P. abrotanoides: Afghanistan–Tibet. Uprt semi-shrubby plant best hard pruned in March. Slightly hry whitish branching stems, small dissected grey-green lvs and violet-blue fls in 1 ft spikes. 'Blue Haze'* and 'Blue Spire' are good. *Ht:* 4 ft; *Spd:* 2 ft; *Fl:* 8–9; *Z:* 4

P. atriplicifolia Russian sage: Afghanistan–Tibet. Has sub-shrubby, tapering, white downy stems and fls more violet than blue. Smaller grey-green lvs are coarsely toothed and the whole plant aromatic. Prop by cuttings as *P. abrotanoides*. *Ht:* 2 ft; *Spd:* 4 ft; *Fl:* 8–9; *Z:* 4

Phalaris

Phalaris

P. arundinacea 'Picta' Gardener's garters, Ribbon grass: Temp N Hem. Vigorous, vivid creeping grass with lvs striped green and white lengthwise. Good in half shade but invasive. *Ht:* 2 ft; *Spd:* 4 ft; *Fl:* 6–7; *Z:* 3

Phlomis

P. russelliana (= samia, viscosa)★: Syria. Striking, useful with coarse broad basal lvs and 1½ in fls in whorls up the stems. Fls dry to buff and stay until winter. Prop by seed, div. *Ht:* 3 ft; *Spd:* 2 ft; *Fl:* 6–7; *Z:* 6

Phlox

Phlox

North American meadow-flowers much bred for garden use. Almost essential for color and scent in mid- or late summer. They like fertile soil and need moisture.

P. maculata★: E N Amer. Less frequently planted than the summer or gdn phloxes but an especially good plant with lvs pointed in pairs up red-spotted stems and light purple fls *c.* 1 in wide. The cv 'Alpha' is mauve-pink and fragrant. Prop by div, rt cuttings. *Ht:* to 3 ft; *Spd:* 18 in; *Fl:* 7–8; *Z:* 4

P. paniculata 'Brigadier'

P. paniculata (= decussata)★ Summer phlox, Garden phlox: E N Amer. The summer phloxes are a range of cvs of the sp ranging in col from white through all shades of pink to red and purple and including orange and mauve to blue sorts. Swooningly scented fl heads of many round 1 in fls often have a deep or contrasting eye. 'Dresden China' is shell pink with a deeper eye, 'Vintage Wine' a rich claret col. Prop by div, basal or rt cuttings. *Ht:* to 3 ft; *Spd:* 2 ft; *Fl:* 7–9; *Z:* 4

P. paniculata 'Rheinlander'

Phormium

Phormium

Essentially shrubby in effect with upright evergreen sword-shaped leaves forming substantial clumps in time.

P. cookianum★: NZ. Like a large evergreen iris in habit with green lvs and striking stems of buff-colored 2 in fls succeeded by twisted seed pods. There are also variegated and tricolored-leaved forms. *Ht:* 4 ft; *Spd:* 18 in; *Fl:* 7–8; *Z:* 9

P. tenax New Zealand flax lily: NZ. Similar to *P. cookianum* but much bigger, reaching 9 ft × 4 ft. Lvs are a metallic grey-green, fl stems tall and tough bearing warm red 2 in fls followed by shining black seed pods. Worthwhile cvs inc 'Purpureum'★ lvs bronze-purple; 'Variegatum' lvs yellowish-white striped and new cvs from NZ: 'Sundowner' lvs grey, green and light red striped; 'Dazzler' lvs yellow and green. Prop sp from seed, cvs by div. *Fl:* 7–9; *Z:* 9

P. tenax

Phygelius

P. capensis★ Cape figwort: S Africa. Loosely bushy, sometimes shrubby plant with oval deep green lvs and fascinating terminal heads of several pendulous horn-shaped orange-red fls 1½ in long. Will thrive in shade in a warm climate. Prop by seed, cuttings. *Ht, Spd:* 3 ft; *Fl:* 8; *Z:* 7

P. capensis

Physalis

P. franchetii Chinese lantern: Japan. Jagged-leaved running per with uninteresting small white fls but seeds enclosed in large bright orange lantern-shaped inflated structures to 2½ in long which are highly ornamental. Prop by seed, div. *Ht:* 2 ft; *Spd:* 3 ft; *Fl:* 7; *Z:* 4

P. franchetii

Physostegia

P. virginiana The Obedient plant: E USA. Uprt; lvs narrow. Fls pink tubes in terminal 5 in spikes, staying put when touched, hence common name. 'Speciosa' is rose-pink. *Ht:* 3 ft; *Spd:* 18 in; *Fl:* 8–9; *Z:* 3

Phytolacca

P. americana Poke weed, Red ink plant: Florida. Coarse oval-lvd plant with substantial purplish branching stems and terminal 4 in shrubby spikes of white fls. Juicy, deep purple berries and rts poisonous but early spr stks cooked and eaten like asparagus. Self-seeds freely. *Ht:* 9 ft; *Spd:* 3 ft; *Fl:* 6–10; *Z:* 3

P. americana

Balloon flower, Chinese bellflower

P. grandiflorus★: China, Manchuria, Japan. Like a small campanula of notably trim and pleasing design. Fl buds the shape of hot air balloons open into 5-lobed bells *c.* 1½ in wide. Named forms, e.g. 'Mother of Pearl' can be white, blue or pink. The lvs turn yellow in autumn. Prop by div, seed. *Ht:* to 2 ft; *Spd:* 1 ft; *Fl:* 8–9; *Z:* 4

P. grandiflorus

Podophyllum

P. peltatum May apple, Lady's parasol. N Amer. Much prized. Has 1 large round lf with 1 water lily-like 1½ in fl. Plum-shaped fr edible, lvs and rts poisonous. Prop by seed. *Ht:* 15 in; *Spd:* 1 ft; *Fl:* 5–6; *Z:* 3

Polemonium

P. caeruleum Jacob's ladder, Greek valerian: N Hem. Branching slender stems, bright green divided lvs and blue, bell-shaped ½ in fls freely borne. Also a white form. *Ht:* 2 ft; *Spd:* 18 in; *Fl:* 6–7; *Z:* 3
***P. foliosissimum*:** W N Amer. Larger all over; a better choice with rich blue or lavender fls. *Ht:* 30 in; *Spd:* 18 in; *Fl:* 6–8; *Z:* 4

P. caeruleum

Solomon's seal, Lady's seal

***P. multiflorum of gdns (= P. × hybridus)*:** Eur, N Asia. Graceful arching stems with wing-like horizontal lvs to 5 in long. Fls are greenish-white bells each 1 in long in clusters dangling from the lf axils followed by black berries. Variegated and double-flowered forms also available. Prop by div. *Ht:* 30 in; *Spd:* 1 ft; *Fl:* 6; *Z:* 4

P. multiflorum

Knotweed

A genus with valuable long and late-flowering members but also some dangerously invasive and weedy ones.

P. affine: Nepal. Mat-forming sp with narrow rich evergreen lvs that col well in aut. Fls red massed in sturdy spikes 6 in long. 'Darjeeling Red' and 'Lowndes's Variety' are recommended. Prop by div. *Ht:* 10 in; *Spd:* 1 ft; *Fl:* 8–10; *Z:* 4
P. amplexicaule: Him.. Vigorous, with long heart-shaped lvs and thin stems bearing narrow 6 in spikes of pink or red fls. 'Atrosanguineum'* is crimson. Prop by div. *Ht:* 3 ft; *Spd:* 3 ft; *Fl:* 7–10; *Z:* 6
P. campanulatum: Him. Pretty non-invasive knotweed with pale pink fls in bunches 3 in wide. Lvs are elliptic, pale green and deeply veined. Prop by div. *Ht:* to 3 ft; *Spd:* 30 in; *Fl:* 7–10; *Z:* 6

P. affine

P. amplexicaule

Cinquefoil

P. gdn hybs*: gdn origin. Loud, cheerful mid-smr fls derived from sev more discreet spp. Lvs strawberry-like, fls to 1½ in wide. Good ones include 'Gibson's Scarlet' single, bright scarlet, 1 ft; 'Glory of Nancy' orange-crimson, semi-double, 18 in; 'William Rollison' orange, flame and yellow, 15 in. Prop by div. *Spd:* 1 ft; *Fl:* 6–9; *Z:* 2

P. gdn hybrid 'Gibson's Scarlet'

Primula

Primula, primrose

The primrose genus, with 500 species, embraces alpines, meadow-flowers and bog plants, all spring flowering and of almost childish charm. All like peaty soil: some drained, some wet, and all are perennials growing rapidly from seed but sometimes short lived. They have a tendency to "mealiness", a floury coating that adds to their crisp, laundered look.

P. denticulata

P. denticulata Drumstick primula, Himalayan primrose: Him. V early, often starting into fl before lvs. Globular fl heads to 3 in wide are composed of masses of single lilac or pale purple fls each with yellow eye. *Ht, Spd:* 1 ft; *Fl:* 3–5; *Z:* 5
P. florindae*: Tibet. Tall stems of drooping bell-shaped sulfur-yellow frag ¾ in fls in clusters above broad lvs. Ptls powdered with a white farina. Likes wet ground. *Ht, Spd:* 2 ft; *Fl:* 6–7; *Z:* 6
P. japonica*: W Him. A type of "candelabra" primula with red, pink or white ¾ in fls arranged in whorls up the stem. 'Miller's Crimson' and 'Postford White' are reliable old cvs. *Ht:* 20 in; *Spd:* 1 ft; *Fl:* 3–5; *Z:* 4
P. pulverulenta: W Szechwan. Also a candelabra. The ¾ in fls are deep red with a purple eye in whorls up the mealy stems. The lvs are broader at the tip. Likes wet ground. *Ht, Spd:* 1 ft; *Fl:* 6; *Z:* 6
Polyanthus: gdn origin. Hybs between the primrose (*P. acaulis*) and cowslip (*P. veris*). Fls like bigger primroses and sev on a stem. Many cols inc white, crimson, pink, blue, orange and yellow sometimes laced with gold and occasionally double. *Ht, Spd:* 1 ft; *Fl:* 3–4; *Z:* 4

P. florindae

Polyanthus hybrids

Prunella

Self heal

P. grandiflora: Eur. Showy per with divided dark green hry lvs and pink 1 in fls in terminal 3 in spikes. 'Loveliness' is a richer color. Prop by div. *Ht:* 7 in; *Spd:* 1 ft; *Fl:* 7; *Z:* 5

Lungwort, Soldiers and sailors

P. angustifolia Blue cowslip: Eur. V early; lvs bristly, fls funnel-shaped. 'Munstead Blue' is a deeper col. *Ht:* 10 in; *Spd:* 1 ft; *Fl:* 3–4; *Z:* 3

P. rubra: SE Eur. More or less evergreen lvs a lighter shade. V early fls brick red. *Ht:* 1 ft; *Spd:* 15 in; *Fl:* 3–4; *Z:* 3

P. saccharata Bethlehem sage: Eur. Evergreen lvs spotted silvery-pink and grey. Fls pink, becoming blue. *Ht:* 15 in; *Spd:* 2 ft; *Fl:* 3–4; *Z:* 3

P. saccharata

Ranunculus

Buttercup

R. aconitifolius White bachelor's buttons: Eur. Tall, lfy sp with single white ½ in fls. *Ht:* 30 in; *Spd:* 18 in; *Fl:* 5–6; *Z:* 4

R. acris 'Flore-pleno'★ Yellow bachelor's buttons: Eur, N Asia. Well-behaved; double golden yellow fls with dark green wedge-shaped divided lvs. *Ht:* 30 in; *Spd:* 2 ft; *Fl:* 6–8; *Z:* 4

R. ficaria Figwort, lesser celandine: Eur. Gdn forms of this weed worth cultivating esp 'Aurantiaca' with bright orange ½ in fls. *Ht, Spd:* 5 in; *Fl:* 3–5; *Z:* 4

R. acris 'Flore-pleno'

Rheum

Rheum

R. palmatum★: China. Has large green cut or jaggedly-lobed lvs and stout stems of deep red fls in spikes to 3 ft long. The cv 'Atrosanguineum' has the advantage of rich dark red lvs. *Ht, Spd:* 4½ ft; *Fl:* 6–7; *Z:* 3

Romneya

California tree poppy

R. coulteri★: SW Cal. Running plant with blue-green stems and divided lvs the same lovely col. Large white frag poppy fls to 6 in wide with a boss of golden stamens. *R. × hybrida* 'White Cloud' rec. Can be hard to establish. *Ht:* 4 ft; *Spd:* 3 ft; *Fl:* 7–10; *Z:* 7

R. × hybrida

Roscoea

Roscoea

R. cautleoides: China. Glossy green uprt lvs clasp the fl stems each of which bear several clear yellow orchid-like fls to 2 in long. Prop by div of tubers. *Ht:* to 1 ft; *Spd:* 6 in; *Fl:* 6–8; *Z:* 8, LF

Rudbeckia

Coneflower

R. fulgida 'Goldsturm'

R. fulgida var sullivantii 'Goldsturm'* A Black-eyed Susan: E USA. Bristly-lvd with single 2½ in fls like daisies, rich yellow ptls and a central 'eye'. *Ht, Spd:* 2 ft; *Fl:* 7–10; *Z:* 5

R. laciniata 'Golden Glow': N Amer. Double golden yellow cv. *Ht:* 7 ft; *Spd:* 30 in; *Fl:* 7–9; *Z:* 4

R. nitida: N Amer. Tall sp to 4 ft; a central black cone prominently displayed by drooping yellow ptls. 'Herbstonne'* pale yellow, green center is even taller; 'Goldquelle' dwarf. *Spd:* 30 in; *Fl:* 7–10; *Z:* 7

Salvia

Salvia

Hairy aromatic plants, sometimes shrubby, with spikes of hooded deadnettle flowers in almost every color.

S. nemorosa

S. nemorosa (= S. × superba)*: SE Eur. Many-stemmed uprt plant with small sage-green lvs. Fls in 8 in spikes are violet-blue with crimson bracts. 'Superba' reaches 3 ft × 2 ft; deeper-colored 'East Friesland' 18 in × 15 in. *Fl:* 6–9; *Z:* 6

S. przewalskii: China. Big, lfy plant with large heart-shaped basal lvs and hry stems; ½ in fls purplish-violet. *Ht:* 3 ft; *Spd:* 4 ft; *Fl:* 6; *Z:* 7

Sanguisorba

Burnet

S. canadensis

S. canadensis (= Poterium canadense): E N Amer. Strong clump-forming per with eau-de-nil lvs and fluffy 6 in spikes of white fls like bottle brushes. Prop by div, seed. *Ht:* 4 ft; *Spd:* 30 in; *Fl:* 7–8; *Z:* 4

Saponaria

Soapwort, Bouncing Bet

S. officinalis: Eur. Sprawler with small opp lvs and spreading rts (stolons). Fls to 1½ in wide are pink or white in frilly heads; double red, white or pink ones are better plants. *Ht, Spd:* 30 in; *Fl:* 7–9; *Z:* 3

Saxifraga

Saxifrage

S. × umbrosa* London pride, St Patrick's cabbage: Eur. Rosettes of leathery evergreen lvs and slim fl stems to 18 in with myriads of pink starry fls. 'Variegata' has yellow mottled lvs. *Spd:* 1 ft; *Fl:* 5–7; *Z:* 7

Scabious, Pincushion flower

S. caucasica: Caucasus. Long-lived light lavender-blue fls like frilly pincushions on a pale green plant. Lvs on the long stems are divided, at the base lance-shaped. 'Clive Greaves' is a reliable cv; 'Moerheim Beauty' deep blue; 'Miss Willmott' white. Prop by div. *Ht, Spd:* 2 ft; *Fl:* 6–9; *Z:* 5

S. caucasica

Figwort

S. aquatica 'Variegata': GB. Spectacular dark green and white variegated lvs make this plant effective from June–Oct. Fls are inconspicuous russet brown. Basal lvs large, white, stem lvs smaller. *Ht:* 3 ft; *Spd:* 18 in; *Z:* 6

S. aquatica 'Variegata'

Sedum

S. 'Autumn Joy'*: gdn origin. Outstanding late-flowerer; flattish pink 8 in fl heads turn to mahogany. *Ht, Spd:* 2 ft; *Fl:* 9; *Z:* 4
S. maximum 'Atropurpureum': Eur. Maroon lvs and stems with smaller heads of dusky reddish-pink fls. *Ht, Spd:* 18 in; *Fl:* 8–9; *Z:* 4
S. spectabile: China. Forms 7 in domes of pink fls. 'Brilliant' is deep rose-pink; 'Carmen' carmine. *Ht, Spd:* 18 in; *Fl:* 9–10; *Z:* 4

S. spectabile

Sidalcea

S. malviflora False mallow: Cal. Silky 2 in fls and abundant fresh green lvs. Many forms, inc 'Elsie Hough' satin pink, 40 in; 'Rose Queen' rose-pink, 30 in; 'William Smith' salmon, 3 ft. *Spd:* 18 in; *Fl:* 7–8; *Z:* 6

Sisyrinchium

S. striatum: Chile. Like a small iris in habit but with tiny ½ in fls bell-shaped and creamy-yellow with purple dash on back of each ptl. Frs amber berries. Seeds itself. *Ht:* to 2 ft; *Spd:* 10 in; *Fl:* 6; *Z:* 10

Solidago

Golden rod

S. brachystachys 'Goldenmosa': Eur. Fluffy yellow golden rod for the front of the border with fl plume to 8 in long and light green lvs. Prop by division. *Ht:* 30 in; *Spd:* 18 in; *Fl:* 8–9; *Z:* 4

Solidaster

Solidaster

S. hybridus (= × Solidaster luteus, × Asterago luteus): gdn origin. A cross between an aster and a solidago with narrow lvs and flattened heads up to 4 in across composed of numerous small yellow fls which fade to a creamy-yellow. Prop by division. *Ht:* 2 ft; *Spd:* 1 ft; *Fl:* 7–9; *Z:* 5

S. hybridus

Stachys

Stachys

S. macrantha (= Betonica macrantha): Caucasus. Broad, dark ground-covering wrinkled hry lvs; purple fls. 'Robusta' deeper col. *Ht:* 2 ft; *Spd:* 1 ft; *Fl:* 5–7; *Z:* 3
S. olympica★ Lamb's tongue, Lamb's ears: Iran. Tongue-like woolly lvs and whitish stems with ⅓ in fls. 'Silver Carpet' is non-flowering. Good ground cover. *Ht:* 18 in; *Spd:* 1 ft; *Fl:* 7–9; *Z:* 3

S. olympica

Stokesia

Stoke's aster

S. laevis (= cyanea): N Amer. Narrow lvs form a basal rosette; 3 in fls are open chalices of fringed ptls, blue or mauve with white centers. 'Blue Star' is a better shade. Prop by div. *Ht, Spd:* 18 in; *Fl:* 8–9; *Z:* 6

S. laevis

Symphytum

Comfrey

S. caucasicum: Caucasus. Comfreys all have bold hry oval lvs; this one has pale blue tubular 1 in fls rather like borage. *Ht, Spd:* 18 in; *Fl:* 5–6; *Z:* 4

Tellima

Tellima

T. grandiflora★: N–W Amer. Useful evergreen sp with rounded toothed lvs that redden in winter and sprays of 1 in greenish-yellow bell-like fls in April–June. 'Purpurea' has bronze lvs turning purple in winter. Prop by div or seed. *Ht:* 2 ft; *Spd:* 18 in; *Z:* 6

Teucrium

T. chamaedrys* Wall germander: Eur. Creeping dark green sub-shrubby edging plant. Fls are pink-mauve like snapdragons with tiny red and white spots. Prop by div, cuttings. *Ht:* 10 in; *Spd:* 1 ft; *Fl:* 7–9; *Z:* 7

Meadow rue

Most graceful cousins of the buttercups with complex leaves like rue and small flowers airily displayed.

T. delavayii (= dipterocarpum): W China. Exceptionally elegant; slender branching stems, dainty leaflets and fluffy 6 in heads of deep lilac fls with pronounced pale yellow stamens. 'Hewitt's Double' is a rich rosy mauve but less easy. *Ht:* 3 ft; *Spd:* 18 in; *Fl:* 7–8; *Z:* 5

T. speciosissimum*: N Africa, S Eur. Especially valuable for its blue-green lvs effective from May–aut. Fls pale straw yellow in fluffy pyramids to 9 in long. *Ht:* 4 ft; *Spd:* 28 in; *Fl:* 7–8; *Z:* 6

T. speciosissimum

False lupine

T. montana (= fabacea): W N Amer. Almost too easy to grow. Like a slender bright yellow lupine with spikes of fl to 1 ft long. Inclined to run into clumps. Prop by seed. *Ht, Spd:* 3 ft; *Fl:* 6–7; *Z:* 4

T. montana

Tiarella

T. cordifolia Foam flower: E N Amer. Pretty little ground-covering plant. Pale green lvs rounded, lobed, hry becoming bronze in winter. Fls a creamy white froth of tiny stars on 10 in stems. Prop by div, seed. *Spd:* 6 in; *Fl:* 4–6; *Z:* 4

T. wherryi: E USA. Lvs similar to *T. cordifolia* but fl stems to 15 in. Fls foaming white or pink tinged in fluffy 10 in spikes. Prop by div, seed. *Spd:* 7 in; *Fl:* 5–6; *Z:* 4

T. cordifolia

Trachystemon

Trachystemon

T. orientale (= Nordmannia cordifolia): SE Eur, Asia Minor, Caucasus. Giant per borage to 2 ft × 2 ft with long lax lvs and blue fls with prominent anthers. Plant for a wild gdn. Good in dry shade. *Fl: 3–5; Z: 4*

Tradescantia

Tradescantia

T. × andersoniana (= virginiana) Spiderwort: gdn origin. Lush, strap-leaved plants often pink-tinged in young growth. Fls have 3 ptls. Most cvs are hybs of *T. virginiana*. Good ones inc: 'J. C. Weguelin' azure; 'Osprey' white, blue eye; 'Purewell Giant' rich purple-red. *Ht: 22 in; Spd: 18 in; Fl: 6–9; Z: 4*

T. × andersoniana

Tricyrtis

Toad lily

T. hirta: Japan. Graceful and intriguing rather than eye-catching. Lvs to 6 in long are thin and hry, fls narrow-petaled, bell-shaped, white, smothered with purple spots. For moist soil. *Ht, Spd: 2 ft; Fl: 6–7; Z: 9*

Trollius

Globe flower

T. × cultorum: gdn origin. Hybs often listed as *T. europaeum*. Lvs are lobed, fls gold, globe-shaped, 2½ in. 'Alabaster' is pale cream; 'Orange Princess' orange; 'Princess Juliana' yellow. Prop by div. *Ht: to 3 ft; Spd: 18 in; Fl: 5–6; Z: 3*
T. ledebourii: E Asia. Taller with lvs more deeply divided. 'Golden Queen' is rich orange-yellow. *Ht: 3 ft; Spd: 18 in; Fl: 5–6; Z: 3*

T. × cultorum 'Orange Globe'

Valeriana

Valerian

V. officinalis All heal: Eur. Bushy plant beloved of cats. Lvs are bright green, heart-shaped, stems fluted, fls pink in 6 in heads. White and carmine forms are available. Prop spp by seed. *Ht, Spd: 40 in; Fl: 6; Z: 4*

X *Venidio-arctotis*

Venidio-arctotis

× ***Venidio-arctotis hybs:*** gdn origin. Brilliantly colored daisy flowered hybs of African parents. Cols red, orange, salmon pink, yellow, crimson. Only hardy in frost-free areas. Prop by cuttings. *Ht: 18 in; Spd: 2 ft; Fl: 5–11; Z: 9*

× *Venidio-arctotis*

Veratrum

False hellebore

V. album White hellebore: Eur, N Africa, Siberia. Exciting pleated lvs with greenish-white waxy fls in branched 1 ft spikes. *V. nigrum* has nearly black fls. Not difficult. *Ht:* 4 ft; *Spd:* 2 ft; *Fl:* 7; *Z:* 5

Verbascum

Mullein

V. bombyciferum (= broussa): Asia Minor. Eye-catching spire-like biennial with silvery woolly lvs and a 3 ft spike studded with yellow fls. *Ht:* 6 ft; *Spd:* 2 ft; *Fl:* 6–7; *Z:* 4

V. phoenicium Purple mullein: Eur, N Asia. Basal rosette of deep green lvs; 2 ft spikes of purple fls. Hybs inc 'Cotswold Gem' buff, purple center; 'Pink Domino' rose-pink. *Ht:* 4 ft; *Spd:* 2 ft; *Fl:* 5–9; *Z:* 4

V. bombyciferum

Verbena

Verbena

***V. bonariensis*:** S Amer. Long-stemmed lanky per to 4 ft with thin lvs in pairs up branching stems. Tiny bright purple fls in 3 in tufts. *Spd:* 28 in; *Fl:* 7–9; *Z:* 5

V. rigida: S Amer. Tuberous-rooted, often used for bedding out. Lfy stems divided into 3 spikes of frag, purple fls. Prop by div. *Ht:* 2 ft; *Spd:* 18 in; *Fl:* 7–10; *Z:* 5

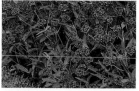

V. rigida

Veronica

Speedwell

Narrow spire-flowers for a long summer season. Easy plants for mixed and herbaceous borders.

V. gentianoides: Caucasus. Lvs a shining deep green, fls pale blue in pointed 10 in spires. There is a creamy-white variegated form. *Ht, Spd:* 2 ft; *Fl:* 5; *Z:* 4

V. incana: USSR. Silvery-grey hry-lvd plant for front of sunny border. Light blue fls in 6 in spires. *Ht, Spd:* 1 ft; *Fl:* 7; *Z:* 4

V. spicata: Eur. A neat edging plant with bright blue fls in short spikes. Hybs inc × 'Wendy' blue fls, silvery lvs; × 'Bacarolle' rose-pink; × 'Red Fox' rich plum red; × 'Icicle' white. Prop by div. *Ht, Spd:* 18 in; *Fl:* 6–8; *Z:* 4

V. virginica (= Veronicastrum virginica, Leptandra virginica): N Amer. Strong spires with regular whorls of horizontal lvs make a unique pattern of light and shade. Fls pale blue but white in the best one 'Alba'*; *Ht:* 4 ft; *Spd:* 18 in; *Fl:* 8–9; *Z:* 4

V. incana

V. spicata

Pansy, Violet

Little woodland-edge plants with sweet faces best in light shade and leafy soil. Some species flower all summer.

V. cornuta 'Alba'

V. labradorica

V. cornuta: Pyrenees. A plump green cushion of lvs smothered in pale blue 1 in pansy fls. Can also be grown in rock gdns. 'Alba' white and 'Lilacina' pale lilac are good cvs. Prop by div, seed. *Ht:* 1 ft; *Spd:* 18 in; *Fl:* 5–10; *Z:* 6

V. labradorica*: N USA, Canada, Greenland. Small creeping violet with dusky purplish-green lvs and violet-blue fls ¾ in across. Will tolerate dry shade. *Ht:* 3 in; *Spd:* 10 in; *Fl:* 4–5; *Z:* 6

V. tricolor Heartsease: Eur. Sprawling wildling with small fls often half black-purple, half yellow. Self-sows. *Ht:* to 6 in; *Spd:* to 15 in; *Fl:* 5–9; *Z:* 7

V. × wittrockiana Garden pansy: gdn origin. Huge range bred for big fls in many cols inc wtr, spr and smr-flowering selections, usually grown as anns and per "tufted pansies" e.g. 'Maggie's Mott' mauve. *Ht:* 9 in; *Spd:* 1 ft; *Z:* 7

Viscaria

Catchfly

V. vulgaris

V. vulgaris: Eur. Siberia, Japan. The name comes from the sticky stem. Sp superseded as a gdn plant by the knicker-pink double-flowered form 'Splendens Plena'. The lvs are narrow. Prop by division. *Ht:* 15 in; *Spd:* 1 ft; *Fl:* 5–7; *Z:* 4

Zauschneria

California fuchsia, Humming bird's trumpet

Z. californica

Z. californica: Cal, Mexico. Sub-shrubby plant also with a place in the rock gdn. Small grey lvs and tall dainty sprays of bright scarlet 1½ in fls. There is a v rare white form. *Z. cana* has needle-like silver lvs and smaller scarlet fls. Prop by cuttings, division or seed. *Ht:* 1 ft; *Spd:* 18 in; *Fl:* 8–10; *Z:* 8

Alpines, rock garden plants

True alpine plants are those that grow naturally on mountains above about 10,000 feet. The plants described in this section as for use in the rock garden are those small bushy or trailing perennials that look at home among rocks, whatever their natural origin. Although spring (after snow melt) is the main flowering season, plants can be found to provide interest all summer.

Acaena

New Zealand burr-weed

A. novae-zealandiae: New Zealand. One of the prettiest of a group of vigorous plants forming bronze carpets to 2 in under reddish fls. All acaenas are ideal for paved areas and difficult sunny sites on poor soil. Fls are petalless but worthwhile, taking the form of club-like burrs on stems held above the lvs. *A. buchananii* has pea-green lvs; the larger lvs of *A. adscendens* are nearly blue. *Spd:* 2 ft; *Fl:* 6–9; *Z:* 7

A. novae-zealandiae

Achillea

Achillea

A. clavenae Alpine achillea: E Alps. Neat, mat-forming. Useful tufty mat of lvs. White fls to ⅓ in diam are held aloft on 6 in stems. Prop by div. Contrasts well with campanulas. *Spd:* 8 in; *Fl:* 5–6; *Z:* 6

Aethionema

Stone cress

A. 'Warley Rose': Cv found in the garden of Miss Ellen Willmott at Warley, Eng, early this century. The brightest member of a generally rather dim genus, having deep pink fls. Forms shrublets only 6 in high. All aethionemas are attractive for their fls in spikes to 3½ in long and the slightly succulent texture of their tiny leaves. *Spd:* 15 in; *Fl:* 4–5; *Z:* 6

A. 'Warley Rose'

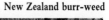

Alchemilla

Lady's mantle

A. erigena (=conjuncta): Swiss Alps. One of the few alpine alchemillas. Forms a neat clump of mid-green lvs with silvery backs and greenish-yellow fls. The genus contains many similar spp, some half dozen of which have gdn value. Prop by seed or div. *Ht:* 6 in; *Spd:* 15 in; *Fl:* 6–8; *Z:* 3

Allium

Flowering onion

A. beesianum China onion: W China. An onion with china-blue fls to 2 in freely produced on 9 in stems from fibrous clumps rather than true bulbs. Grassy lvs and characteristic onion smell. Prop by div or seed. One of more than 300 ornamental onion spp. *Spd:* 6 in; *Fl:* 7–9; *Z:* 5

Alyssum

*A. saxatile** Basket of gold: Eur. One of the basic rock gdn plants. Strong clumps of greyish-green lvs hidden by myriads of brilliant yellow fls. Commonly seen in company of blobs of mauve *Aubretia*. Good cvs include 'Dudley Neville' biscuit-yellow; 'Citrinum' pale yellow; 'Plenum' double yellow, and dwarfs such as 'Compactum'. *Ht:* to 1 ft; *Spd:* to 18 in; *Fl:* 4–6; *Z:* 3

A. saxatile

Androsace

Rock jasmine

A. lanuginosa: Him. The thin stems of this excellent plant link the grey rosettes of lvs and allow them to travel over rocks and crevices showing the ½ in white fls to advantage. 'Leitchtlinii' has exquisite pink-eyed fls. Sev other forms only suitable for the alpine house. *Ht:* 2 in; *Spd:* to 18 in; *Fl:* 6–10; *Z:* 6

A. lanuginosa

Antennaria

Catsear

A. dioica: Eur, Asia, N Amer. A valuable plant, but uncommon in gdns and the wild. Forms pewter-grey rosettes of lvs with whitish fls to ½ in diam. Ideal over patches of crocuses. Also a useful carpeting plant for filling pockets in paving. *Ht:* 1 ft; *Spd:* 18 in; *Fl:* 5–6; *Z:* 3

Arabis

Wall cress, Rock cress

A. caucasica (= A. albida): Eur. A universally grown spring fl with white blooms to ¾ in diam that cool the brassy yellows of the season and continue sporadically into summer. 'Flore Plena' is double, *A. c. variegata* a variegated form. Lvs like grey flannel. *Ht:* 8 in; *Spd:* to 2 ft; *Fl:* 2–6; *Z:* 6

Arenaria

Sandwort

A. ledebouriana: Armenia. A tufty crevice plant with white fls over narrow grey-green lvs. The shade-loving *A. balearica**, which grows like pale green moss on rock faces, is v pretty but so natural-looking that it fails to attract attention. Deserves wider use. *Ht:* 1½ in; *Spd:* 1 ft; *Fl:* 5–7; *Z:* 6

Arisarum

Mouse-tail plant

A. proboscidium: Eur Alps. Tuberous-rooted aroid happy in any cool moist spot. Small clumps of arrow-shaped lvs to 4 in partially conceal brownish-white spathes whose tips give the impression of field mice diving for cover. Fascinating for children. *Ht:* 4 in; *Spd:* 6 in; *Fl:* 6; *Z:* 6

Armeria

Thrift, Sea pink

A. maritima: GB. Densely packed narrow lvs form dark mats which are the perfect foil for the light pink fls to 1 in. Gdn forms include 'Laucheana' a rich pink; 'Alba' white and 'Vindictive' a fierce red. All spp are equally at home on the shore and in the mountains. Their use is not confined to the rock gdn— they can form useful cover or edging plants. *Ht, Spd:* to 1 ft; *Fl:* 5–7; *Z:* 3

A. maritima

Artemisia

Wormwood

A. stellerana* Beach wormwood: N Amer NE Asia. One of a genus ranging from tiny alpine house or scree plants to valuable shrubs. Most have lively silver foliage. This one is a trailing plant strong enough to engulf any defenseless neighbors but needs to be replaced by rooted cuttings every 2–3 yrs to preserve its health and vigor. Looks good with scarlet geums or against nodding campanulas. *Ht:* 20 in; *Spd:* 18 in; *Fl:* 8–9; *Z:* 4

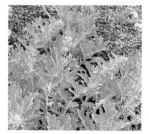

A. stellerana

Asarina

Asarina

A. procumbens Trailing snapdragon: Italy, S France. A charming trailer with cream fls and soft grey-green lvs ideal for cool crevices and rock faces. Short-lived but self-seeding. *Ht:* 20 in; *Spd:* 3 ft; *Fl:* 6–9; *Z:* 9

Asperula

Woodruff

A. odorata Sweet woodruff: GB. Vig members of a pretty minor genus. Forms small rugs of lvs with cross-shaped sweet-scented white or pink ¼ in fls. Keep roots cool. *Ht:* to 1 ft; *Spd:* to 18 in; *Fl:* 5–6; *Z:* 4

Aster

Aster

A. alpinus Alpine aster: Eur Alps. A rock gdn representative of a vast gp inc Michaelmas daisies of the autumn herbaceous border. Easy to grow, reaching 10 in high and twice as wide. Blue and gold fls to 1¾ in freely produced in smr. 'Albus' is a useful albino; 'Beechwood' a good purplish cv. *Fl:* 7; *Z:* 5

A. alpinus

Aubrieta

Aubrietia

A race of about 12 species which have crossed to produce the named cultivars that flower for weeks on end in spring.

A. deltoidea and gdn hybs★: Sicily E to Asia Minor. Varieties do not come true from seed so named sorts must be propagated by cuttings. Popular ones include 'Crimson Bedder' red; 'Dawn' rose-pink; 'Gurgedyke' light blue. There is also a less vigorous cream-variegated one with blue fls. *Ht:* 2½ in; *Spd:* to 2 ft; *Fl:* 3–6; *Z:* 6

A. deltoidea 'Godstone'

Bellis

English daisy

B. perennis 'Dresden China': Eur. The prettiest daisy in intentional cultivation, with elegant soft pink double fls. 'Pomponette' is a deeper pink. Much nicer than the once-popular 'Alice'. *B. p. prolifera* the 'Hen and Chicken' daisy has been cultivated since the 17th century. 'White Pearl' is a worthy albino. *Ht, Spd:* to 4 in; *Fl:* 3–10; *Z:* 6

B. perennis 'Pomponette'

Borago

Borage

B. laxiflora Baby borage: Corsica. One of the bohemians of the rock gdn, forming trails of clear blue fls among shrubs and heathers. Related to the bigger borage of the herb gdn and like it has hry lvs. Easy from seed and good with yellow alpine hypericums. *Ht, Spd:* to 1 ft; *Fl:* 7–8; *Z:* 6

Campanula

Bellflower

C. garganica★: Italy, Yugoslavia. An excellent free-flowering late-summer species found in crevices in the wild and therefore useful for dry walls and similar sites. Star-shaped clear blue fls are in heads to 6 in long. Forms with white centers include 'W. H. Payne'. All are in the white-blue-purple color range. *Ht:* to 6 in; *Spd:* to 1 ft; *Fl:* 8–9; *Z:* 5

C. garganica

Cerastium

Cerastium

C. tomentosum★ Snow-in-summer: Eur. The most rampageous of a v vig bunch but well loved for its sheets of grey-green lvs and waves of white fls to ¾ in. *C. lanatum* is less invasive. *Ht:* to 6 in; *Spd:* 2 ft; *Fl:* 5–7; *Z:* 2

Ceratostigma

Plumbago, Leadwort

C. plumbaginoides★ Perennial plumbago: China. A creeping plant for late smr when the lvs become bronzed as the intense gentian-blue fls begin a lengthy display. Deeper in color than the shrubby sp *C. willmottianum*. The two look good together. *Ht:* to 1 ft; *Spd:* to 16 in; *Fl:* 7–11; *Z:* 5

C. plumbaginoides

Convolvulus

Bindweed

C. mauritanicus Baby bellbind: N Africa. Inclined to wander but less invasive that the clear pink *C. althaeoides* which is worth growing only where paths or walls stop its trespass. Funnel-shaped fls open and close with the sun. *Ht:* 3 in; *Spd:* 3 ft; *Fl:* 6–9; *Z:* 7

Cornus

Dogwood

C. canadensis★ Bunchberry: N Amer. The conspicuous bracts form a white layer followed by cheerful red berries over a carpet of dark green lvs. Only 6 in high in fl. Best in semi-shade with an occasional small fern growing through it. *Spd:* 2 ft; *Fl:* 6; *Z:* 3

C. canadensis

Corydalis

Fumitory

C. wilsonii: China. Forms clumps of prettily dissected grey-green lvs with gps of bright yellow fls over a long period. Sev others weedy but good ones are quite lovely. *Ht:* 10 in; *Spd:* 1 ft; *Fl:* 5–9; *Z:* 5

Cytisus

Broom

C. × beanii Dwarf broom: A hyb found at Kew, London in 1900 and forming a small spreading shrub with pea-like yellow fls to ½ in. *C. × kewensis★* taller at 1 ft but also trails and has creamy-white fls. *C. purpureus* has pink and purple fls in frothy sprays. Looks good with heathers. *Ht:* 10 in; *Spd:* 3 ft; *Fl:* 5–6; *Z:* 6

C. × beanii

Daphne

Daphne

D. cneorum Garland flower: S Eur. Low spreading shrub smothered with headily frag bright rose-pink fls ½ in. *Ht:* 6 in; *Spd:* 30 in; *Fl:* 5–6; *Z:* 6

Dianthus

Pink

Country cousins of the carnation with much more natural grace. Invaluable plants for their evergreen leaves, which are often grey and grassy, and for their usually pink, fragrant flowers.

D. alpinus Alpine pink: Eur Alps. One of the many alpine pinks. Makes low cushions of green lvs with large rosy-red fls to 2¼ in. *Ht:* 4 in; *Spd:* 6 in; *Fl:* 5–8; *Z:* 2
D. deltoides Maiden pink: Eur. Reaches 6 in high and has a mass of small pink fls to ¾ in. Easy from cuttings in July or from seed. *Ht:* 8 in; *Spd:* 10 in; *Fl:* 6–10; *Z:* 2

D. deltoides

Dodecatheon

Shooting star

D. meadia★: N Amer. Striking and memorable fls from the grassy slopes of mountains, particularly in California. In gdns they like moisture and a little shade. Pink and white fls are poised like tiny comets on long elegant stems to 18 in. Increase by division or seed. *Spd:* 1 ft; *Fl:* 5–6; *Z:* 6

D. maedia

Dryas

Mountain avens

D. octopetala★: GB. Mat-forming, woody-stemmed. Little oak-like dark green lvs overlap and smother weeds. White, golden-centered single rose-like fls to 1 in arise in spring and summer. Silky seed heads. There is a miniature form *D. o. minor.* *Ht:* to 4 in; *Spd:* 2 ft; *Fl:* 5–6; *Z:* 2

D. octopetala

Erinus

Erinus

E. alpinus Summer starwort: Eur. Only 2 in high has mauve pink or red starry fls to ⅓ in. Named forms inc 'Dr Hanelle' crimson and 'Mrs Charles Boyle' pink. *Spd:* 6 in; *Fl:* 3–8; *Z:* 5

Euphorbia

Spurge

E. myrsinites★: S Eur. A fleshy glaucous trailer with terminal heads of greenish-yellow fls in heads to 4 in. Exudes a characteristic milky sap if broken. Easy from seed. *Ht:* 6 in; *Spd:* 18 in; *Fl:* 3–4; *Z:* 7

Gentian

Synonymous with the Alps and rock gardens. Sometimes unpredictable; not all are dwarf. All gardens should have one.

G. acaulis Trumpet gentian: Eur Alps. Pure blue trumpet fls in spr held proudly over mats of green lvs. Likes lime while, as a rule of thumb, autumn-flowering ones (e.g. *G. sino-ornata*) hate it. *Ht:* 3 in; *Spd:* 14 in; *Fl:* 5–6; *Z:* 4

G. septemfida*: Caucasus. V easy, smr-flowering. Not fussy about soil. Good from midsmr on, conveniently between spr and aut sorts. *Ht:* 8 in; *Spd:* 1 ft; *Fl:* 7–8; *Z:* 5

G. septemfida

Cranesbill

G. cinereum: Pyrenees. Grey-green lvs are a perfect foil for the rosy-purple fls with dark-veined ptls. *G. dalmaticum* has neat glossy lvs and clear pink fls. *Ht:* 6 in; *Spd:* to 1 ft; *Fl:* 5–10; *Z:* 5

Gypsophila, Baby's breath

G. repens: Eur Alps. Fleshy-rooted per. Branched stems support frothy clouds of fls. Miniatures of the herbaceous kinds; × 'Letchworth Rose' good long-flowering pink hyb. *Ht:* 10 in; *Spd:* to 2 ft; *Fl:* 6–8; *Z:* 5

Haberlea

H. rhodopensis: Balkans. Tricky but rewarding plants related to ramondas and like them best grown on their sides in damp walls where their rosettes of lvs can be seen to advantage and water will drain off, preventing rotting. Lf rosettes are dark green and closely packed. Stems of fls *c.* 1 in diam in lavender flecked with gold in spr. *H. ferdinandi-coburgii* is a better form less frequently seen. *Ht:* 5 in; *Spd:* 8 in; *Fl:* 5; *Z:* 7

H. rhodopensis

Everlasting flower, Straw flower

H. bellidioides: New Zealand. One of a genus of sun-loving plants mainly grown in alpine houses but this sp is hardier than most gardeners think. Makes silvery lf mats all summer. *Ht:* 3 in; *Spd:* 1 ft; *Fl:* 5–8; *Z:* 7

Hepatica

H. transsilvanica*: E Eur. The best sp in a genus deserving wider use. Lvs are puckered, kidney-shaped, fls a distinctive blue. Look for rare white, pink or double forms. *Ht:* 6 in; *Spd:* 10 in; *Fl:* 2–4; *Z:* 4

Hieraceum

Hawkweed

H. villosum: C Eur. Yellow–flowered sp that can be invasive. Shaggy silvery lvs in rosettes support fl stems to 10 in; *Spd:* 18 in; *Fl:* 6–8; *Z:* 4

Hypericum

St John's wort

H. olympicum: S Eur. V easy member of a large sun-loving genus. Has blue-grey lvs and freely produced golden-yellow fls. Invasive *H. cerastoides* (= *H. rhodopeum*) also good. *Ht:* 1 ft; *Spd:* 10 in; *Fl:* 7–8; *Z:* 6

Iberis

Candytuft

I. sempervirens* Evergreen candytuft: S Eur. Per version of more colorful border anns. Fol in big mats good in wtr. 'Snowflake' is best cv with pure white fls. *Ht:* 10 in; *Spd:* to 2 ft; *Fl:* 5–6; *Z:* 6

Iris

Iris

I. pumila

I. cristata Crested iris: N Amer. A 3 in charmer with blue and gold fls in May and June. The tiny rhizomes like a little sun and cool root conditions. *Spd:* 6 in; *Z:* 4

I. pumila*: Eur, Asia Minor. A wide range of excellent cvs. Cols inc white, pale or indigo blue and yellow. A yellow/brown one received an AGM in 1958 as *I. attica*. *Ht:* to 4 in; *Spd:* 6 in; *Fl:* 4; *Z:* 5

Leontopodium

Edelweiss

L. alpinum

L. alpinum: C Eur, Asia. An unspectacular plant associated with the high Alps, gentians, yodeling and lederhosen, but not difficult to grow in lowland gdns given sufficient drainage. Fls 2 in wide are whitish-grey with a flannel-like texture, the lvs thin and grey-green. Fls last for sev weeks. *Ht:* 8 in; *Spd:* 9 in; *Fl:* 6–7; *Z:* 4

Lewisia

Lewisia

L. cotyledon

L. cotyledon: N Amer. Forms rosettes of fleshy green lvs. Best grown in crevices with the rosettes placed vertically to let water drain off. *L. cotyledon* cvs are easiest and will tolerate some lime. Fls are pink to apricot, often striped. Easy from seed but prop cvs by div to maintain their identity. *Ht:* 1 ft; *Spd:* 6 in; *Fl:* 5–6; *Z:* 7

Lithospermum

L. diffusum: Med. Popular spreading sp with small dark green leaves. Produces sheets of exquisite gentian–blue ½ in fls for weeks on end in June through to October. The best form is 'Heavenly Blue'*. The rampant European spp *L. purpureocaeruleum* will tolerate lime unlike the N. American ones. *Ht:* 6 in; *Spd:* 2 ft; *Z:* 8

L. diffusum 'Heavenly Blue'

Lysimachia

Loosestrife

L. nummularia 'Aurea': Creeping Jenny, Moneywort: GB. A golden-leaved form less vigorous than the type but good as ground cover. Bears small yellow fls *c.* ½ in across in summer. *Ht:* 2 in; *Spd:* 18 in; *Fl:* 6–7; *Z:* 4

L. nummularia

Onosma

Donkey plant

O. tauricum: Med. Low clumps with rather coarse lvs from which stems of pendant, tubular, soft yellow fragrant fls arise. Particularly useful for its long flowering season. All onosmas like to grow in rocky fissures and object to being disturbed. *Ht, Spd:* 10 in; *Fl:* 4–8; *Z:* 7

Oxalis

Oxalis

O. adenophylla: Chile. One of about 1,000 spp, most of which are invasive and should be avoided: never accept one as a gift. Has crinkly grey lvs and lavender or pink fls. The tuber is like a small coconut wrapped in fibrous scales and breaks up into bulbils easily used for propagation after flowering. *Ht:* 2½ in; *Spd:* 6 in; *Fl:* 5–7; *Z:* 8

O. adenophylla

Penstemon

Penstemon

P. rupicola: N Amer. Prostrate woody per with grey-green lvs. Good in sinks and troughs as well as rock gdns. Rosy-carmine fls to 1 in. Prop by seed or cuttings. *Ht:* 4 in; *Spd:* 1 ft; *Fl:* 5–7; *Z:* 6
P. newberryi: W N Amer. Larger than *P. rupicola* with pink or mauve fls. *Ht:* to 18 in; *Spd:* 18 in; *Fl:* 6; *Z:* 5

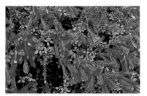

P. newberryi

Phlox

Phlox

P. douglasii

P. douglasii Alpine phlox: Rocky Mts. Hummock-forming. Fls pink, mauve or white. 'Boothman's Variety' is mauve with a violet eye. *Ht:* 2 in; *Spd:* 18 in; *Fl:* 5–6; *Z:* 4
P. subulata★ Moss pink: E USA. Carpet-forming. Good cvs inc 'Appleblossom' pale pink; 'G. F. Wilson' mauve; 'Temiscaming' magenta. *Ht:* 2 in; *Spd:* to 18 in; *Fl:* 4–5; *Z:* 4

Polygonum

Knotweed

P. vaccinifolium: Him. From Aug to Oct trailing stems are adorned with pink candles of fls to 2 in. Dense mat of shining evergreen lvs. Useful on flat surfaces or dry walls. *Ht:* 4 in; *Spd:* 3 ft; *Z:* 7

Potentilla

Cinquefoil

P. × 'Tonguei'

P. alba: C, S Eur. Useful as a specimen or in gps as ground cover. Lvs glossy, dark green. Single fls white. *Ht:* 4 in; *Spd:* 15 in; *Fl:* 6–9; *Z:* 5
P. × 'Tonguei': gdn origin. Fls rich apricot, crimson blotched. Plant prostrate. *Ht:* 4 in; *Spd:* 15 in; *Fl:* 8–9; *Z:* 6

Pulsatilla

Pulsatilla

P. vulgaris 'Budapest'

P. vulgaris (= Anemone pulsatilla)★ Pasque flower: Eur. Fls borne in Apr and May are 2–3 in across with silky purple ptls and hry stems to 8 in. 'Budapest' is excellent and good nurserymen occasionally offer a red-flowered var. Loves lime. High alpine spp such as *P. alpina* have white or sometimes yellow fls. Raise from seed. *Spd:* 15 in; *Z:* 6

Ramonda

Ramonda

R. myconi: Pyrenees. Dark green rosettes of thick crinkled lvs with stems of lilac-blue, golden-eyed fls in sprays. Likes peaty soil. Plant on its side in a crevice or dry stone wall. *Ht:* 6 in; *Spd:* 10 in; *Fl:* 4–5; *Z:* 2

Sanguinaria

Bloodroot

S. canadensis★: N Amer. A crawler of great class. Blue-grey lvs act as wrappers for the buds of exquisite single white fls to 1½ in diam. The rare double 'Flore Pleno' is superb. *Ht:* 6 in; *Spd:* 14 in; *Fl:* 4–5; *Z:* 5

Saponaria

Soapwort

S. ocymoides: Eur Alps. Good mat or wall-hanging to 20 in. Cheerful pink fls. Hyb × 'Bressingham Pink' is richer col. *Spd:* 1 ft; *Fl:* 6–9; *Z:* 4

Saxifraga

Saxifrage

Silvery encrusted saxifrages like full sun but *S. umbrosa* and mossy ones need partial shade. All prefer lime.

S. cochlearis: Mar Alps. Forms mounds of silvery lime-encrusted lf rosettes. White fls on 5 in red stems. *S. aizoon* is larger but equally easy. *Spd:* 10 in; *Fl:* 6; *Z:* 6

S. fortunei★: China, Japan. Aut-flowering gem; glossy lvs with mahogany-red backs. Red stems to 18 in bear dainty white fls. 'Wada's Variety' has strikingly red lvs. Needs some shade and much moisture. *Spd:* 14 in; *Fl:* 10–11; *Z:* 6, LF

S. fortunei

S. moschata: Eur. Forms soft carpets in partial shade. The many cvs include 'Dubarry' crimson; 'Flowers of Sulphur' yellow; 'Mother of Pearl' white. *Ht:* 6 in; *Spd:* 18 in; *Fl:* 4–5; *Z:* 6

S. stolonifera: China, Japan. Rounded veined lvs with little plantlets on runners. Hardy in gdns. *Ht, Spd:* 1 ft; *Fl:* 7–8; *Z:* 5

S. moschata 'Edie Campbell'

Sedum

Stonecrop

A vast variety of fleshy rosette plants from a tiny cliff-top one to hearty herbaceous perennials. Many worth growing.

S. spurium: Caucasus. A mat-former. The species has bright crystalline pink fls. 'Schorbusser Blut' is an old deep red cv, 'Green Mantle' rarely flowers but is excellent ground cover. Divides easily. *Ht:* 2½ in; *Spd:* 1 ft; *Fl:* 7–8; *Z:* 6

S. spurium

Sempervivum

Houseleek

S. tectorum: Eur. The best known of these clump-forming plants with succ lf rosettes. Has red fls and stout stems. *S. arachnoideum★* has cobweb-like covering of white hrs. Good for dry places. *Ht:* 6 in; *Spd:* 1 ft; *Fl:* 7; *Z:* 5

Silene

Campion, Catchfly

S. schafta: Caucasus. Strong magenta-pink fls in sprays to ¾ in freely displayed from July to Oct when they give welcome relief from autumn's orange and gold tints. 'Robusta' is a bit bigger. *Ht:* 6 in; *Spd:* 1 ft; *Z:* 4

Sisyrinchium

Sisyrinchium

S. angustifolium Blue-eyed grass: N Amer. Has tufts of thin iris-like lvs and charming round fls on 6 in stems. *S. graminifolium*, 8 in, has yellow fls; *S. bermudiana*, 10 in, has violet-blue fls. *Spd:* 10 in; *Fl:* 5–10; *Z:* 4

Tanacetum

Tanacetum

T. bipinnatum (= densum amani): Asia Minor. The only interesting sp in the genus and one that botanists have continuously renamed. Makes humps of exquisite filigree silver fol. The yellow fls are pleasing but not of great value. Propagate by cuttings. *Ht:* 8 in; *Spd:* 18 in; *Fl:* 8; *Z:* 4

T. bipinnatum

Teucrium

Teucrium, Germander

T. chamaedrys★ Wall germander: S, C Eur. The best-known sp, often classified as a herb and only suitable for the larger rock gdn or a border edge, but try dwarf 'Nana'. Fls pink. *Ht:* 8 in; *Spd:* 16 in; *Fl:* 7–9; *Z:* 7

Thymus

Thyme

T. serpyllum★ Creeping thyme: Eur. Prostrate carpeter; lvs dark green. Select from 'Annie Hall' pale pink; 'Pink Chintz' deep pink; 'Coccineus' crimson; 'Albus' white to give a mass of fls. *Spd:* 20 in; *Fl:* 6–7; *Z:* 3

Veronica

Speedwell

V. prostrata: Eur–USSR. An easy plant to 4 in with tiny fls in spires of brilliant blue and trailing mats of green lvs. 'Spode Blue' is brighter than the type while 'Mrs Holt' is pink and 'Alba' white. Other spp notorious lawn weeds. *Spd:* 16 in; *Fl:* 5–7; *Z:* 4

V. prostrata

Waldsteinia

Waldsteinia

W. ternata: Eur. A mat-forming sp for the slopes and plains of the rock gdn or as ground cover on a larger scale. Has 3-lobed lvs which color in autumn and back up the showers of buttercup-yellow fls to ½ in diam. Has surface rooting stems and is easily divided. *Ht:* 2½ in; *Spd:* 18 in; *Fl:* 4–5; *Z:* 4

W. ternata

Bog, waterside and pond plants

Plants that live in water or in permanently saturated soil are distinct from those that like moisture, but also need drainage. The latter need oxygen in the soil; the former can dispense with it. Some water plants, in fact, can do without soil altogether and live afloat. This section includes plants for the water itself and for the boggy brink.

 Acorus

Acorus

A. calamus Sweet flag: Eur, S Asia, N Amer. Iris-like plant; sword-shaped lvs with wavy edges. Fls curious, greenish-yellow in 4 in spikes like stubby thumbs. *A. c. variegatus* more decorative with creamy-yellow and green lvs. Prop by div. *Ht:* to 3 ft; *Spd:* 2 ft; *Fl:* 6; *Z:* 3

A. calamus

 Alisma

Water plantain

A. lanceolatum: N Temp zones. Lvs spear-shaped and veined like lawn plantain. Fls ½ in wide, pale pink to white in loose clouds on branching stems. Prop by div, seed. *Ht:* to 3 ft; *Spd:* 20 in; *Fl:* 7; *Z:* 6

 *Aponogeton*

Aponogeton

A. distachyus Water hawthorn: S Africa. Floating narrow lively green lvs. Stubby forked fl stems bear white, single-petaled frag fls with brown/purple anthers. *Ht:* 6 in; *Spd:* 20 in; *Fl:* 4–10; *Z:* 8

 *Butomus*

Flowering rush

B. umbellatus: Temp Eur and Asia. Uprt plant with tough narrow pointed lvs with a purplish sheen in infancy, becoming green as they develop. Fls rose-pink, 1 in wide, borne in a terminal umbrella on green stems. Rootstock edible. Prop by div. *Ht:* to 3 ft; *Spd:* 20 in; *Fl:* 6–8; *Z:* 3

B. umbellatus

 *Calla*

Calla

C. palustris Water arum: E N Amer, N Asia, N Eur. Wandering marginal or shallow-water plant with dark green spear-shaped lvs and white arum-lily-like 4 in fls followed by attractive red berries. Prop by div of creeping rhizomes. *Ht:* to 8 in; *Spd:* 2 ft; *Fl:* 6; *Z:* 3

C. palustris

Caltha

Marsh marigold, Cowslip

C. palustris*: Eur, N Amer–Arct, Caucasus. Marginal plant with heart-shaped lvs to 10 in wide when mature. Fls like large golden buttercups 2 in wide on pale green stems. There are single white and an excellent double yellow-flowered form 'Plena'. Prop by div, seed. *Ht:* 1 ft; *Spd:* 18 in; *Fl:* 3–4; *Z:* 3

C. palustris

Cyperus

Sedge

C. longus Galingale, Umbrella grass: GB. Decorative, grass-like shining green lvs in umbrella-like whorl. Prop by div, seed. *Ht:* to 4 ft; *Spd:* 1 ft; *Fl:* 7–10; *Z:* 5
C. papyrus Papyrus: Egypt. Lvs narrow, v small. Stems to 9 ft support mop-like heads of slender threads. Needs warmth. *Spd:* 2 ft; *Fl:* 7–9; *Z:* 10

C. papyrus

Eichhornia

Water hyacinth

E. speciosa (=crassipes)*: S Amer, Trop Africa. Lvs shiny, heart-shaped; swollen lf stks act as support. Fls funnel-shaped, lavender-blue with gold markings in spikes to 1 ft. Long, trailing purplish rts spread by runners. Prop by div. *Ht:* to 18 in; *Spd:* 1 ft; *Fl:* 6–7; *Z:* 8

Glyceria

Manna grass

G. aquatica variegata: N Hem. Lvs flat, pale green to 3 in wide, striped white. Fls grass-like. *Ht:* to 1 ft; *Spd:* 18 in; *Fl:* 7–9; *Z:* 6

Gunnera

Gunnera

G. manicata*: Brazil. Colossal coarse rhubarb-like lvs to 6 ft wide, on stout, rough, warty stems. Fl spike from base is greenish-brown and club-like to 3 ft long, but the lvs are the main attraction. Prop by div, seed. *Ht:* to 14 ft; *Spd:* 20 ft; *Fl:* 7–10; *Z:* 7

G. manicata

Houttuynia

Houttuynia

H. cordata: Him, China, Japan. Lvs alternate, heart-shaped, bluish-green. Stems uprt, angular, lfy. Fls tiny below elliptical white lflts in 4s. Smells of orange peel when crushed. *Ht:* 18 in; *Spd:* 1 ft; *Fl:* 6; *Z:* 6

Iris

***I. kaempferi*★** Clematis-flowered iris: Japan. Fls to 8 in wide, purple, white, pink or red, may be blotched. *Ht:* 3 ft; *Spd:* 18 in; *Fl:* 7; *Z:* 6
***I. laevigata*★:** Japan. Tall, fine, strap-like lvs. Fls rich blue, gold mark at ptl base, also white forms. *Ht:* 2 ft; *Spd:* 18 in; *Fl:* 7; *Z:* 6
***I. sibirica*★:** Eur, USSR. Elegant; narrow lax lvs, neat blue fls. *Ht:* 3 ft; *Spd:* 2 ft; *Fl:* 6; *Z:* 6

I. kaempferi

 *Juncus*

Rush

J. effusus 'Spiralis' Corkscrew rush: gdn origin. Writhing green stems spiral from the water's surface. 'Vittatus' has lvs striped yellow. Fls insignificant. Prop by div. *Ht:* to 18 in; *Spd:* 15 in; *Z:* 6

Ligularia

Ligularia

L. dentata (=clivorum): China. Rounded dark green toothed lvs. Fls daisy-like bright orange to 4 in wide. 'Desdemona'★ is magnificent with shining maroon-backed lvs. Prop by div. *Ht:* to 7 ft; *Spd:* 3 ft; *Fl:* 7–8; *Z:* 6

Lobelia

Lobelia

L. cardinalis Cardinal flower: N Amer. Brilliant rich-scarlet fls, snapdragon-like on 1 side of lfy stems. Lvs smooth, flat, deep green or purple. *L. syphilitica* has clear bright blue fls in lf axils in Aug–Sept; there is also a white-flowered form. Prop both spp by div. *Ht:* 3 ft; *Spd:* 1 ft; *Fl:* 7–8; *Z:* 5

 Lysichitum (=Lysichiton)

Lysichitum

Dramatic growth of a dazzling yellow or white flower from ground level. Often (wrongly) called Skunk cabbage.

L. americanum Bog arum: W N Amer. Noble bright green lvs, uprt or flopping, to 3 ft × 8 in with sturdy center rib. Fls like arum lilies to 2 ft, light yellow with green spadix. *Ht:* to 3 ft; *Spd:* 6 ft; *Fl:* 4; *Z:* 5
L. camtschatcense: Kamtschatka, Japan. Sim to above but white fls 1 ft long. Less easy to prop by seed but both easy by div. *Ht, Spd:* to 3 ft; *Fl:* 5; *Z:* 5

L. americanum

Lysimachia

Lysimachia

L. punctata: Asia Minor. Erect, lightly hry plant bearing whorls of oblong pointed lvs and bright blue fls in 8 in spikes. Prop by div or seed. *Ht:* 3 ft; *Spd:* 2 ft; *Fl:* 7–9; *Z:* 5

Mentha

Mint

M. citrata (=aquatica citrata) Water mint: Eur. Smooth-leaved lemon-scented mint. Fls lavender-blue in 4 in spikes in July–Sept. Prop by division. *Ht:* 1 ft; *Spd:* 2 ft; *Z:* 4

Mimulus

Monkey flower

M. guttatus (=lutens guttatus) Monkey musk: N Amer. Spreads and clambers freely. Lvs light green, main stems hollow; 2 in fls are 5-lobed funnels, yellow spotted brown/purple. *Ht, Spd:* 20 in; *Fl:* 6–7; *Z:* 4

Myosotis

Forget-me-not

M. scorpioides (=palustris) Water forget-me-not: Eur, Asia. Fls to $\frac{1}{2}$ in wide typical forget-me-not-blue with a yellow eye. Rounded lvs a shining rich green. Prop by seed, div or cuttings. *Ht:* to 1 ft; *Spd:* to 18 in; *Fl:* 5–6; *Z:* 5

M. palustris

Nelumbo

Lotus

N. nucifera★ E Indian lotus: Asia. Rhizomatous plant for warm water with rounded blue-green wavy-edged lvs to 15 in diam on stems to 6 ft. Chalice-shaped fls white with pink tips or all pink, frag. Seed heads conical, v decorative. *N. lutea* (American lotus) sim but fls yellow. Prop by div or seed. *Ht:* to 6 ft; *Spd:* 30 ft+; *Fl:* 7–9; *Z:* 9

N. nucifera

Nuphar

Water lily

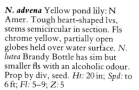

N. advena Yellow pond lily: N Amer. Tough heart-shaped lvs, stems semicircular in section. Fls chrome yellow, partially open globes held over water surface. *N. lutea* Brandy Bottle has sim but smaller fls with an alcoholic odour. Prop by div, seed. *Ht:* 20 in; *Spd:* to 6 ft; *Fl:* 5–9; *Z:* 5

N. advena

Water lily

The loveliest of water-plants are remarkably easy to grow. They can be planted in a weighted sack or perforated container.

*N. alba**⋆ European white water lily: Eur. Young lvs deep red. Fls waxy white, full petaled, green stripe on backs. *Ht:* 1 ft; *Spd:* 6 ft; *Fl:* 7–9; *Z:* 4

*N. gdn hybs**⋆: gdn origin. V many good ones. Tender/trop sorts inc: 'Mrs G.H.Pring' white; 'St Louis' yellow; 'Mrs C.W.Ward' pink; 'Blue Beauty'; 'Glorie de Temple sur Lot' double; 'Darwin' striped. More vig red cvs are 'Escarboucle'; 'James Brydon'. *Ht:* to 15 in; *Spd:* to 6 ft; *Fl:* 6–9; *Z:* 6

N. gdn hybrid 'Escarboucle'

N. × laydekeri: gdn origin. Small hybs with fls *c.* 4 in diam. The two best are 'Lilacea' pink, deepening to crimson and 'Purpurata' red. *Ht:* 15 in; *Spd:* 3 ft; *Fl:* 6–9; *Z:* 6

N. × marliacea: gdn origin. Blanket name for many hybs inc 'Albida' white, frag; 'Chromatella' yellow; 'Rosea' soft pink. *Ht:* to 4 ft; *Spd:* 3 ft; *Fl:* 6–9; *Z:* 5

N. alba 'Gladstone'

N. odorata: N Amer. Frag white fls. Cvs inc 'Sulphurea' yellow. *Ht:* 15 in; *Spd:* 3 ft; *Fl:* 6–9; *Z:* 6

N. × pygmaea: gdn origin. Miniatures with fls 2–3 in wide. Rec are 'Alba' white; 'Helvola' yellow. *Ht:* 1 ft; *Spd:* 18 in; *Fl:* 6–9; *Z:* 6

N. × marliacea 'Rosea'

⊜ ⊛

Peltiphyllum

Umbrella plant

P. peltatum: Cal. Lvs large, nearly circular, lobed, roughly hry. Fls white or pale pink in a flat head on substantial stem before lvs fully developed. Prop by div. *Ht, Spd:* to 2 ft; *Fl:* 4; *Z:* 5

P. peltatum

⊛ ⊜ ⊛

Pontaderia

Pontaderia

P. cordata Pickerel weed: N Amer. Vigorous plant. Lvs arrow-head-like, smooth green on erect stks. Fls 5-petaled, light blue in 4 in spikes. Prop by div. *Ht:* 18 in; *Spd:* 1 ft+; *Fl:* 7–9; *Z:* 3

P. cordata

Primula

Primula, Primrose

P. sikkimensis: SE Asia. Frag pale yellow fls in long terminal head; lvs oval, glossy green. Many spp listed under herbaceous pers also suitable (except *Polyanthus* hybs). *Ht:* 30 in; *Spd:* 18 in; *Fl:* 5–6; *Z:* 5

Rheum

Ornamental rhubarb

R. palmatum: China. Elegant rhubarb with large roughly heart-shaped lvs cleanly cut and lobed. Fls red in 3 ft spikes. The cvs 'Atro-sanguineum'★ and 'Bowles' Form' have rich red young lvs; lf undersides also red fading to green during the season. *Ht:* 8 ft; *Spd:* 6 ft; *Fl:* 6; *Z:* 3

R. palmatum

Rodgersia

Rodgersia

R. aesculifolia★: China. Lvs horse-chestnut-shaped to 18 in across, coarsely toothed with brown highlights. Stems covered with brown hrs. Fls tinted white or pink in broadly based panicles to 18 in. Prop by seed, div of rhizomes. *Ht:* to 4 ft; *Spd:* 20 in; *Fl:* 7–10; *Z:* 6

R. aesculifolia

Thalia

Thalia

T. dealbata: Carolina, Texas. Tall, slender plant. Lvs grey/green with whitish bloom. Fls sev per group, violet-purple, hanging from tall stems. Prop by div. *Ht:* to 2 ft; *Spd:* 15 in; *Fl:* 6–9; *Z:* 9

Trollius

Globe flower

T. europaeus: Eur. Bigger, better buttercups; fls globe-shaped to 2½ in wide. Lvs hrlss. Cvs, esp of *C.* × *cultorum* rec, e.g. 'Alabaster' white; 'Canary Bird' yellow. Prop by div. *Ht:* 2 ft; *Spd:* 18 in; *Fl:* 5–6; *Z:* 4

Zantedeschia

Zantedeschia

Z. (=Calla) aethiopica★ Arum lily, Lily of the Nile: S Africa. Bulbous plant with rich dark green arrow-shaped lvs and typical white fl spathes to 9 in with golden yellow spadix. Tender in many areas. Cv 'Crowborough' considerably more hardy. Prop by div. *Ht:* to 4 ft; *Spd:* 2 ft; *Fl:* 6–8; *Z:* 9

Z. aethiopica

Herbs

A non-botanical classification of plants found useful for flavoring, medicinal or cosmetic purposes rather than for actual food or decoration. Most are aromatic and/or flavorsome and few are showy "flowers". They can be shrubby, perennial or annual. Generally the shrubs prefer dry soil, annuals relatively moist conditions and the perennials are not particular.

Allium

Allium

A. sativum Clove garlic: Med. Pungent hardy per. Fls star-shaped, white or purplish. Plant 2 in deep in spr, harvest in late Aug. *Ht:* to 3 ft; *Spd:* 1 ft; *Fl:* 6; *Z:* 5
A. schoenoprasum Chives: N Hem. Clumps of grassy lvs with onion flavor. Remove mauve fl heads to encourage lf growth. Good edging. *Ht:* 8 in; *Spd:* 1 ft; *Fl:* 6–7; *Z:* 3

A. schoenoprasum

Anethum

Dill

A. graveolens: Eur. Fennel-like ann to 3 ft. Lvs finely dissected, fls mustard-yellow in flat heads to 3 in wide. Lvs and seeds used in cooking and to flavor vinegar. Prop by seed. *Spd:* 1 ft; *Fl:* 6–8

Angelica

Angelica

A. archangelica*: Eur. Stately short-lived per (sometimes only biennial) usually *c.* 7 ft tall. Stems hollow, lvs rich, fresh green 2 ft or more long. Fls yellow-green in rounded heads 3 in wide. Candied angelica made from stems. Prop by seed in spring or late summer. *Spd:* 3 ft; *Fl:* 7–8; *Z:* 5

A. archangelica

Anthemis

Chamomile

A. nobilis: Eur. Low-growing with rich green lvs. Fls daisy-like. Non-flowering 'Treneague' used as lawns. *Ht, Spd:* 15 in; *Fl:* 6–8; *Z:* 4

Anthriscus

Chervil

A. cerefolium: E Eur. Lvs lacy and bright green, slightly aniseed in flavour. Used in sim way to parsley. Stems hollow, fls tiny. Hardy ann or per; prop by seed at regular intervals. *Ht:* 18 in; *Spd:* 1 ft; *Fl:* 6–8

Artemisia

Artemisia

A. dracunculus Tarragon: Eur, Asia. Two types in cultivation—Russian: hardier, to 4 ft, fresh matt green thin lvs; French: More flavor, to 2 ft, lvs darker, glossier. Prop by div, seed. *Spd:* 15 in; *Fl:* 8; *Z:* 4

Borago

Borage

B. officinalis: Eur. Easy ann with cucumber-flavored lvs; an essential garnish for summer drinks. Lvs and stks coarsely hry. True-blue 5-petaled starry fls to 1 in diam can be candied. Sow seed in April, thin out to 15 in. *Ht:* to 3 ft; *Fl:* 6–9

B. officinalis

Carum

Caraway

C. carvi: Eur–N India. Slim v branched ann to 2 ft with finely cut lacy green lvs and flat heads of white fls. Lvs and seeds are used for their flavor and are said to "relieve flatulence". *Spd:* 1 ft; *Fl:* 6–7

Coriandrum

Coriander

C. sativum: Eur. Ann *c.* 18 in tall. Finely divided shining green lvs with an aniseed flavor. Fls white or pale lilac in a 5–10-rayed cartwheel. Seeds aromatic but smell unpleasant until dry. Reputedly aphrodisiac. Prop by seed in April. *Spd:* 1 ft; *Fl:* 6–8

C. sativum

Crocus

Crocus

C. sativus Saffron: S Eur–Kurdistan. Aut-flowering small crocus with bright lilac fls 4 in high from whose prominent scarlet stigmas saffron is obtained for use as a flavoring and coloring. Pinch out and dry them. Lvs typically crocus-like to 18 in. Prop by corms planted in July–mid Aug. *Spd:* 4 in; *Fl:* 10; *Z:* 6

C. sativus

Cuminum

Cumin

C. cyminum: Egypt. Ann to 1 ft with v branched stems. Lvs finely cut, deep green. Fls pale rose-pink or white in small heads. Seeds used as flavoring in Arabian, Levantine and Indian cooking. *Spd:* 8 in; *Fl:* 6–7

Foeniculum

Fennel

F. vulgare*: Eur. Graceful per. Branched green stems; finely cut rich green lvs and seeds with aniseed flavor. Often used with fish. Fls yellow; prop by seed. Also a good brown-lvd form. *Ht:* 5 ft; *Spd:* 2 ft; *Fl:* 7–8; *Z:* 4

Hyssop

H. officinalis: S Eur. Semi-evergreen bushy shrub to 2 ft, good as edging plant. Lvs narrow, dark green, aromatic. Fls blue, white or pink *c.* ¾ in wide. Prop by cuttings or sow seed in April. *Spd:* 1 ft; *Fl:* 7–9; *Z:* 3

H. officinalis

Levisticum

Lovage

L. officinale (= Ligusticum scoticum)★: Eur. Uprt per, celery-like in looks and flavor but taller. Lvs rich green, fls white in July (remove when plant grown as herb). Prop by seed. *Ht:* to 3 ft; *Spd:* 15 in; *Z:* 6

Lippia

Lippia

L. citriodora Lemon verbena: Chile. Decid shrub with pointed coarse lvs 3–4 in long, intensely lemon-scented. Not often seen more than 5 ft tall but can reach 9 ft in a warm sheltered spot. Fls faded purple in panicles to 4 in long. Prop by cuttings in late smr. *Spd:* 4 ft; *Fl:* 8; *Z:* 8

L. citriodora

Mentha

Mint

M. spicata Spearmint: Eur. The most common mint with smooth lvs. All mints are vig plants: any rooted piece will grow if planted in March or Apr. Most gardeners have a favorite sort. *M. rotundifolia* (Apple mint) with hry lvs and purplish-white fls rec. There is a pretty white-variegated form★. *Ht:* 3 ft; *Spd:* 2 ft; *Fl:* 8; *Z:* 3

M. rotundifolia 'Variegata'

Myrrhis

Myrrhis

M. odorata Sweet cicely: GB. Hardy per with aromatic pale green foliage like pressed lace. Used in salads and omelets: not unlike chervil (p 77). Stems 2–3 ft tall bear sev flat heads of white fls in May–June. Prop by seed in March/April. *Spd:* 2 ft; *Z:* 5

M. odorata

Nasturtium (= Rorippa)

Watercress

N. officinale: Eur. Hardy per salad vegetable or herb. Best in a wet place or shallow stream. Lvs dark green with a peppery flavor. Land or American cress needs less moisture. *Spd:* 2 ft; *Fl:* 6; *Z:* 4

Ocimum

Basil

O. basilicum Common or sweet basil: Trop Asia. Tall ann. Small oblong lvs have a unique flavor excellent with tomatoes. Fls white, tubular. Prop by seed. Only flourishes in hot smrs. *Ht:* 18 in; *Spd:* 1 ft; *Fl:* 8

Origanum

Origanum

O. marjorana

O. majorana (= Majorana hortensis) Sweet marjoram: N Africa. Nearly hardy sub-shrub. Small blunt hry lvs used to flavor veal, poultry. Fls white or faded maroon. Wild marjoram (*O. vulgare*) v sim; pot marjoram (*O. onites*) is a hardy per. Prop all by seed. *Ht:* to 2 ft; *Spd:* 1 ft; *Fl:* 6; *Z:* 9

Petroselinum

Parsley

P. crispum

P. crispum: C, S Eur. Hardy biennial, slow and sometimes hard to germinate, with curled lflts. French or flat-lvd parsley has a better flavor and is easier to grow. Sow only fresh seed. *Ht:* to 2 ft; *Spd:* 9 in; *Fl:* 6–8; *Z:* 3

Rosmarinus

Rosemary

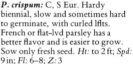

R. officinalis

R. officinalis*: S Eur, Asia Minor. Shrub with narrow aromatic lvs used particularly to flavor pork and lamb. Usually *c.* 4 ft but can be taller. Fls pale blue, 2-lipped, ¾ in long, on last year's growth in March–April. Prop by cuttings taken in mid-Aug. Uprt and variegated forms grown ornamentally. *Spd:* 6 ft; *Z:* 7

Ruta

Rue

R. graveolens: Eur. Small shrub with unpleasant-smelling pungent green lvs. Used medicinally and in claret cup. Fls mustard-yellow in flat heads. Do not confuse with blue-lvd border rue. *Ht, Spd:* 18 in; *Fl:* 6–9; *Z:* 5

Sorrel

R. acetosa: W Asia, N Africa, Eur. Easy strong-growing per to 2 ft. Spear-shaped lvs like spinach pleasantly acid-tasting and make excellent soup. Remove fls. French sorrel (*R. scutatus*) less inclined to run to seed. Prop by div or seed in spr. *Spd:* 9 in; *Fl:* 5–8; *Z:* 3

 *Salvia*

Sage

S. officinalis Garden sage: S Eur. Low evergreen branching shrub 1 ft × 18 in, inclined to layer. Lvs oblong like wrinkled grey-green felt, strong-flavored and often used with pork. Purple, blue or white 2-lipped fls to 1½ in. Sev colored-lf forms grown ornamentally but taste the same. Others grown as anns, herbaceous pers. *Fl:* 5–7; *Z:* 4

S. officinalis

 Satureia

Savory

S. montana: S Eur, N Africa. Semi-evergreen sprawling shrub, can be used as an edging plant. Narrow lvs and pale purple fls. Prop by div or seed. *S. hortensis* is a shorter hardy ann. Both can be used as an alternative to thyme. *Ht:* to 15 in; *Spd:* 1 ft; *Fl:* 6; *Z:* 4

S. montana

Symphytum

Comfrey

S. officinale: Eur, E to Siberia, Turkey. Roughly hry per. Fleshy pale green shoots and sim lvs used in same way as spinach. Fls tubular, white, blue purple or pink in clusters. *Ht:* 4 ft; *Spd:* 20 in; *Fl:* 6; *Z:* 4

Trigonella

Fenugreek

T. foenum-graecum Classical fenugreek: S France. Uprt ann to 2 ft, many divided lvs. Small white fls followed by seeds with strong celery flavor in sickle-shaped pods. Prop by seed in Apr. *Spd:* 1 ft; *Fl:* 6–8

Thymus

Thyme

T. vulgaris Common thyme: S Eur. Small densely branched wiry spreading bush 6–9 in tall good for edging paths. Tiny deep green lvs, hry on underside, strongly aromatic, excellent for flavoring. Lilac fls in closely packed 2 in heads from June–Aug. Prop by cuttings in May or June in cold frame, or by div, seed. *Spd:* 1 ft; *Z:* 4

T. vulgaris

Ferns

Flowerless, leafy plants reproducing by spores, usually found on their frond undersides, and mostly preferring shade. Only a few of the many excellent species are listed here.

Adiantum

Maidenhair fern

A. pedatum American maidenhair fern: N Amer. Perfectly hardy decid fern with pale green lfts on shining black wiry stems to 18 in. Forms light frothy clumps to 10 in wide. Needs moist but well-drained soil. Prop by div or spores. *Z: 3*

A. pedatum

Dryopteris

Dryopteris

D. filix-mas★ Male fern: Temp zones. Esp useful for dry shady places but naturally better where there is more moisture. Has tapered feather-shaped fronds to 3 ft tall and 9 in wide at the base, making clumps 2–3 ft across. Decid. Prop by division or spores. *Z: 3*

D. filix-mas

Matteuccia

Matteuccia

M. struthiopteris★ Ostrich plume fern: N Hem. Graceful fern; 3 ft tapering fronds form a green funnel or shuttlecock shape *c.* 2 ft wide at the mouth. Decid but some fronds stay brown until spr. Prop by div, spores. *Z: 3*

Onoclea

Onoclea

O. sensibilis Sensitive fern, Bead fern: N Amer, N Asia. Good ground cover in moist soils, spreading by rhizomes. Lvs to 18 in, usually arching, thick cut with rounded lobes. *Ht:* 2 ft; *Spd:* 5 ft; *Z: 3*

Osmunda

Osmunda

O. regalis★ Royal fern: Worldwide except Australasia. Bold stately decid fern esp attractive in early spr when unfurling fronds resemble meditating monks. Lvs 4 ft high with large blades over tough, fibrous rootstock. Prop by div or spores which germinate rapidly when fresh. *Ht, Spd:* 4 ft; *Z: 3*

O. regalis

Bulbs, corms and tubers

"Bulb" is taken as the group term for plants with swollen underground parts for the storage of supplies, and includes corms (as in crocuses), tubers (as in cyclamen) and rhizomes (as in irises). These parts make a highly convenient package for transplanting and sale, since many have a dormant period when they need no moisture (lilies are an important exception). Most of these plants reproduce by both offsets and seed.

           Achimenes

Achimenes

A. hybs: C, S Amer. Curious tuberous plants; those commonly grown are hybs with rough or hairy lvs and funnel-shaped red, pink, white, mauve or deep blue fls. Start in heat. *Ht:* 1 ft; *Spd:* 8 in; *Fl:* 7–8; *Z:* 10

          Acidanthera

Acidanthera

A. bicolor: Ethiopia. V like a white gladiolus with fls 2 in wide. It differs in having the tube of ptl-like parts at right angles to the stem and flowers in late Sept–Oct. *A. b. murielae* is hardiest in the gdn and has a purple blotch at the base of each ptl. Prop by corms or seed. Also good in pots. *Ht:* 3 ft; *Spd:* 6 in; *Z:* 10

A. bicolor murielae

   *Allium*

Ornamental onion

A large genus including chives and garlic. All are easy in well-drained borders; most smell of onions if bruised.

A. christophii (= albopilosum)*: Turkestan. The biggest drumstick heads of any onion with 8 in globes of lilac fls. Equally valuable when dry. The strap-shaped lvs are more substantial than others in the genus. Prop by seed or bulblets. *Ht:* 20 in; *Spd:* 8 in; *Fl:* 6; *Z:* 5

A. giganteum: Him. A splendid globular purplish fl head 4 in wide on a sturdy stem to 4 ft in June. Can be planted to come through low pers. Prop by seed or offsets. *Spd:* 1 ft; *Z:* 5

A. giganteum

A. moly: Med. Has bright yellow clusters of star-fls in July on 8 in stems over bluish-green lvs. Spreads and sows itself freely; easy to naturalize. Prop by seed or division. *Spd:* 1 ft; *Z:* 3

A. moly

Amaryllis

Belladonna lily

A. belladonna: S Africa. Plant these large bulbs *c.* 8 in deep in a warm well-drained place as at the foot of a south facing wall, then leave undisturbed. Pink, mauve-tinted, trumpet-shaped fls 4 in wide with a paler throat appear in Sept–Oct followed by strap-shaped lvs in early spring. Prop by dividing clumps or from seed. *Ht:* 30 in; *Spd:* 1 ft; *Z:* 9

A. belladonna

Anemone

Anemone, Windflower

Daisy-like flowers of simplicity and charm. Those listed are woodland plants with rhizomes or tubers flowering in spring.

A. blanda

A. apennina: S Eur. Rhizomatous March–April flowering sp. Naturalizes happily in the light shade of trees or the open border. Has sky-blue circular fls like larger daisies. Prop by division. *Ht:* 6 in; *Spd:* 4 in; *Z:* 6

A. blanda*: Greece–E Eur. Often in fl in Feb with pale to deep blue, pink or white fls 1½ in wide and soft, finely dissected lvs. Best left to naturalize. Divide tubers to increase. *Ht:* 6 in; *Spd:* 4 in; *Z:* 6

A. coronaria: S Eur. A range of strongly colored hybs including the semi-double or full-petaled 'St Brigid' race and the single-flowered 'De Caen' strain plus sev named cvs. Need a warm protected site to be really effective. Good cut fls. Prop by dividing tubers. *Ht:* 1 ft; *Spd:* 6 in; *Fl:* 3–4; *Z:* 6

A. coronaria

Anthericum

St Bernard's lily

A. liliago*: S Eur (Alpine meadows). Clump-forming, fleshy tuberous-rooted per with narrow 1 ft grass-like lvs and elegant clusters of pure white 1½ in fls. Prop by division. *Ht:* 18 in; *Spd:* 16 in; *Fl:* 6–7; *Z:* 6

Antholyza (= Curtonus)

Antholyza

A. (= Curtonus) paniculata Aunt Eliza: S Africa. Like a giant montbretia with pleated lvs and an arching stem. Burnt orange/red fls are a narrow trumpet shape to 2 in long in a zig-zag. *Ht:* 4 ft; *Spd:* 10 in; *Fl:* 8–9; *Z:* 7

Arisaema

Arisaema

A. candidissimum*: W China. Enchanting sugar-pink and pale green fls to 3 in and 3-lobed lvs make this a v decorative plant. Needs moist but not wet soil. Slow from seed. *Ht:* 10 in; *Spd:* 1 ft; *Fl:* 6; *Z:* 4

Arum

Flowers arranged on a central proboscis or spadix are shielded by a leafy cloak or spathe—these parts are the main attraction.

A. italicum Italian arum: Eur inc Med. A larger version of the hedgerow Lords and ladies with yellow spathes 7 in high appearing in aut. *A. i. marmoratum* has variegated lvs and a marbled spathe, purplish at the base. Prop by seed or division of tubers. *Spd:* 6 in; *Fl:* 9–10; *Z:* 6
A. pictum★: Spain, Corsica. Flowers a little later before lvs appear. Stouter and with larger lvs lasting all winter. Glistening red berries make a striking aut group. *Ht:* 10 in; *Spd:* 6 in; *Fl:* 9–10; *Z:* 6

A. italicum

 Babiana

Baboon root

B. stricta hybs: S Africa. Gladiolus-like, open tubular fls for a dry place; wiry stems *c.* 1 ft. Fls are brilliantly coloured and can be blue, violet, pink, crimson or yellow, often with a blotch at the base of each ptl and a sweet scent. Prop by corm offsets. *Spd:* 4 in; *Fl:* 6–5; *Z:* 6

Begonia

Begonia

Two tuberous-rooted begonias are commonly planted in gardens; many others are used in greenhouses or as house plants. The fibrous-rooted sorts are used for edging and carpeting.

B. grandis evansiana Hardy begonia: E Asia. Has heart-shaped lvs green above, red below and single pinks fls to 1¾ in wide on lax branching stems to 2 ft in light shade and warmth. Prop by bulblets. *Spd:* 1 ft; *Fl:* 6–9; *Z:* 6
B. stricta hybs (B × tuberhybrida)★: gdn origin. The big bedding sorts with fls to 6 in. Many named cvs in a wide variety of colors. *Ht:* 20 in; *Spd:* 16 in; *Fl:* 6–9; *Z:* 10

B. grandis evansiana

Brodiaea (= Tritelia)

Ithuriel's spear

B. laxa: Cal. One of a range of graceful spp and part of the supporting cast of the July gdn. Has agapanthus-like clusters of widely spaced funnel-shaped violet-blue or white fls 1¾ in long on slender stems to 2 ft. Prop by offsets. Do not disturb once planted. *Spd:* 4 in; *Z:* 6

Caladium

Caladium

C. bicolor: S Amer. Variable but gorgeous with lvs generally deep pink in the center merging to white then green. Several cvs also have violet and red stems. Lift in aut when the foliage collapses. Feed often in growth. Should not dry out completely in storage. *Ht:* 1 ft; *Spd:* 10 in; *Z:* 10

Calochortus

Mariposa lily

C. venustus: Cal. Each of the 3 ptls is yellow at the base with a purple blotch and often a pink blotch near top. *Ht:* 2 ft; *Spd:* 1 ft; *Fl:* 5–6; *Z:* 6

Camassia

Quamash

C. leichtlinii*: W N Amer. The tallest sp; reaches 3 ft with 1½ in spikes of starry violet-blue, blue or white fls and thin strap-like lvs. Slow from seed but long lived; does not easily produce bulblets. Pretty at the edge of light woodland with *C. quamash* (common quamash). Lasts well when cut. *Spd:* 6 in; *Fl:* 6–7; *Z:* 5

C. leichtlinii

Canna

Indian shot plant

C. indica hybs: Trop Amer, Asia. Hyb cannas are generally divided into those with green and those with purple lvs. All lvs are broad, shiny and to 4½ ft long. Gladiolus-like fls to 3 in long in spikes may be red, yellow, pink or white. Prop by division. *Spd:* 18 in; *Fl:* 8–10; *Z:* 7

Cardiocrinum

Cardiocrinum

C. giganteum Giant Himalayan lily: Him. A monster lily to 9 ft with glossy lvs, thick stems and 10 or 12 spectacular glistening white fls each 6 in long hanging from the top. It may take 7 or 8 years from seed to flowering but seedlings give the best flower. *Spd:* 4 ft; *Fl:* 7; *Z:* 6

C. giganteum

Chionodoxa

Glory of the snow

C. luciliae: E Med, Asia Minor. Early bulb 6 in high with up to 10 round starry fls to 1 in diam. Intense blue ptls and a pale to white center. The strap-shaped lvs are shining green. Will seed itself or thick patches can be divided. Best left to naturalize. *Spd:* 4 in; *Fl:* 3–4; *Z:* 5

C. luciliae

Clivia

Clivia

C. miniata: S Africa. Thick fl stems to 15 in, each bearing a cluster of orange/scarlet open funnel-shaped fls to 3½ with a yellow throat. Lightly frag, long lasting. Prop by offsets. Tender. *Spd:* 3 ft; *Fl:* 3–8; *Z:* 10

Colchicum

Meadow saffron

Mainly autumn-flowering—the large glossy green leaves do not appear until spring. Petals may have a checkered pattern.

C. autumnale: Eur. Fls are 2 in long and crocus-like but larger and a pale rose-pink. The lvs die away quickly by July. Single white and double rose-pink vars are known. Increase by offsets. *Spd:* 10 in; *Fl:* 9–11; *Z:* 6

C. speciosum*: Caucasus, Asia Minor. The loveliest and most spectacular with chalice-like fls of rosy lilac or even a deep wine col. 'Album' is a desirable albino. *Ht:* 10 in; *Spd:* 1 ft; *Fl:* 9–10; *Z:* 6

C. speciosum

Convallaria

Lily of the valley

C. majalis: Eur, Asia, N Amer. Hardy genus of a single sp well known as a cut fl of delicious fragrance. Spreading thong-like roots have thick nodes from which sheathed, pointed lvs arise. White, nodding bell-shaped ¼ in fls are borne on arching stems to 8 in. Named forms inc 'Fortin's Giant' pale pink and rare varieg cvs. *Spd:* 2 ft; *Fl:* 4–5; *Z:* 3

C. majalis

Corydalis

Corydalis

C. solida: Eur. Per with pale green dissected lvs and purple fls. With the blue-flowered *C. cashmeriana** hard to grow but a useful color change in spr gdn. Prop by seed or division. *Ht:* 6 in; *Spd:* 10 in; *Fl:* 4–5; *Z:* 6

Crinum

Crinum

C. × powellii*: S Africa, S Asia. A hardy hyb except in v cold or badly drained gdns. Has dark green strap-shaped lvs and stout stems to 3 ft with terminal gps of lily-like fls to 6 in wide. *Spd:* 1 ft; *Fl:* 7–9; *Z:* 8

Crocosmia

Crocosmia

C. × crocosmiiflora Montbretia: S Africa. Makes spreading clumps of 32 in sword-shaped lvs. Wiry fl stems have yellow/orange funnel-shaped fls to 1¾ in long in a flat zig-zag cluster in Aug and Sept. *C. masonorum** has larger fls of fierce reddish-orange on curving stems with fls facing upwards. Increase by division or seed. *Spd:* 3 ft; *Z:* 7

C. masonorum

Crocus

Among the most common and loveliest spring flowers. But some crocus species flower in autumn. For easy reference they have been divided into spring flowering species, hybrids and the autumn flowering species often confused with colchicums.

C. tomasinianus

C. Dutch

C. chrysanthus*: Greece, Turkey. Fls in mid-Feb are orange or old gold with purplish flecks or feathering outside. Excellent cvs include 'E. A. Bowles' deep yellow; 'Snow Bunting' white inside, cream and deep lilac inside. *Ht:* 3½ in; *Spd:* 4 in; *Fl:* 2–3; *Z:* 4

C. Dutch*: gdn origin. Larger and more flamboyant fls than above in white, mauve or yellow. A number of striped ones, e.g. 'Winston Churchill' are v decorative. *Ht, Spd:* 4 in; *Fl:* 3–4; *Z:* 4

C. speciosus*: S USSR–Iran. Glorious autumn-flowering sp. Slightly globular fls 3½ in high are bright lilac with 3 prominent dark veins and a yellow center. Plant by July. *Spd:* 4 in; *Fl:* 8–10; *Z:* 4

C. tomasinianus: Dalmatia. Delightfully invasive spr flowering sp. Slim silvery-mauve buds open to reveal rich purple ptls. 'Whitwell Purple' is darker. *Ht:* 3½ in; *Spd:* 4 in; *Fl:* 2–3; *Z:* 4

Cyclamen

Cyclamen vary more in timing than looks. All have typically long-eared flowers and are best increased by seed.

C. coum

C. persicum

C. coum: E Med–N Iran. Rarely over 3½ in in fl with rounded plain dark green lvs. Fls ¾ in long are rich carmine with deep spots at ptl bases. *Spd:* 6 in; *Fl:* 12–3; *Z:* 6

C. europaeum: S Eur. Has deep carmine fls to 1½ in in late smr and often in spr. Distinctive lvs are marked with a silvery zone. *Ht:* 4 in; *Spd:* 6 in; *Fl:* 4, 7–9; *Z:* 5

C. hederifolium (= neapolitanum)*: S Eur. Has angular toothed lvs with variable markings and rose-pink fls 1 in long with a deep carmine blotch at the base. There is also a white form. *Ht, Spd:* to 6 in; *Fl:* 8–11; *Z:* 5

C. persicum: E Med. Fragrant white or pale pink to carmine fls 1½ in long are held over dark green, often marbled lvs. *Ht:* 10 in; *Spd:* 8 in; *Fl:* 3–4; *Z:* 10

C. repandum Ivy-leaved cyclamen: S Eur. Distinctive lobed lvs have silvery markings and reddish undersides. Frag fls 1 in long are usually bright carmine. *Ht:* 6 in; *Spd:* 8 in; *Fl:* 4; *Z:* 6

Dahlia

Tuberous-rooted daisy-flowered plants, none hardy enough to treat as a perennial in zones 1 to 8, although tubers may survive a mild winter. Dahlias are usually classified in groups: Single-flowered; Anemone-flowered; Colarette, Peony-flowered; Decorative; Ball; Pompon; Cactus; Mignon; Orchid-flowered; Duplex and Miniature. Some of the groups are further subdivided by flower size. All the dahlias generally grown are derived from Mexican species.

D. Single-flowered. Attractive simple fls often used for bedding: 18in–2ft tall. Some, e.g. 'Yellow-hammer' have dark coppery foliage. 'Bishop of Landaff'* possibly a form of *D. coccinea*, is scarlet with red lvs. Mignon dahlias have single fls but are less than 18in tall. Orchid-flowered types are also single but with slightly tubular rays. Duplex vars are like Singles with 2 rows of rays. *Ht:* to 5ft; *Spd:* 2ft; *Fl:* 8–10; *Z:* 9

D. Decorative 'Polly Peachum'

D. Anemone-flowered: Fls to 2in wide; center of small tubular ray florets set in a ring of ptls. *Ht:* to 3½ft; *Spd:* 2ft; *Fl:* 8–10; *Z:* 9

D. Collarette: Dressy rather prim fls to 4in wide with 2nd row of short ptls around center disc. Inner and outer ptls often contrast in col giving a delightful effect. *Ht:* 4ft; *Spd:* 30in; *Fl:* 8–10; *Z:* 9

D. Peony-flowered: Full fls with 2 or 3 rows of undisciplined ptls producing a floppy effect. Heads 3–7in across according to cv. Dwarfs reach only 30in, others to 4ft. *Spd:* 2ft; *Fl:* 8–10; *Z:* 9

D. Small cactus 'Klankstad Kerkrade'

D. Decorative: Subdivided into 4 classes, 3 according to fl size and a dwarf section. All have fully double fls with central disc hidden by ptls and are 3–5ft tall. 'Gerrie Hoek' is a silvery-pink small decorative with fls 4–6in diam. The brilliant magenta 'Winston Churchill' is a miniature with fls under 4in diam. *Spd:* to 4ft; *Fl:* 8–10; *Z:* 9

D. Ball: The show dahlias with fully double almost round fls over 3in across. Tightly packed ptls are individually incurved. *Ht:* to 4ft; *Spd:* 30in; *Fl:* 8–10; *Z:* 9

D. Pompon: Neat round heads of fl *c.* 2in diam like pompomed poodles' tails. Vary from miniatures to tall border plants. *Ht:* to 4ft; *Spd:* 30in; *Fl:* 8–10; *Z:* 9

D. Collarette 'Grand Duke'

D. Cactus: Double fl heads but quill-shaped ptls give spiky look. Fls to 10in diam. Grouped as Incurved and Recurved Cactus. *Ht:* to 5ft; *Spd:* to 4ft; *Fl:* 8–10; *Z:* 9

D. Miniature: Any of the above types (except Pompons) with fls less than 4in wide.

D. Miniature ball 'Rothesay Superb'

Dichelostemma

D. ida-maia (= Brodiaea coccinea) California firecracker: Cal. Separated from *Brodiaea* because of its long (2 in) fl tubes, bright yellow tipped green. Of borderline hardiness. *Ht:* 18 in; *Spd:* 6 in; *Fl:* 6; *Z:* 6

Dierama

Venus' fishing rod, Wand flower

D. pulcherrimum*: S Africa. From July, often into aut, silvery-pink or purplish bell-shaped 1 in fls are borne on elegantly arching wiry stems 4 ft high. Lvs thin; corms need deep soil. Prop by seed. *Spd:* to 2 ft; *Z:* 7

D. pumilum: S Africa. Shorter at 30 in with stiff uprt stems. A number of named cvs, e.g. 'Ceres' light blue-violet. *Spd:* 18 in; *Fl:* 6–7; *Z:* 7

D. pulcherrimum

Dracunculus

Dracunculus

D. vulgaris Dragon arum: Med. Sinister arum with a 1 ft spathe dull red within and evil purplish-green outside. Fleshy spotted stem, purplish-white tube striped at mouth. Smells fetid. *Ht:* 2 ft; *Spd:* 18 in; *Fl:* 5–6; *Z:* 8

Eranthis

Eranthis

E. hyemalis* Winter aconite: Eur. Gleaming buttercup-yellow fls in Feb and March. Single fls 1 in wide on 2–4 in stems backed by a frilled ruff of bright green lvs. Naturalize freely if undisturbed and look well with snowdrops. Soak tubers in water for sev hours then plant 3 in deep. Prop by div or seed. *Spd:* 3 in; *Z:* 6

E. hyemalis

Eremurus

Foxtail lily

Spectacular soaring spikes of little lilies above an eruption of broad green strap-leaves. Sometimes classed as hardy perennials.

E. robustus: Turkestan. Magnificent sp with pokers of peach fls to 8 ft tall over a rosette of lvs each 3 ft × 4 in. Prop by div of starfish-like tuberous rts or fresh seed. *Spd:* 4 ft; *Fl:* 6–7; *Z:* 6

E. hybs: gdn origin. The 'Shelford Hybrids'* which fl earlier in June and reach 4–6 ft are frequently seen. Fls buff, pale yellow or shades of pink to white in spikes to 3 ft. Prop by div. *Spd:* 3 ft; *Z:* 6

E. robustus

Erythronium

E. dens-canis★ Dog's tooth violet:
Eur–Japan. Violet-like fls purplish-
rose, sol, 2 in wide, nodding over
beautifully marked lvs. *Ht:* 8 in; *Spd:*
6 in; *Fl:* 3–4; *Z:* 2
E. revolutum Mahogany fawn lily,
Trout lily: N Amer. Cream fls
turning purplish. In 'White Beauty'★
they remain white, 1–3 per stem.
Lvs veined white, faintly mottled.
Ht: to 1 ft; *Spd:* 6 in; *Fl:* 4–5; *Z:* 5
E. tuolumnense: Cal. Sim to above
but 8–12 smaller yellow fls on a
stem. Lvs plain yellowish-green.
Prop by div, seed. *Fl:* 4–5; *Z:* 5

E. revolutum

Freesia

Freesia

F. hybs: S Africa. Fls funnel-shaped,
strongly frag, purple, blue, orange,
yellow, pink or white on wiry stems
to 18 in with narrow lvs. Generally
grown under glass or in pots but
there are outdoor kinds that need
partial shade in a warm gdn. Plant
2 in deep; prop by seed or div of
named sorts. *Spd:* 4 in; *Fl:* 3–4;
Z: 10

F. hybrids

Fritillaria

Fritillary

F. imperialis★ Crown imperial: W
Him. Spectacular whorl of 2 in
nodding orange or yellow bells
topped by a tuft of short green lvs.
Each fl exquisitely marked inside.
Prop by seed. *Ht:* 4 ft; *Spd:* 15 in; *Fl:*
4; *Z:* 5
F. meleagris Guinea-hen flower:
Eur. Of more modest charm. Fls
1–2 per stem, bell-like, veined and
checked in varying shades of purple,
sometimes white. Lvs narrow. *Ht:*
to 15 in; *Spd:* 6 in; *Fl:* 4; *Z:* 6

F. imperialis

Galanthus

Snowdrop

G. elwesii★: Asia Minor. Among
the best spr flowering sp. Big
glaucous lvs. Fls 1¼ in, each white
inner ptl with conspic green blotch
at base and tip. Prop by div, seed.
Ht: 8 in; *Spd:* 8 in; *Fl:* 1–2; *Z:* 5
G. nivalis★ Common snowdrop:
Eur–USSR. Ptls white, 1 in, green
streaked inside, green marking near
tip. Narrow lvs. Sev selected forms
and named hybs inc doubles. *Ht:*
8 in; *Spd:* 6 in; *Fl:* 2–3; *Z:* 4

G. elwesii

Summer hyacinth

G. candicans: S Africa. Useful
Aug/Sept flowering bulb bearing
15–20 white nodding fls each 1½ in
long on a 3–4 ft stem. Lvs strap-
shaped, uprt, glaucous to 32 in.
Slow from seed, better from
bulblets. *Spd:* 8 in; *Z:* 7

G. princeps: S Africa. Shorter and
smaller in all its parts. Fls are
greenish and useful for cutting. Like
G. candicans v useful if planted 6 in
deep among low pers or ground
cover plants. *Ht:* 2 ft; *Spd:* 6 in; *Fl:*
8–9; *Z:* 7

G. candicans

Gladiolus

Gladiolus

Funnel-flowered relations of the iris, growing from corms.
Mostly South African and tender in frost areas, with a few
exceptions from the Mediterranean. The showiest are highly bred
hybrids, often artificial and plastic-looking, used for summer
bedding and as cut flowers. The hybrids want rich but well-
drained soil and sun. Many of the species are winter-flowering
and need a greenhouse.

G. byzantinus

G. byzantinus: Med. Good gdn per
to 30 in high; 6–10 fierce magenta fls
per spike, each 2½ in wide. A highly
desirable but less hardy rare white
form known. Lvs sword-shaped,
grey green. Prop by seed or div of
clumps (which tend to spread). *Spd:*
6 in; *Fl:* 6; *Z:* 7

G. × colvillei: gdn origin. 'The
Bride' is one of the better known of
this group of hybs which were some
of the first gladiolus crosses made.
Colville was the nurseryman who
brought them into popularity.
White fls 3 in wide with a deep
crimson blotch mark. Plant in early
aut in mild areas or in pots under
glass. Protect in borders in wtr.
Prop by cormlets. *Ht:* 30 in; *Spd:*
6 in; *Fl:* 4–6; *Z:* 7

G. × hortulanus gdn hybs: gdn
origin. Bulb merchants, catalogues
and flower show judges usually list 5
main types of hybs. Large flowered,
to 4 ft tall, have roughly triangular
fls each to 7 in wide; Primulinas are
free-flowering hybs to 3 ft tall with
fls to 3 in wide and a hooded top ptl;
Miniatures, averaging 18 in high,
have smaller fls 2 in wide in
Primulina shape and usually
attractively ruffled or frilled;
Butterfly gladioli to 4 ft tall have
close-packed fls often with striking

G. gdn hybrid 'Ravel'

Gladiolus

contrasting markings in the throat; Mid-season hybs to 4 ft flower in June–July. Between them these hybs cover all shades of the color card including purple, blue and brown as well as the primary cols. Good examples inc 'Ravel' and 'Red Cascade' as illustrated. Fls to 7 in wide. Each corm can produce 2 spikes each lasting for about 10 days, lvs grow until frosted. Plant 4–6 in deep, lift in aut. *Spd:* to 6 in; *Fl:* 7–9; *Z:* 7

G. Butterfly gdn hybrid

G. tristis Yellow marsh afrikander: S Africa. Elegant but tender May-flowering sp, sweetly frag. To 18 in tall with 3 or 4 pale yellow fls each 2–3 in long and tinted red on ptl reverses. Prop by seed or cormlets. *Spd:* 6 in; *Z:* 8

G. gdn hybrid 'Red Cascade'

Gloriosa

Creeping or climbing lily

G. rothschildiana: Africa, Trop Asia. Tender, but can be treated like a dahlia in gdns. Climbs by lf-tip tendrils to 7 ft. Exotic fls 4 in wide with lower half of each ptl yellow, top crimson, reflexed in a turban shape. Start in pots, handle carefully because of brittle rts. Prop by seed, offsets. *Spd:* 2 ft; *Fl:* 6–8; *Z:* 9

G. rothschildiana

Haemanthus

Blood flower, Blood lily

H. coccineus: S Africa. Bulbs produce 2 wide tongue-shaped 18 in lvs dying in smr. Fl clusters 3 in wide in Sept surrounded by fleshy scarlet bracts. Best in pots but will do well in a v warm spot. *Ht:* 10 in; *Spd:* 4 in; *Z:* 10

Hippeastrum

"Amaryllis"

H. hybs: gdn origin. Large funnel-like fl trumpets often 10 in wide; 1–4 on a thick stem 1–2 ft high. Lvs strap-shaped. Easy in pots but only suitable for v warm gdn as they need a minimum temp of 55°F, higher to fl, in Feb–April, and rich, loamy soil. Die down in late smr and need to be dried off in the pots. *Spd:* 6 in; *Fl:* 1–4; *Z:* 10

H. hybrid 'Jenny Lind'

Hyacinthoides (= Endymion)

Bluebell

H. hispanicus (= Scilla hispanica)* Spanish bluebell: Spain, Portugal. Fls deep blue to pale pink, ¾ in long. Named forms inc 'Mount Everest' white; 'Queen of the Pinks' pink. Prop by div. *Ht:* 1 ft; *Spd:* 6 in; *Fl:* 5; *Z:* 5

Hyacinthus

Hyacinth

H. Roman*: gdn origin. April-flowering with a loose 4 in gp of white bells on a 9 in stem. Deliciously frag and useful for early forcing in bowls after which they can be planted out and allowed to naturalize. Lvs bright green. Prop by offsets. *Spd:* 9 in; *Z:* 6

H. Roman 'Eros'

Hymenocallis

Spider lily

H. narcissiflora (= calanthina): Peru. Nearly hardy curious bulbous fl with a long white-green faintly striped ptl tube finely feathered at the edge. Fls 1–5 per 18 in stem and 6 in wide. Prop by offsets. *Spd:* 15 in; *Fl:* 3–4; *Z:* 7

Ipheion (= Brodiaea, Milla, Tritelia)

Ipheion

I. uniflorum: S Amer. Pretty little spring-flowering bulb bearing 1 (sometimes 2) star-shaped white, pale mauve to deep purple-blue frag fls 2 in wide on a 6 in stem. Lvs thin, pale green and smelling of onions when bruised. V easy in a sunny border. Increase by div of clumps. *Spd:* 3 in; *Fl:* 4–5; *Z:* 7

I. uniflorum

Iris

Iris

All irises have food-storage organs at or below soil level. The border irises and some others (see p 37) have rhizomes but the miniature winter and spring-flowering and taller summer-flowering English, Spanish and Dutch kinds arise from bulbs. All bulbous irises need good drainage for a summer period of dry dormancy; moisture is necessary only in the flowering season.

I. danfordiae: Turkey. Fls in March, deep yellow with a green tinge to 3 in wide and honey fragrance. Plant 3 in deep. Inclined to split into tiny bulblets after flowering. Maintain a clump by adding a few bulbs each year. *Ht:* 4 in; *Spd:* 6 in; *Z:* 6

I. Dutch: gdn origin. *I. xiphium × tingitana* hybs. Fls to 5 in wide produced in May–June make rich patches of col in the early border and

I. danfordiae

good cut fls. Wide range of named forms and cols inc white, yellow, orange, blue, purple or bronze and bicolors. Pale blue 'Wedgwood' v popular. Can be left for several years. Prop by seed or separation of bulbs which are smooth unlike the reticulate (wtr/spr flowering) gp. *Ht:* 1–2 ft; *Spd:* to 4 in; *Z:* 5

I. English: gdn origin. Follow on from the Dutch irises in late June and overlap with the Spanish ones in early July. Ptls close, giving elegant appearance, and are white, blue, mauve or purple. Can be left to colonize. Not English: derived from Spanish parents. Prop by seed or division of clumps. *Ht:* to 2 ft; *Spd:* 4 in; *Z:* 6

I. histrioides*: Turkey. Fls before even lf tips show above soil from late wtr. Fls to 3½ in wide, intense royal blue with an orange crest and paler spotting are seemingly weatherproof. Fls followed by taller, glaucous lvs. Prop by separation of bulbs or seed. *Ht:* to 4 in; *Spd:* 4 in; *Z:* 5

I. reticulata: Turkey, Caucasus, Iran. The most reliable and popular winter iris for general gdn planting. Fls to 3 in wide from March, deep violet–purple with gold markings and a velvety sheen. Lvs present at flowering time reach twice the height of the fls and have 4 prominent veins. Sev named cvs available. Prop by seed or separation of bulbs. *Ht:* to 8 in; *Spd:* 4 in; *Z:* 5

I. Spanish: gdn origin. Succeed Dutch irises in mid-July. Should be treated in the same way but lift and dry bulbs when lvs start to wither. Fls to 4½ in. wide. Cvs offered under names in the following cols: blue, white, yellow and purple, also bicolors, often with a golden blotch as in Dutch types. Plant in Sept. *Ht:* 2 ft; *Spd:* 6 in; *Z:* 6

I. tuberosa (= Hermodactylus tuberosus) Snake's head iris: Eur. Curious rather than beautiful fls with velvety yellow-green standards and purplish-black falls to 2 in. Thin lvs 1 ft tall and fl stems a little shorter. Sometimes a little shy-flowering once established in colonies. Prop by div. *Spd:* to 10 in; *Fl:* 4–5; *Z:* 5

I. Dutch

I. histrioides

I. reticulata

I. Spanish

I. tuberosa

Corn lily

I. gdn hybs: gdn origin. Brightly colored fls to ¾ in wide are cream, orange or pink, usually with pronounced central disc, and open only in direct sun. Useful in pots. Plant 3 in deep in aut, protect in wtr, remove in spr. Prop by bulblets or save seed. *Ht:* to 1 ft; *Spd:* 4 in; *Fl:* 5–6; *Z:* 9

Lachenalia

Lachenalia

L. aloides

L. aloides Cape cowslip: S Africa. Barely hardy enough for the gdn but easy in pots if kept frost free. Tubular fls in fls on 1 ft stems spotted brown like the lvs. 'Lutea' is yellow; 'Nelsonii' green tinged. *Spd:* 6 in; *Fl:* 3–4; *Z:* 9

Leucojum

Snowflake

L. vernum

L. aestivum Summer snowflake*: Eur. Forms large clumps of narrow dark green 2 ft lvs; 2–8 clean white bell-shaped fls 1 in diam, green at ptl tips. 'Gravetye Giant' good. Prop by div. *Spd:* 8 in; *Fl:* 4–5; *Z:* 4
L. vernum Spring snowflake: Eur. One or 2 white ¾ in fls with pronounced green spot on outer tip of each ptl. Lvs narrow, strap-shaped to 10 in. Naturalizes easily; likes damp. *Spd:* 4 in; *Fl:* 2–3; *Z:* 4

Lilium

Lily

The most glamorous of bulbs, but also the most demanding. Lilies like a combination of plentiful moisture and rapid drainage, which is often hard to provide. They are vulnerable to disease and suffer from drying out when moved. Woodland conditions and leafy lime-free soil are best for most unless otherwise noted.

L. auratum

L. auratum* Goldband lily. Japan. Glorious lily to 8 ft tall with 20 + fls to 1 ft, each ivory white and opening with a central inner gold band and lots of purplish spots. Heavily scented. Plant 4–6 in deep. Stem-rooting; needs support. Prop by scales, bulblets or virus-free stock. *Spd:* 1 ft; *Fl:* 8; *Z:* 4
L. candidum* Madonna lily: E Med. The common white lily of cottage gdns, 2–6 ft high. Intensely frag 4 in fls with pronounced golden anthers. Transplant bulbs after flowering in early Aug. Plant shallowly; prop by scales or div. Likes sunshine and

Lily

some lime. *Spd:* 9 in; *Z:* 4

L. gdn hybs: gdn origin. Hybrids (there are hundreds) can be more or less divided into categories according to their parentage or to the arrangement and formation of the fls and stem heights. Most are June/July flowering, some Aug. Consult a good catalog and choose what suits from the wide variety of shapes and sizes available. *Ht:* to 8 ft; *Spd:* to 1 ft; *Z:* 4

L. martagon Martagon or Turk's cap lily: Eur. Usually 2–3 ft tall but can reach 5 ft; 30–50 frag purplish-red, purple-spotted fls. There is an enchanting white form. Lvs in whorls up the stem. Plant 4–6 in deep; prop by bulblets, slow from seed. *Spd:* 10 in; *Fl:* 6–7; *Z:* 3

L. pyrenaicum: Pyrenees. Also "Turk's cap" in type. The acid-greenish-yellow purple-spotted 2 in fls have recurved ptls revealing orange pollen on the anthers. Early June-flowering, unpleasant scent. Lvs narrow, grassy up stems 2–3 ft high. Prop by bulbs, scales or seeds. Likes lime. *Spd:* 10 in; *Z:* 4

L. regale★: W China. Large trumpet-shaped glistening white fls in July sometimes 5 in long, with bright yellow throat and rosy-maroon on ptl outsides. Strongly frag. Excellent border plant reaching 6 ft in good conditions. Remarkably easy to grow and raise from seed, happy on lime *Spd:* 1 ft; *Z:* 3

L. tigrinum 'Fortunei'★ Tiger lily: sp China, Japan. Distinct orange-red black-spotted 4 in fls on purplish black hry stems to 6 ft bearing bulblets (for prop) in lf axils. *Spd:* 10 in; *Fl:* 8–9; *Z:* 3

L. candidum

L. regale

L. pyrenaicum

Muscari

Grape hyacinth

M. armeniacum★: N Asia Minor. V easy forming dense clumps with grassy lvs to 18 in. Tiny pitcher-shaped blue fls in clusters 1–3 in long on 8–10 in stems produce a noticeable effect. *M. racemosum* less tall and more common in gdns. Prop by seed, div of bulbs. *Spd:* 4 in; *Fl:* 4–5; *Z:* 5

M. racemosum

Daffodil

"Daffodils" are narcissi with trumpets as long as their petals (technically perianth segments) or longer. Sixty-odd species, mainly from round the Mediterranean, have produced over 8,000 cultivars, including many of the easiest and hardiest of all the bulbs in the garden.

N. Double 'Mary Copeland'

N. Dwarf (*N. cyclamineus*)

N. Large-cupped 'Ceylon'

N. poeticus

N. Double daffodils: gdn origin. The plain yellow double daffodil 'Van Sion' found in borders and old orchards is v ancient in cultivation. Newer, better forms, but less weatherproof, inc 'Mary Copeland' with creamy-white ptls interspersed with shorter ones of apricot-buff. *Ht:* 18 in; *Spd:* 6 in; *Fl:* 3–5; *Z:* 3

N. Dwarf: Spain, Portugal. Botanically *N. bulbocodium* (Hoop petticoat) and *N. cyclamineus*. The former is a March/early April flowering 6 in miniature with a wide-flared trumpet (hence the common name) with only rudimentary ptls. Likes moist soil and naturalizes easily. *N. cyclamineus* is 4–8 in tall with a long, thin perianth tube and swept back ptls. Likes damp soil, can take semi-shade, seeds freely. 'February Gold'★ is an excellent cv. *Spd:* 4 in; *Fl:* 2–3; *Z:* 3

N. jonquilla Jonquil: Portugal, Spain–N Africa. Jonquils consist of 5 *Narcissus* spp and sev cvs. Mainly March/April flowering, rush-lvd 6–10 in tall, 1–5 v frag fls per stem. For a sheltered gdn or a cold greenhouse. 'Bobbysoxer' is a cv with yellow ptls and an orange cup. *Spd:* 4 in; *Z:* 3

N. Large and small cupped: gdn origin. March/April flowering and often 2-colored. One fl to a stem, the cup is not more than one third the width of the ptls. 'Flower Record' is a good large-cupped one, 'Edward Buxton' a good small-cupped. *Ht:* to 18 in; *Spd:* 6 in; *Z:* 3

N. poeticus Poet's narcissus: S Eur. Flowers in mid spr with white ptls forming a flat saucer to 3 in wide (except in *N. p. recurvus*, Pheasant's eye narcissus) and a small red-rimmed yellow or bright red cup. Deliciously frag; valuable as the last narcissus to flower. *Ht:* 18 in; *Spd:* 6 in; *Z:* 3

N. tazetta: Med–China, Japan. One of the most desirable and sweetly scented of all narcissi but too early and tender for most gdns. Enjoyed best in pots and bowls (for which 'Paper White' is the most common choice) with gps of entirely white fls to 3 in wide on stems to 2 ft tall. *Spd:* 6 in; *Fl:* 3–4; *Z:* 6

N. triandrus: Spain. Perfectly hardy little 6 in–1 ft sp with 1–3 nodding white fls per stem. Ptls are about

Daffodil

twice the length of the ½ in trumpet and slightly reflexed. Ideal for rock gdns and the front of the border. 'Albus'★ white is called Angels' tears; 'Thalia'★ is an excellent taller cv with the same grace and is later flowering. *Spd:* 6 in; *Fl:* 4–5; *Z:* 3

D. Trumpet: gdn origin. Common-or-garden trumpet daffodils comprise a large gp which have 1 large fl on a stem and a trumpet equal in length or longer than the width of the ptls. They may be in 1 or 2 cols and are 18–20 in tall. Plant 6 in deep and leave undisturbed for several years. *Spd:* 6 in; *Fl:* 3; *Z:* 3

N. triandrus

Nerine

N. bowdenii★: S Africa. Spidery icing-sugar-pink fls in late Sept–Nov in loose terminal clusters 6 in wide on 1–2 ft stems. Strap-shaped fresh green lvs appear at flowering time but die away by following aut. Just about hardy: need warmth to fl really well. Plant no more than 6 in deep. 'Mark Fenwick' is taller. Prop by div but best undisturbed. *Spd:* 6 in; *Z:* 6

N. bowdenii

Star of Bethlehem

O. nutans: E Eur, Asia Minor. Drooping white 1 in fls pale green on outside. Floppy lvs to 18 in. Prop by div, seed, naturalizes well. *Spd:* 6 in; *Fl:* 4–5; *Z:* 6

O. umbellatum: Asia Minor, Eur. 10–20 open starry fls form flat pyramid to 1 ft tall. Fls shining white, green striped ptl backs. *Spd:* 8 in; *Fl:* 4–5; *Z:* 5

O. umbellatum

Sea lily

P. maritimum: S Eur. V frag white fls 3 in wide in a loose umbel on 1 ft stems in July–Sept. Glaucous lvs virtually ever-grey. Plant 3 in deep, protect in winter. Prop by separation of bulbs. *Spd:* 1 ft; *Z:* 7

Pleione

P. bulbocodioides: Asia. A group of small hardy orchids often cataloged under older individual names. Lvs narrow, longitudinally pleated. Fls orchid-like to 4 in wide, rose-purple often with whitish lip. Exquisite but not easy. Prop by div of pseudo bulbs. *Ht:* 6 in; *Spd:* 4 in; *Fl:* 3–5; *Z:* 8

Polianthes

P. tuberosa Tuberose: Mexico. Rarely seen in gdns nowadays but well worth growing. Strongly frag fls white, open, star-shaped on stems to 4 ft. Lvs narrow, smell v nasty when bruised. Plant new bulbs each season. *Spd:* 5 in; *Fl:* 7–8; *Z:* 9

P. tuberosa

Ranunculus

Buttercup

R. asiaticus Garden ranunculus, Persian buttercup: Orient. Nearly all double-flowered in a wide range of attractive cols and *c.* 3 in wide. Lvs dissected. Lift and divide annually. *Ht:* to 15 in; *Spd:* 6 in; *Fl:* 5–6; *Z:* 4

Rhodohypoxis

Rhodohypoxis

R. baurii: S Africa. Rts fleshy. Brightly colored white, pink or red fls to 1½ in diam, 6-petaled. Sev named cvs available and many fl from May–Sept. Also good in rock gdns. *Ht:* 4 in; *Spd:* 6 in; *Z:* 7

Schizostylis

Kaffir lily

S. coccinea★ Crimson flag: S Africa. Oct–Nov flowering per with fleshy or rhizomatous rtstock. Buds open to form 6-petaled fls 1½ in wide, 10–14 on a spike 18 in–2 ft tall. Pale green lvs sheathing the base of the stem. Good for cutting. Named clones with larger or deep pink or red fls available. Prop by offsets or div. *Spd:* 1 ft; *Z:* 9

S. coccinea

Scilla

Squill

Relations of the lily with close-packed little flowers, generally blue. *S. sibirica* is early, easy and in fact essential.

S. peruviana★ Cuban lily: Med. Fine plant with broad green lvs 6–10 in long and domed 6 in heads of lilac-blue fls, 50–100 closely packed. Also a white form. Prop by seed, div. *Spd:* 8 in; *Fl:* 5–6; *Z:* 8

S. sibirica★ Siberian squill: E USSR, Siberia. One of the easiest and best early blue fls; 3–4 slightly drooping fls ½ in wide, deep gentian-blue. Lvs squeaky to touch. Prop by seed, offsets. *Ht:* to 8 in; *Spd:* 4 in; *Fl:* 3; *Z:* 3

S. peruviana

Gloxinia

S. speciosa: Brazil. Not hardy but common indoors. Soft hry lvs, bell-shaped 4 in fls deep blue to pink and deep red. *Ht:* 10 in; *Spd:* 1 ft; *Fl:* 5–9; *Z:* 10

S. speciosa

Sparaxis

S. tricolor Harlequin flower: S Africa. Most bulbs offered are hybs of this and *S. grandiflora* with the influence of *Streptanthera*. They have 3–6 brightly colored fls of red, yellow, purple, orange, white or a mixture on wiry stems. Lvs uprt. Prop by seed. *Ht:* 15 in; *Spd:* 4 in; *Fl:* 4–5; *Z:* 10

Sternbergia

S. lutea★: C Eur. Rather like a yellow aut crocus but lvs and fls appear together. Lvs narrow, deep shining green, gradually reach 6 in; fls 2 in, golden, shining on 5 in stems. Transplant in lf or when dormant in midsummer. Reasonably hardy in all but v cold areas. Prop by div of clumps. *Spd:* 6 in; *Fl:* 8–9; *Z:* 6

S. lutea

Tigridia

T. pavonia★ Peacock or tiger flower: Mexico, Peru. Exotic 6-petaled fls 4 in wide, inner ptls crimson spotted. Sp orange/scarlet, other forms red, crimson, pink, orange and yellow. Fls last 1 day, but 6–10 in succession. Sadly only hardy in warm gdns. *Ht:* 18 in; *Spd:* 4 in; *Fl:* 7–9; *Z:* 6

Trillium

T. erectum Birth root: E N Amer. Symmetrical 3-petaled fls 1½ in wide which can be white, yellow or pink but are usually mahogany; ptls separated by 3 small green sepals. Lvs broad in stalkless whorl of 3 on the stem. Prefers peaty soil. Prop by seed or div of tubers but slow to increase. *Ht, Spd:* 1 ft; *Fl:* 5; *Z:* 4

T. grandiflorum Wake robin: E N Amer. The best known and most useful gdn plant of the genus producing clean white fls to 3 in wide on a 2 ft single stem. There is also a sumptuous rare double-flowered form★. Prop by div, seed. *Spd:* 1 ft; *Fl:* 4–6; *Z:* 4

T. erectum

Tritonia

T. crocata 'White Beauty'

T. crocata Blazing star: S Africa. Usually best under glass. Glowing orange open fls 1½ in wide, shaded yellow throat. Fls of 'White Beauty' white, may have yellow center. Lvs narrow. Prop by seed, div. *Ht:* to 2 ft; *Spd:* 6 in; *Fl:* 5–6; *Z:* 6

Tulbaghia

Tulbaghia

T. violacea

T. violacea Violet tulbaghia: S Africa. Tubular fls are violet-colored and frag. 8–16 at the tip of 1 ft fl stems displayed like a partly opened umbrella. Lvs to 15 in. Prop by seed, offsets. *Spd:* 15 in; *Fl:* 7–9; *Z:* 9

Tulipa

Tulip

Tulips have been garden plants since the sixteenth century in Holland and much earlier in the East. Their classification is thus horticultural and artificial, by shape and flowering period. Smaller, often earlier flowering, natural "botanical" species were more recently collected. Many can become permanent.

T. clusiana

T. greigii 'Red Riding Hood'

T. clusiana Lady tulip: Iran, Iraq, Afghanistan. Slender elegant "botanical" tulip with 1½ in white fls with violet blotch in center and broad rosy-pink stripe on ptl outside. Lvs to 10 in, slightly glaucous, sometimes with a thread of red along edge. Plant 5 in deep. *Ht:* 8 in; *Spd:* 3 in; *Fl:* 4; *Z:* 3

T. Darwin: gdn origin. Popular tall May flowering tulips often used for bedding out. Large squarish fls to 5 in across in wide col range from pale yellow through pink, scarlet, crimson, mauve and purple to near-black. Plant 6 in deep in aut. *Ht:* to 2 ft; *Spd:* 8 in; *Z:* 3

T. fosteriana: Samarkand. V big fls to 9 in wide with long blunt ptls which open flat. Sp is rich shiny scarlet and 8–18 in tall. Cvs have red, pink, yellow or white fls all with characteristic grey lvs. *Spd:* 4 in; *Fl:* 3–4; *Z:* 3

T. greigii*: Turkestan. The sp is brilliant scarlet, its hybs a colorful range 8–10 in tall and long-lasting in fl. The mottled glaucous lvs have attractive brown-purplish streaks. *Spd:* 6 in; *Fl:* 4; *Z:* 3

Tulip

T. kaufmanniana Water lily tulip: Turkestan. The sp is cream with a pink and yellow flush; hybs range from yellow to scarlet and have 3–5 lvs, the longest, lowest ones to 10 in. All are *c.* 1 ft tall with 3½ in fls in March–early April according to type and severity of wtr. Can be left to colonize. *Spd:* 6 in; *Z:* 3

T. kaufmanniana

T. Lily-flowered: gdn origin. Tall late-flowering tulips with distinct long, slightly waisted fls to 8 in diam and pointed reflexed ptls. Good col range, mainly in deep shades. *Ht:* 2 ft; *Spd:* 6 in; *Fl:* 5; *Z:* 3
T. Parrot★: gdn origin. Tulips 18 in–2 ft tall with large fringed and ruckled ptls forming heavy, often floppy fls 8 in wide. Brightly colored and inc strange mixtures such as salmon-pink with streaks of green, orange and yellow. *Spd:* 8 in; *Fl:* 5; *Z:* 3

T. Parrot 'Sunshine'

Vallota

V. capensis Scarborough lily: S Africa. Like a more elegant amaryllis with 4 in fls of similar funnel shape but smaller with up to 10 fls per 18 in stem. Broad lvs 18 in at flowering time. *Spd:* 1 ft; *Fl:* 8–9; *Z:* 10

Veltheimia

V. capensis: S Africa. Something like a squat red hot poker. Many strap-shaped, bright green wavy-edged lvs to 1 ft. Fls reddish-pink or yellowish, spotted pendulous tubes on purplish spotted stems. *Spd:* 18 in; *Fl:* 4–7; *Z:* 10

Watsonia

W. pyramidata (= rosea): S Africa. Botanically close to gladioli. Can be divided for gdn purposes into decid and evergreen sorts. *W. pyramidata* is decid with red fls, *W. beatricis*, one of the best evergreens, also with red fls in spikes to 5 ft. Prop from corms. Not reliably hardy; can be lifted in aut. *Spd:* 8 in; *Fl:* 6; *Z:* 8

W. pyramidata

Zephyranthes

Z. candida Flower of the West Wind: S America (along La Plata River). Single white funnel-shaped fls 1½ in wide and narrow green lvs. Colonizes readily in warm borders. Prop by offsets. *Ht:* 8 in; *Spd:* 6 in; *Fl:* 9–10; *Z:* 7

Roses

The conventional classification of roses, with such evocative terms as China and noisette, Portland and damask, reflects their ancient history in cultivation. In modern practice, broader distinctions are sufficient guide to general character. Here we classify them simply into natural species and old-fashioned shrubs; modern (mainly 20th century) shrubs; hybrid teas; floribundas, with the similar grandifloras; climbers and ramblers; and miniatures.

Species and old roses

These roses may not be such efficient "flowering machines" as the latest bedding varieties but have more grace and charm, distinction of habit, leaf and fragrance, and more character. Most flower only once but many produce ornamental hips.

R. × alba 'Semi-plena'

R. centifolia

R. gallica 'Versicolor'

R. damascena 'Madame Hardy'

R. × alba★ "White Rose of York", "Jacobite Rose": gdn origin. Famous old rose, long in cultivation. Flat semi-double richly frag white fls to 3 in wide. Lvs pale, 5–7 greyish-green lflts. 'Celestial' clear pink double; 'Great Maiden's Blush' pale pink double. *Ht:* 6 ft; *Spd:* 6 ft; *Fl:* 6–7; *Z:* 4

R. centifolia★ Cabbage or Provence rose: gdn origin. Head of a group of richly scented forms and cvs. Fls of sp deep pink, round, 3 in wide. Lvs have 5–7 lflts. 'Muscosa' the Moss rose sim, fls double, sticky glandular "mossy" buds and shoots. *Ht, Spd:* 4 ft; *Fl:* 6–7; *Z:* 5

R. chinensis★ China rose: China. Elegant sp, seemingly always in fl. Ptls translucent, crimson or old rose pink. Form 'Old Blush' China, fls to 2½ in wide, most common. Lvs have 3–5 lflts. *Ht:* to 5 ft; *Spd:* 3 ft; *Fl:* 6–9; *Z:* 6–7

R. damascena★ Damask rose: Asia. V old in cultivation, many forms and hybs. Lvs greyish-green, 5–7 lflts; stems prickly. Fls richly frag, red, 3 in wide. 'Versicolor' is the semi-double white-striped "York and Lancaster" rose. *Ht, Spd:* to 6 ft; *Fl:* 6–7; *Z:* 4

R. gallica★ French rose: S Eur–W Asia. Dwarf, bushy spp. Stems bristly, lvs coarse, leathery, 3–5 lflts. Fls single, deep pink to crimson, 3 in wide. Hips (frs) round, brick red. *R. g. officinalis* the "Apothecary's Rose" or "Red Rose of Lancaster" has frag, semi-double, bright crimson fls with prominent yellow stamens. Lvs dark green. *R. g.* 'Versicolor' or "Rosa Mundi" is a sport of *R. g. officinalis* with semi-double fls but in deep rosy red splashed and striped blush pink. *Ht, Spd:* 3 ft; *Fl:* 6; *Z:* 5

R. hugonis★: China. Fls pale yellow, single, to 2½ in wide. Lvs have 5–11 lflts. Hips round, dark red. Forms delicate arching shape. *Ht, Spd:* 6 ft; *Fl:* 6; *Z:* 4

R. moyesii★ China. Vig, uprt shrub. Fls single, blood red, 2 in wide followed by bottle-shaped red hips to 2½ in. Parent of shorter 'Geranium' with lighter, brighter red fls. *Ht:* to 12 ft; *Spd:* 8 ft; *Fl:* 6–7; *Z:* 4

R. pimpinellifolia (= spinosissima)★ Scotch or Burnet rose: Eur–USSR. Suckering prickly-stemmed bush; lvs have 5–9 small, apple-green lflts. Fls small but generously produced and with exquisite scent, white or pale pink in sp. Hips round, blackish, shiny. Cvs inc double, pink, red, white and yellow forms, e.g. 'William's Double Yellow'. *Ht:* 3 ft; *Spd:* 5 ft+; *Fl:* 5–6; *Z:* 4

R. rubiginosa (= eglantaria)★ Sweet briar, Eglantine: Eur. Thorny, stout shrub, good hedging. Fls small, single, bright pink; lvs deliciously frag, esp after rain. Lvs have 5–9 lflts. Hips oval, orange. *Ht, Spd:* 8 ft; *Fl:* 6; *Z:* 4

R. rubrifolia★: C, S Eur. Decorative in lf, fl and fr. Lvs have 5–9 steely blue-grey lflts with hint of crimson. Fls single, 1½ in wide, rose-pink, paler towards center. Hips oval, glistening browny-red. Comes true from seed. *Ht:* 7 ft; *Spd:* 6 ft; *Fl:* 6; *Z:* 4

R. rugosa★ Ramanas rose: E Asia. Suckering on light soils. Lvs have 5–9 handsome round, veiny dark green lflts with useful yellow aut col. Fls single, red or white, 3 in diam. Hips orange-red, tomato-shaped. Sev excellent (AGM) cvs inc 'Fru Dagmar Hastrup' dwarf, single, pale pink; 'Roseraie de l'Hay' semi-double crimson-purple; 'Blanc Double de Coubert' semi-double white; 'Sarah van Fleet' masses of semi-double mallow-pink fls. *Ht:* to 7 ft; *Spd:* 6 ft; *Fl:* 6–7; *Z:* 4

'Frau Karl Druschki'★: gdn origin. Hybrid perpetual. Splendid white repeat-flowering uprt rose with bright green lvs. Fls to 4 in wide. *Ht:* 5 ft; *Spd:* 4 ft; *Fl:* 6–10; *Z:* 5

'Hugh Dickson'★: gdn origin. Hybrid perpetual. Wonderfully vig. Long shoots can be wall-trained. Fls bright scarlet-crimson to 4 in wide. *Ht:* 9 ft; *Spd:* 10 ft+; *Fl:* 6–9; *Z:* 5

'Mrs John Laing'★: gdn origin. Hyb perpetual. V popular. Strong growth and large pink frag fls freely borne. *Ht:* 5 ft; *Spd:* 5 ft; *Fl:* 6–9; *Z:* 5

'Reine des Violettes'★: gdn origin. Hyb perpetual. Fls burgundy-purple to 4 in wide, fading to a wine-stained col. *Ht:* 6 ft; *Spd:* 5 ft; *Fl:* 6–9; *Z:* 5

R. hugonis

R. moyesii

R. moyesii fruits

R. rugosa 'Sarah van Fleet'

'Frau Karl Druschki'

'Reine des Violettes'

The bedding roses par excellence, in which individual flowers 4–6 in wide, from long pointed buds, have been brought to perfection in the nursery; flowering is almost continuous all summer and autumn. Disadvantages are awkward little angular bushes and proneness to disease.

Hybrid tea 'Fragrant Cloud'

Hybrid tea 'Peace'

Hybrid tea 'Super Star'

Hybrid tea 'Sutter's Gold'

'Charlotte Armstrong'*: Long, pointed dark red buds open to rose-pink fls of modest frag. Vig, bushy, profuse bloomer. *Ht:* 4 ft; *Spd:* 30 in; *Fl:* 6–7(–9); *Z:* 3

'Chrysler Imperial'*: High-centered, strongly frag, crimson fls do not darken with age. Stiff, uprt bush; fol dark green. *Ht:* 4 ft; *Spd:* 40 in; *Fl:* 6–7(–9); *Z:* 3

'Crimson Glory'*: Velvety, dark red fls with strong clove scent. Forms spreading bush. *Ht:* 4 ft; *Spd:* 40 in; *Fl:* 6–7(–9); *Z:* 3

'Eclipse'*: V long tapered buds open to chrome yellow fls. Fol leathery. *Ht:* 4 ft; *Spd:* 30 in; *Fl:* 6–7(–9); *Z:* 3

'First Prize'*: Deep pink frag fls lighter at center, darker at ptl margins. *Ht:* 4 ft; *Spd:* 30 in; *Fl:* 6–7(–9); *Z:* 3

'Fragrant Cloud'*: V frag coral red fls. A good bush seemingly resistant to all weathers and diseases. *Ht:* 3 ft; *Spd:* 30 in; *Fl:* 6–7(–9); *Z:* 3

'Garden Party'*: Frag fls yellowish-ivory, flushed delicate pink. *Ht:* 4 ft; *Spd:* 30 in; *Fl:* 6–7(–9); *Z:* 3

'Helen Traubel'*: High-centered fls of gentle pink flushed with apricot. Long buds and stems. Vig. *Ht:* 3 ft; *Spd:* 30 in; *Fl:* 6–7(–9); *Z:* 3

'John F. Kennedy'*: Lemon-white buds open to pure white fls. Lvs big, dark. *Ht:* 4 ft; *Spd:* 30 in; *Fl:* 6–7(–9); *Z:* 3

'Mister Lincoln'*: Long-lasting deep red fls strongly frag. Fol shiny, dark green. *Ht:* 4 ft; *Spd:* 30 in; *Fl:* 6–7(–9); *Z:* 3

'Oregold'*: Unfading rich yellow fls have high centers. Buds long, pointed. V vig. *Ht:* 3 ft; *Spd:* 30 in; *Fl:* 6–7(–9); *Z:* 3

'Peace'*: Strong growing. Large frag fls yellow with ptls edged pink. Lvs dark shining green. *Ht, Spd:* 6 ft; *Fl:* 6–7(–9); *Z:* 3

'Super Star'*: Frag fls a fluorescent vermilion—an overpowering col needing careful placing. *Ht:* 5 ft; *Spd:* 3 ft; *Fl:* 6–7(–9); *Z:* 3

'Sutter's Gold'*: Frag rose of good stamina for bedding. Fls rich yellow, buds and ptl backs shaded reddish-orange. Lvs dark green, glossy coppery hue. *Ht, Spd:* 3 ft; *Fl:* 6–7(–9); *Z:* 3

'Tiffany'*: Buds golden at base; fls rich pink, frag. V vig. *Ht:* 4 ft; *Spd:* 30 in; *Fl:* 6–7(–9); *Z:* 3

Old-fashioned roses had a narrow range of ancestors. Modern shrubs draw on the inheritance of a wide range, including recently-introduced species, to produce plants of great character, some flowering repeatedly. The hybrid musks, nearest to floribundas, are ideal as shrubs for bedding.

'Canary Bird'*: Rich yellow early single making tall vase-shaped bush. Lvs have 7–13 pretty little lflts. *Ht:* 8 ft; *Spd:* 6 ft; *Fl:* 5–6; *Z:* 4

'Complicata'*: Forms dome-shaped bush of sage green lvs. Fls single, bright pink, to 4 in wide. *Ht:* 5 ft; *Spd:* 8 ft; *Fl:* 6–7; *Z:* 4

'Fritz Nobis'*: Has beautifully formed bright shell-pink clove-scented fls in profusion and orange hips. One main burst of fls then continues blooming sporadically until autumn. *Ht:* 6 ft; *Spd:* 5 ft; *Fl:* 6(–9); *Z:* 4

'Fruhlingsgold'*: Tall arching shrub rose. V free flowering, once. Fls creamy-yellow, frag, single. Its sister plant is 'Fruhlingsmorgen'. Produces a few dark hips. *Ht, Spd:* 7 ft; *Fl:* 5–6; *Z:* 4

'Fruhlingsmorgen'*: Single fls to 4 in, 5–7 ptls cherry pink with yellow centers and dark red stamens. Moderately frag. Hips big, red. *Ht:* 7 ft; *Spd:* 5 ft; *Fl:* 6–7 (–9); *Z:* 4

'Golden Wings'*: Large single yellow fls over a long period and matt green lvs. *Ht:* 6 ft; *Spd:* 5 ft; *Fl:* 6–7; *Z:* 4

'Nevada'*: Strong grower with few thorns and graceful arching stems. Buds pale pink, fls creamy white flushed pink in heat, single with prominent stamens. Dying fls hang on which is the only disadvantage. *Ht:* 6 ft; *Spd:* 8 ft; *Fl:* 5–6; *Z:* 4

'Sea Foam'*: Shrubby polyantha hyb, also makes a climber or ground cover. Foamy clusters of 2 in double fls starting white, fading to cream. Everblooming; v disease resistant. *Ht:* 2 ft; *Spd:* 6 ft; *Fl:* 6–7(–9); *Z:* 4

'The Fairy'*: Big clusters of small delicate pink fls. Lvs small, shiny, lacy. V resistant to disease and insects. Use as shrub or hedge. *Ht:* 3 ft; *Spd:* 6 ft; *Fl:* 6–7(–9); *Z:* 4

Hybrid musks

'Belinda'*: Big clusters of semi-double, pink frag fls less than 1 in across. Uprt bushes make good hedges. *Ht:* 8 ft; *Spd:* 6 ft; *Fl:* 6–7 (–9); *Z:* 4

'Buff Beauty'*: Dark green lvs start coppery. Soft apricot fls fade to buff. Makes a spreading bush or good against a wall. *Ht, Spd:* 6 ft; *Fl:* 6–7(–9); *Z:* 4

Modern shrub 'Canary Bird'

Modern shrub 'Complicata'

Modern shrub 'Fruhlingsgold'

Modern shrub 'Golden Wings'

Modern shrub 'Nevada'

Modern shrub and Hybrid musk roses ⊛ ⊖ ⊕ ⊛

Hybrid musk 'Buff Beauty'

'Felicia'*: One of the most rewarding of all shrubs. More compact than other hyb musks and bearing great quantities of shapely double fls, apricot-pink in bud, opening to clear silvery pink. *Ht:* 5 ft; *Spd:* 6 ft+; *Fl:* 6–7(–9); *Z:* 5

'Penelope'*: Deep pink buds open to creamy pink, then fls become off-white. Hips coral pink with a grey bloom. *Ht:* 4 ft; *Spd:* 5 ft; *Fl:* 6–7 (–9); *Z:* 5

'Prosperity'*: Dark green lvs on stems with a reddish cast. Fls borne in large trusses with pale yellow tinge in center. *Ht:* 6 ft; *Spd:* 4 ft; *Fl:* 6–7(–9); *Z:* 5

Hybrid musk 'Prosperity'

Floribundas and Grandifloras ⊛ ⊖ ⊕ ⊛

In contrast to the hybrid teas with their emphasis on the single, perfect bloom on each shoot, floribundas carry smaller flowers, 2½–3½ in wide, in greater numbers, usually in clusters, over an equally long period. In practice the distinction between the two classes is rapidly being eroded by further breeding.

Floribunda 'All Gold'

'All Gold'*: V reliable long-established bedding rose with glossy lvs and unfading, frag, semi-double bright yellow fls. *Ht:* 3 ft; *Spd:* 30 in; *Fl:* 6–10; *Z:* 3

'Apricot Nectar'*: As good as it sounds. Vig, free-flowering; big, shapely full-petaled fls of soft apricot. Deliciously frag. *Ht:* 4 ft; *Spd:* 3 ft; *Fl:* 6–10; *Z:* 3

'Betty Prior'*: V hardy disease-resistant. Ideal for tall hedge. Dogwood-shaped, single, mid-pink, 5 petaled fls in loose clusters have moderate frag. *Ht:* 5 ft; *Spd:* 4 ft; *Fl:* 6–7(–9); *Z:* 3

'Carrousel'*: Semi-double deep red fls to 4 in wide moderately frag. Lvs big, dark, shiny. *Ht:* 4 ft; *Spd:* 30 in; *Fl:* 6–7(–9); *Z:* 3

'Elizabeth of Glamis'*: Handsome in bud. Frag fls coral-pink and hold their col well. Good fol. *Ht, Spd:* 30 in; *Fl:* 6–10; *Z:* 3

'Fashion'*: Distinctive coral-peach double fls moderately frag. Sturdy, spreading, bushy plant. *Ht, Spd:* 3 ft; *Fl:* 6–7(–9); *Z:* 3

'Frensham'*: Fls rich crimson red but no scent. Lvs dark green, glossy.

Floribunda 'Elizabeth of Glamis'

Bushy shrub that maintains its vigor. *Ht, Spd:* 3½ ft; *Fl:* 6–10; *Z:* 3
'Gruss an Aachen'*: Good mixer in any company. Fls frag, double, pearly-white aging to parchment col. Low bushy habit; clean fol. *Ht, Spd:* 30 in; *Fl:* 6–10; *Z:* 3
'Iceberg'*: Strong growing; good shining lvs, shapely buds and clean white fls sometimes developing pink flush with age. Sweetly frag. 'Ice White' more fully double. *Ht, Spd:* 3 ft; *Fl:* 6–10; *Z:* 3
'Masquerade'*: Yellow in bud, opening to salmon-pink and becoming deep red. The effect is so striking that it must be used with great care to avoid loud col clashes. *Ht, Spd:* 4 ft; *Fl:* 6–10; *Z:* 3
'Motezuma'*: High-centered, double red-orange fls to 4 in produced singly or in clusters. *Ht:* 4 ft; *Spd:* 30 in; *Fl:* 6–7(–9); *Z:* 5
'Queen Elizabeth'*: Head and 7 ft with tapering buds opening to clear pink, frag fls. Lvs clean dark green. Also good hedging. *Spd:* 4 ft; *Fl:* 6–10; *Z:* 3
'Spartan'*: Double fls ranging from orange-red to deep coral have good scent. Tolerant of heat, cold, drought and pests. *Ht:* 3½ ft; *Spd:* 30 in; *Fl:* 6–7(–9); *Z:* 3

Floribunda 'Iceberg'

Floribunda 'Masquerade'

Floribunda 'Queen Elizabeth'

Climbers are roses that produce relatively few very long and stiff stems and often flower repeatedly over a long period. Ramblers usually have more pliable and shorter shoots in large numbers and flower only once but with overwhelming generosity. Again there is no hard and fast distinction, particularly among the huge-growing sorts.

R. banksiae* Banksian rose: China. V vig small-flowered climber for warm (and high) walls, blooming in late spr. Sev forms: 'Lutea' double, yellow with tight rosettes in generous bunches, is hardiest but least frag; *R. b. normalis* (the wild subsp) is single, white, v frag and rather tender; 'Albo-plena' is double, white, frag; *R. b. lutescens* single, pale yellow, frag. Lvs pale with 7–9 lflts; few thorns. *Ht:* 20 ft; *Spd:* 20 ft; *Fl:* 5–6; *Z:* 7
R. bracteata* Macartney rose: China, Formosa. Rather tender white rose, evergreen with v dark

R. banksiae 'Lutea'

Rambler 'American Pillar'

Rambler 'Albertine'

Climber 'Dorothy Perkins'

Climber 'Golden Showers'

Climber 'Mermaid'

glossy lvs divided into 5–11 lflts with unusual blunt tips. Habit like a tall shrub; downy shoots with thorns in 1s and 2s. Single fls 3 in wide, prominent stamens, lemon scent. Named for the lfy bracts behind fls. Parent of the excellent 'Mermaid' (see below). *Ht:* 15 ft; *Spd:* 8 ft; *Fl:* 6–9; *Z:* 6

R. filipes★: W China. Sensationally vig climber capable of 20 ft shoots. Small creamy-white single fls in sprays of 100 or more at a time have prominent stamens and musk fragrance. Lvs have 5–7 narrow green lflts. 'Kiftsgate' has copper new wood and extra vigor in fl. Small oval red hips. *Ht:* to 60 ft; *Spd:* 30 ft; *Fl:* 6–7; *Z:* 6

R. wichuraiana★ Memorial rose: E Asia. Trailing evergreen rambler. Excellent ground cover, easily trained. Fls white, yellow stamens, frag, in small clusters, v late. Important parent of many cvs inc 'Dorothy Perkins' (see below). *Ht:* to 25 ft; *Spd:* 10 ft; *Fl:* 7–8; *Z:* 6

'Albertine'★: Rambler especially good when allowed to froth over a wall or down a bank. Free flowering. Semi-double fls open coppery-pink from deep red buds. Well scented, prone to mildew. *Ht, Spd:* 20 ft; *Fl:* 6; *Z:* 6

'America'★: Climber. Pointed salmon buds open to 4 in double deep salmon fls with silvery sheen; v profuse. Frs spicy. *Ht:* 15 ft; *Spd:* 6 ft; *Fl:* 6–7(–9); *Z:* 6

'American Pillar'★: Rambler excluded from some gdns and books because of its dazzling shocking-pink single fls each with white eye, borne in extravagant clusters. No scent. For best results prune hard immediately after flowering. Best on a pergola. *Ht:* to 15 ft; *Spd:* to 30 ft; *Fl:* 6–7; *Z:* 6

'Dorothy Perkins'★: Well established old favorite rambler, hyb of R. wichuraiana. Covered in bright rose-pink double or semi-double fls in full smr. Blooms once. Mildew-prone. *Ht, Spd:* 10ft; *Fl:* 6–7; *Z:* 6

'Blaze'★: Most pop US climber. Fls scarlet, semi-double to 3 in wide best in spr and aut. *Ht:* 15 ft; *Spd:* 6 ft; *Fl:* 6–7(–9); *Z:* 6

'Dr J.H.Nicolas'★: Everblooming, spreading climber. Fls double, rose pink, 3–4 per cluster with moderate frag. *Ht:* 8 ft; *Spd:* 10 ft; *Fl:* 6–7(–9); *Z:* 6

'Dr W. Van Fleet'★: Old vig climber, needs little attention. Double pinks fls to 3½ in wide on long stems. Fr slim. *Ht:* 20 ft; *Spd:*

10 ft; *Fl:* 6–7; *Z:* 6

'Don Juan'*: Velvety red, double 5 in fls strongly frag. Lvs glossy, dark. *Ht:* 10 ft; *Spd:* 6 ft; *Fl:* 6–7(–9); *Z:* 6

🌼 **'Golden Showers'*:** Weatherproof with rich golden-yellow, double, lightly frag fls. Clean, glossy, deep green fol. *Ht:* 12 ft; *Spd:* 8 ft; *Fl:* 6–8; *Z:* 6

🌼 **'Mermaid'*:** V vig climber. Coppery young lvs become glossy green. Fls single, pale yellow; pronounced boss of deep buff stamens. *Ht, Spd:* to 25 ft; *Fl:* 6–10; *Z:* 6

Rambler 'New Dawn'

'New Dawn'*: Strong, recurrent-flowering rambler. Lvs glossy. Fls full petaled, soft pink with silvery sheen v attractive when half open. Shorter than average if grown against a tree or allowed to sprawl. *Ht, Spd:* 20 ft; *Fl:* 6–7; *Z:* 6

🌼 **'Paul's Scarlet Climber'*:** Moderately vig with 1 main flowering in late June and a few late blooms. Lightly frag rich crimson-scarlet fls becoming purplish with age. *Ht:* 20 ft; *Spd:* 15 ft; *Z:* 6

Climber 'Paul's Scarlet Climber'

'Zéphirine Drouhin'*: Tall shrub. Cerise-pink perpetual-flowering semi-double deliciously frag rose. Stems virtually thornless; young shoots reddish. Useful hedging. *Ht, Spd:* 10 ft; *Fl:* 6–10; *Z:* 5

Climber 'Zéphirine Drouhin'

Miniatures   ⚙ 🌼 🌱 🌿

Miniature roses are difficult to place in a garden scene, but can be enchanting grown in pots. They are mainly derived from a dwarf perpetual China rose which gave them a long flowering season.

'Baby Betsy McCall'*: Double pearl-pink fls to 1 in long lasting with moderate fragrance. *Ht:* 10 in; *Spd:* 8 in; *Fl:* 6–7(–9); *Z:* 6

'Baby Masquerade'*: Smaller in all its parts but otherwise an exact copy of the flame and gold floribunda of the same name (p 108). Like other miniatures it needs full sun and good drainage. *Ht:* to 1 ft; *Spd:* 8 in; *Fl:* 6–7; *Z:* 6

'Ocaru' (= 'Angela Rippon')*: A shapely, frag salmon pink rose with fls to 2 in wide. *Ht:* 1 ft; *Spd:* 8 in; *Fl:* 6–7; *Z:* 6

Miniature 'Baby Masquerade'

'Pixie' (= 'Little Princess'): Double white fls prettily flushed in shades of deep and pale pink. *Ht, Spd:* 9 in; *Fl:* 6–7; *Z:* 6

'Yellow Doll': Double fls opening yellow, fading to ivory-white. *Ht:* to 1 ft; *Spd:* 9 in; *Fl:* 6–7; *Z:* 6

Miniature 'Ocaru'

Climbers

The gardner's idea of a climber is a plant best suited for walls, fences and trellises. In nature such plants are adapted for climbing trees (and usually hang on by twining or with aerial roots) or for scrambling through shrubs to the light. They often just throw out long shoots needing support. Roots in shade, head in light is a good rule for cultivation.

Aconitum

Monkshood

A. volubile: SE Asia. Unusual slender herbaceous climber with typical helmet-shaped purple-blue 3 in fls in a loose gp. Valuable in late smr. Likes shade at rts. *Ht:* 14½ ft; *Spd:* 4 ft; *Z:* 7

Actinidia

Actinidia

A. kolomikta

A. chinensis Chinese gooseberry: China. Shs and young lvs v hry. Parchment-colored fls and (in heat) edible frs if ♂, ♀ plants grown. *Ht:* 30 ft; *Spd:* 15 ft; *Fl:* 6; *Z:* 7

A. kolomikta*: China, Japan. Curious, decorative with oval lvs green at base then red with white band at tip. Fls lightly frag. *Ht:* 20 ft; *Spd:* 15 ft; *Fl:* 6; *Z:* 4

Akebia

Akebia

A. quinata

A. quinata*: China, Japan. Elegant, easy semi-evergreen with pale green lflts and vanilla-scented purplish-green and light crimson fls in drooping gps. Frs elongated. Prop by cuttings, seed. *Ht:* 32 ft; *Spd:* 30 ft; *Fl:* 4–5; *Z:* 5

Allamanda

Allamanda

A. cathartica

A. cathartica: S Amer. Spectacular tropical climber. Yellow fls 3 in wide, periwinkle shape on a plant to 13 ft once established. Needs pinching out to make it branch low down; best trained on wires inside. More exotic forms like 'Grandiflora' best grafted on to common stock. *Spd:* 20 ft; *Fl:* 7–9; *Z:* 9

Aristolochia

Dutchman's pipe

A. macrophylla (= durior): N Amer. Vig, climbs by twining. Fls yellowish-purple, pipe-shaped, lidded, 1½ in long and concealed by mass of rounded lvs. Can reach 30 ft on a tree or wall. *Spd:* 8 ft; *Fl:* 6; *Z:* 4

Berberidopsis

B. corallina Coral plant: Chile. Barberry-like tough lvs, deep green with a pale underside, contrast prettily with the orange/coral red fls in Aug and Sept. Has no grip of its own; needs support on a sheltered wall or in partial shade. Prop by seed, layers, cuttings. *Ht:* 20 ft; *Spd:* 10 ft; *Z:* 10

B. corallina

Bougainvillea

Tall scramblers needing support. Brilliant bracts make them most spectacular for hot gardens or conservatories.

B. glabra: Brazil. V showy with richly colored pointed deep magenta bracts. Sev recent hybs with pale blue, white, orange or pink bracts. Hardy in warmer areas of Cal and Florida and quite happy in pots (outdoors in smr) in cooler climates. *B. spectabilis* has hooked spines, hry lvs and rosy bracts. *Ht:* to 13 ft; *Spd:* 20 ft; *Fl:* 8–9; *Z:* 10

B. spectabilis

Trumpet vine, Trumpet creeper

C. radicans: SE USA. Vig, lfy, climbs with aerial rts. Intense orange and scarlet 3 in fls in a hot spot. Seedlings variable. *Ht:* 13 ft+; *Spd:* 10 ft; *Fl:* 8–9; *Z:* 4

C. × tagliabuana 'Madame Galen'*: gdn origin. The best clone of the hyb with bunches of salmon-red trumpet-shaped 3 in fls. Best if given reflected heat of a hot wall. *Ht:* 13 ft; *Spd:* to 25 ft; *Fl:* 8–9; *Z:* 5

C. × tagliabuana 'Madame Galen'

Bittersweet

C. orbiculatus Oriental bittersweet: NE Asia. Splendid vig climber happiest growing over a tree. Wonderful in aut when lvs turn yellow and brown/red frs split to reveal scarlet seeds against bright yellow skins. Fls green, inconspic, in June–July. Prop by seed, not fussy about soil. *Ht:* to 40 ft; *Spd:* 18 ft; *Z:* 6

C. orbiculatus

Clematis

Garden hybrid clematis are conventionally classified in botanical groups according to their known or supposed parentage which dictates whether they flower on young or old wood (or both) and hence when they should be pruned. All large-flowered clematis are such hybrids and bloom in early, mid or late summer. A number of smaller-flowered species extend flowering from late winter into autumn. Nearly all can be pruned in late winter.

C. jackmanii

C. viticella purpurea 'Plena Elegans'

C. orientalis

C. alpina: Eur, N Asia. Pale blue fls 1½ in wide, white stamens. 'Frances Rivis' is excellent. *C. macropetala* sim, the 2 spp are known as "atragenes". Prune. *Ht:* 8 ft; *Spd:* 10 ft; *Fl:* 4–5; *Z:* 5

C. armandii: China. Leathery-lvd evergreen; clusters of white fls 2½ in wide. 'Appleblossom' and 'Snowdrift' (both AGM) worth searching for. Try not to prune. *Ht:* to 30 ft; *Spd:* to 10 ft; *Fl:* 3; *Z:* 8

C. flammula★ Virgin's bower: S Eur. From Aug–Oct the little creamy-white strongly frag fls are produced on a tangled mass of stems. Prop by seed; prune. *Ht:* 16 ft; *Spd:* 8 ft; *Z:* 7

C. jackmanii★: gdn origin. Intense violet-purple fls. Prune. Try 'Jackmanii Superba'. *Ht:* 13 ft; *Spd:* 10 ft; *Fl:* 7–10; *Z:* 4

C. montana★: Him. Vig. Pale dusky pink buds, anemone-like white fls 2 in diam. 'Elizabeth' (AGM) soft pink; 'Rubens' (AGM) rose-pink fls. Do not prune. *Ht:* 30 ft; *Spd:* 20 ft; *Fl:* 5; *Z:* 6

C. orientalis★: Caucasus, Him–N China. Mod vig; finely cut pale green lvs, thick-petaled yellow fls 1½ in wide. Hard prune. *C. tangutica* sim. *Ht:* 16 ft; *Spd:* 10 ft; *Fl:* 8–10; *Z:* 6

C. viticella★: Eur. Vig but elegant. Crimson-violet fls 2½ in diam. 'Royal Velours' (AGM) deeper col; 'Alba Luxurians' (AGM) white fls, green or mauve ptl tips; 'Kermesina' wine red. Hard prune. *Ht:* 11 ft; *Spd:* 10 ft; *Fl:* 7–9; *Z:* 5

Clianthus

C. puniceus

C. puniceus Parrot's beak, Lobster's claw: NZ. Exotic-looking climber or wall-trained shrub for a warm garden or a conservatory or sun room. Has brilliant scarlet fls like parrots' beaks in 4 in clusters. Prop by seed or cuttings. *Ht:* 12 ft; *Spd:* 8 ft; *Fl:* 5–6; *Z:* 9

Cobaea

C. scandens Cup-and-saucer vine:
C, S Amer. Can survive mild wtrs
but best as an ann. Will fill a large
space either temporarily or annually.
Has cup-and-saucer-like bell-shaped
3 in fls beginning green and
gradually becoming purplish. Easily
reaches 15 ft in a season. Prop by
fresh seed. *Spd:* 15 ft; *Fl:* 5–10; *Z:* 9

C. scandens

Ornamental gourd

C. pepo: Trop Amer. Blanket name for sev sorts highly prized for their frs
which harden easily and last for months in wtr. Easily grown annually from
seed over twiggy branches or arches; also good ground cover, behaving
(but not tasting) like marrows. *Ht:* 10 ft; *Spd:* 8 ft; *Fl:* 7–9; *Z:* 10

Chilean glory flower

E. scaber: Chile. Almost instant
climber for the impatient gardener
but rather untidy. Tubular 1 in fls
can be orange, yellow or scarlet and
are followed by small inflated pods
generously packed with seed. Clear
yellow fls and claret-colored forms
sometimes seen. *Ht:* to 10 ft; *Spd:*
6 ft; *Fl:* 6–10; *Z:* 9

E. scaber

Ivy

The most adaptable evergreen climbers, equally effective as
ground cover, in a huge range of leaf sizes, shapes and colors.

H. canariensis Canary Is ivy:
Canary Is. Vig; lvs often bronze in
aut with pronounced veins.
'Variegata' (= 'Gloire de Marengo')
has white-edged lvs splashed green
and silver-grey. *Ht:* 40 ft; *Spd:* 20 ft;
Z: 7

H. colchica* Persian ivy: Iran,
Caucasus. V big glossy
drooping lvs. 'Dentata' (AGM) lvs
irregularly toothed; 'Dentata
Variegata' cream/green variegated
and 'Paddy's Pride' yellow-centered
lvs netted gold all rec. *Ht:* 40 ft; *Spd:*
20 ft; *Z:* 9

H. helix Common ivy: Eur,
Asia Minor. Among many cvs
are: 'Buttercup' (AGM) lvs small,
yellow; 'Glacier' lvs silver-grey,
white edges; 'Goldenheart' (AGM)
central gold splash; 'Hibernica' (Irish
ivy) vig plain green lvs; 'Marmorata'
mottled lvs, rosy-grey/green effect.
Ht: to 100 ft; *Spd:* 18 ft+; *Z:* 6

H. colchica

H. helix 'Glacier'

Holboellia

Holboellia

H. (= Stauntonia) latifolia: Him. Deliciously frag climber needing shelter in all but mildest areas. Greenish-white ♂ and greenish ♀ fls in separate clusters on same plant. *Ht:* 12 ft; *Spd:* 10 ft; *Fl:* 6–7; *Z:* 8

Hydrangea

Hydrangea

H. petiolaris

H. petiolaris ★ Climbing hydrangea: Japan–Korea. Bushy shrub with aerial rts to climb trees. Ideal for a north wall but will do equally well in a sunnier spot or up a tree. Large heads 10 in wide of white fls like well-known Lacecaps (p 139). Prop by cuttings or pieces with aerial rts. Slow to establish. *Ht:* to 80 ft; *Spd:* 20 ft; *Fl:* 6; *Z:* 5

Ipomoea

Morning glory

I. purpurea: Trop Amer. Hardy ann best grown from seed. Vivid sky-blue fls of 'Heavenly Blue' to 5 in diam. Also white, pink and purple cvs. Needs light support. *Ht:* 8 ft; *Spd:* 10 ft; *Fl:* 7–9

Jasminum

Jasmine

The jasmines are small-flowered but extremely valuable for their scent in summer and color in winter. They are easy to grow and not fussy about soil.

J. nudiflorum

J. officinale

J. nudiflorum Winter jasmine: W China. Sprawling green-stemmed shrub with myriads of yellow (sadly scentless) fls 1 in wide from mild periods in early winter to early March. Has no climbing equipment but can be wired to a wall, or looks good on a bank. Prune after flowering; prop by cuttings or layers. *Ht:* to 14 ft; *Spd:* 15 ft; *Z:* 7

 J. officinale ★ Common white jasmine: Caucasus–China. Vig, twining climber, needs strong support; tends to be top heavy. Sweetly frag white fls to 3 in. Prop by cuttings, layers. *Ht:* 20 ft; *Spd:* 18 ft; *Fl:* 6–9; *Z:* 7

 J. polyanthum: China. The jasmine of Arabian Nights, powerfully frag fls pale pink in bud. Not hardy but a strong candidate for indoors where it flowers from Nov–April. Prop by cuttings. *Ht:* 24 ft; *Spd:* 18 ft; *Fl:* 4–6; *Z:* 9

J. × stephanense: gdn origin. Vig hyb with frag pale pink fls in 3 in gps. Strongly growing shs often look yellowish and sick but this is natural. Prop by cuttings. *Ht:* to 25 ft; *Spd:* 18 ft; *Fl:* 6; *Z:* 6–7

Lapageria

L. rosea Chilean bell flower: Chile, Argentina. Lustrous waxy bell-shaped 3 in fls of a bright light red in drooping clusters. Needs shade and insists on a lime-free soil. The rare white form is less hardy. Prop by seed. *Ht:* to 16 ft; *Spd:* 8 ft; *Fl:* 7–10; *Z:* 9

L. rosea

Sweet pea

L. latifolius Perennial pea: Eur. Per useful against a wall, over a tough shrub or on a trellis. Large trusses of frag pink fls. Best cvs, e.g. 'White Pearl' have larger fls. *Ht:* 10 ft; *Spd:* 5 ft; *Fl:* 8; *Z:* 5

Honeysuckle

L. japonica: China, Japan. Semi-evergreen, rapidly twining. Flared tubular 1½ in fls white, V frag. 'Aureoreticulata' (AGM) lvs gold-netted, few fls. *Ht:* 20 ft; *Spd:* 12 ft; *Fl:* 6; *Z:* 4
L. periclymenum* Woodbine: Eur, N Africa. Creamy-white fls with purple tinge and heady frag in June–Sept. 'Belgica' fls crimson–purple outside, yellowish inside in May, June; sim 'Serotina' fls July–Oct. *Ht:* 12 ft; *Spd:* 12 ft; *Z:* 4

L. japonica 'Aureoreticulata'

Chilean jasmine

M. suaveolens: Argentina. White fls like periwinkles with sweet smell and elongated heart-shaped lvs. For warm gdns or conservatory. Rarely reaches more than 10 ft. Prop by seed. *Spd:* 4 ft; *Fl:* 8–9; *Z:* 10

Parthenocissus

Leafy self-clinging vigorous climbers often seen covering houses with brilliant red autumn colour. Flowers are insignificant.

P. henryana*: China. Velvety dull green lvs silver-veined turning purplish then bright red. *Ht:* 15 ft+; *Spd:* 18 ft; *Z:* 7
P. quinquefolia: E USA. The true Virginia creeper. Spectacular aut col when large lvs (each with 5 lflts) turn scarlet. Prop by cuttings. *Ht:* 30 ft+; *Spd:* to 30 ft; *Z:* 4
P. tricuspidata Boston ivy: China, Japan. Lvs as above but smaller and coarsely toothed. Burning red aut col. *Ht:* 30 ft+; *Spd:* to 30 ft; *Z:* 4

P. quinquefolia

Passion flower

P. caerulea★: C, SW Amer. The only sp commonly grown. Pliant tendriled climber needing support. Intricate lightly frag fls opening to a saucer shape with prominent central stk holding stigmas and anthers. Named from the elements of the Crucifixion. Frs orange, egg-shaped in a hot year. Prop by cuttings. *Ht:* 20 ft; *Spd:* 18 ft; *Fl:* 7–10; *Z:* 9

P. caerulea

Pileostegia

Pileostegia

P. viburnoides★: India, China. V desirable woody self-clinging shrub. Heads of white fls best in Aug–Sept are appealing in bud when they look pale green against darker lvs. Prop by cuttings. *Ht:* 20 ft; *Spd:* 18 ft; *Z:* 6

Plumbago

Plumbago, Leadwort

P. capensis★ Blue or Cape plumbage: S Africa. Delightful semi-evergreen pale-lvd wall-trained shrub with pale blue phlox-like fls in gps to 1 ft long all smr. Tender, so only suitable under glass or in portable tubs except in v warm areas. Prune hard in wtr, prop by cuttings. *Ht:* to 12 ft; *Spd:* 15 ft; *Fl:* 5–11; *Z:* 9

P. capensis

Polygonum

Knotweed

P. baldschuanicum Russian vine: Turkestan. Rampageous smotherer. Masses of white fls tinged icing-sugar pink. V sim *P. aubertii* (Silver lace vine) has plain white fls. *Ht:* 40 ft; *Spd:* 100 ft; *Fl:* 7–10; *Z:* 4

Schizophragma

Schizophragma

S. integrifolia: China. Hydrangea-like decid climber growing well in shade but producing more fls in sun. Fls white in gps to 1 ft wide, lvs rounded, toothed. Good on stumps. *Ht:* to 40 ft; *Spd:* 18 ft; *Fl:* 7; *Z:* 5

Solanum

Solanum

S. crispum Climbing potato: S Amer. Long-stemmed semi-evergreen; many bluish-purple yellow-eyed fls. 'Glasnevin' (AGM) fls more freely. Needs support. *Ht* *Spd:* to 20 ft; *Fl:* 7–9; *Z:* 8
S. jasminoides Potato vine: S Amer. Less hardy but more vig with grey-blue ¾ in fls. Best on a sunny wall. The white form 'Album'★ is outstandingly beautiful. Prop by cuttings. *Ht:* to 15 ft; *Spd:* 20 ft; *Fl:* 7–10; *Z:* 9

S. jasminoides 'Album'

Thunbergia

Thunbergia

T. alata Black-eyed Susan vine: S Africa. Graceful fast-growing ann summer climber with startling black-centered orange funnel-shaped fls 2 in diam. Prop by seed (save your own). *Ht:* 10 ft; *Spd:* 10 ft; *Fl:* 6–10

Trachelospermum

Trachelospermum

T. asiaticum: Korea, Japan. Tidy, self-clinging, reasonably hardy. Fls small, jasmine-like cream, buff eye, ravishing scent. *T. jasminoides* (Star jasmine, zone 9) has larger fls. *Ht:* 20 ft; *Spd:* 10 ft; *Fl:* 7–8; *Z:* 6

Tropaeolum

Nasturtium

T. peregrinum Canary nasturtium: Peru. Ann; lemon-yellow fls over pale green lvs. Good on a wire fence or twiggy site. Prop by seed. *Ht:* 10 ft; *Spd:* 15 ft; *Fl:* 6–10
T. speciosum★ Flame flower: Chile. Lightweight per needing cool moist soil. Myriads of bright scarlet fls 1½ in wide. Plant in shade. *Ht:* 10 ft; *Spd:* 5 ft; *Fl:* 7–10; *Z:* 9

T. peregrinum

Vitis

Grape vine

V. coignetiae Glory vine: Japan. Handsome huge round lvs woolly below and black grape-like inedible frs. Spectacular orange/yellow-crimson aut col. *Ht:* to 70 ft; *Spd:* to 40 ft; *Z:* 5
V. labrusca Fox grape: E USA. Rampant grower; lvs nearly round; frs thick-skinned, purple-black. Parent of most cultivated grapes in US. *Ht:* 50 ft; *Spd:* 20 ft; *Z:* 4
V. rotundifolia Muscadine grape: USA. Enormous vine needing v sturdy trellis. Lvs coarsely toothed; frs purple, bronze, black or white borne singly or in loose clusters. Best source of table grapes. *Ht:* 90 ft; *Spd:* 25 ft; *Z:* 7

V. coignetiae

Wisteria (= Wistaria)

Wisteria

W. sinensis★ Chinese wisteria: China. Strong stems turn counter-clockwise (unlike *W. floribunda*); 6 in racemes of pale lilac honey-scented pea fls. White fld forms of both known. Smr prune. Can make a small tree. *Ht:* to 70 ft; *Spd:* to 50 ft; *Fl:* 5–6; *Z:* 6
W. venusta: Japan. Less well known and smaller, denser racemes v pale pink. Lvs and shs downy. Prop by layers. *Ht:* 30 ft; *Spd:* 30 ft; *Fl:* 5–6; *Z:* 6

W. sinensis

Shrubs

Shrubs are defined here as any plants with woody, permanent, above ground parts that are not trees. Some of the shrubs described in this section can grow as trees, particularly in warmer climates, but are often seen in gardens as big bushes with many stems, not one long trunk. Trailing, ground-covering woody plants are also included.

Abelia

Abelia

A. × *grandiflora**: gdn origin. Arching evergreen of delicate beauty in late smr. Lvs pointed, oval, pale undersides. Bell-shaped 1 in fls palest pink and white with hry throat and reddish-purple veins. Also a variegated form. Prop by cuttings. *Ht, Spd:* 5 ft; *Fl:* 7–10; *Z:* 6

Abutilon

Abutilon

Fast-growing, soft-wooded tree mallows of great character. *A. vitifolium* with big fragile flowers and jagged leaves is one of the great "instant" shrubs, given moisture and warmth.

A. megapotamicum: Brazil. Lax evergreen. Spls crimson, anthers purple. Lvs of *A. m. variegatum* yellow-blotched. *Ht, Spd:* 8 ft; *Fl:* 5–10; *Z:* 10

A. vitifolium: Chile. More substantial; splendid vine-lvs. Fls of 'Album' white; of 'Veronica Tennant' pale lavender. *Ht:* 12 ft; *Spd:* 8 ft+; *Fl:* 6–7; *Z:* 10

A. megapotamicum

Acacia

Wattle

A. dealbata Silver wattle, Mimosa: Aust. Silvery-green feathery lvs. Fls frag, soft yellow, fluffy 9 in balls. Good in conservatories in cold zones. Prop by seed, cuttings. *Ht:* 60 ft; *Spd:* 18 ft+; *Fl:* 1–4; *Z:* 9

Acer

Maple

A. Japonicum Fullmoon maple: Japan. Slowly forms round bush to 20 ft. Lvs serrate, nearly round; fls wine red in bunches; frs key-like. Glowing aut col. Sev cvs of great quality inc 'Aconitifolium' (AGM) lvs deep cut; 'Aureum' (AGM) lvs soft yellow. *Spd:* 20 ft; *Fl:* 4–5; *Z:* 5

Aesculus

Horsechestnut

A. parviflora*: SE USA. Shrubby, spreading horsechestnut with typical compound hand-shaped lvs. Elegant white candles of fls to 1 ft high, stamens pink and showy. Prop by suckers, seed. *Ht:* to 13 ft; *Spd:* 13 ft+; *Fl:* 8; *Z:* 3

A. parviflora

Shadbush, Shadblow

 A. canadensis*: E N Amer. Large bush/small tree. Lvs oblong, emerging woolly, fiery in aut. Fls starry, white in pendulous bunches to 4 in. Frs purple in June. *Ht:* to 30 ft; *Spd:* 15 ft; *Fl:* 4; *Z:* 4

Aralia

 **A. elata** Japanese angelica tree: Asia. Spiny-stemmed suckering shrub/ small tree. Oversize palm-like lvs; white fls in long plumes. Lf markings in 'Variegata' white. *Ht, Spd:* 15 ft; *Fl:* 8–9; *Z:* 3

Arbutus

A. × andrachnoides: gdn origin. Big bush/small tree. Stems warm cinnamon col. Fls white, pitcher-shaped, bunched; frs small, orange-red. *Ht, Spd:* 15 ft; *Fl:* 4–5; *Z:* 7

 **A. menziessi** Madrone: W N Amer. Bark peeling, stems richer col. Frs orange. Acid soil. *Ht:* 25 ft; *Spd:* 20 ft; *Fl:* 4–5; *Z:* 7

A. unedo* Strawberry tree: Eur, Asia Minor. More lfy and bushy, lime-tolerant. Red frs and white fls borne together. *Ht:* 10 ft+; *Spd:* 8 ft+; *Fl:* 8–10; *Z:* 8

A. menziesii

Manzanita, Bearberry

A. manzanita: Cal. Uprt shrub, stems reddish, lvs evergreen, hard, bluish-grey, pointed. Fls pitcher-shaped in nodding 2 in bunches. Frs small, brown. *Ht:* to 20 ft; *Spd:* 9 ft; *Fl:* 2–4; *Z:* 7

A. uva-ursi: N Hem. Prostrate evergreen, lvs glossy, fls pale pink, vase-shaped; frs round, bright red. Prop by seed, cuttings. *Ht:* 4 in; *Spd:* 2 ft; *Fl:* 4–5; *Z:* 2

A. manzanita

Artemisia

Fine-foliage shrubs related to wormwood, absinthe, tarragon and sage-brush. Good in sun and dry soil.

A. abrotanum Southernwood: S Eur. Uprt sub-shrub often used for low hedges. Lvs grey-green, finely cut, v aromatic. Fls insignificant. Prop by cuttings. *Ht:* to 4 ft; *Spd:* 30 in; *Z:* 4

 **A. arborescens:** S Eur. Grown for the intricate fol which is shining pewter-grey, white below. Stems whitened. Soft fluffy shrub tender in hard wtrs. Prop by cuttings. *Ht, Spd:* 3½ ft; *Z:* 8

A. abrotanum

Bamboo

A. japonica (=Bambusa metake): Japan. Forms broad suckering clump of dull green canes under pale brown sheaths. Lustrous lvs to 1 ft. *Ht:* 15 ft; *Spd:* 20 ft+; *Z:* 7

A. (=Sinarundinaria) nitida: China. Makes clump of purplish stems. Paler shining evergreen lvs in 2nd yr greyish below. Prop by div. *Ht, Spd:* 10 ft; *Z:* 7

A. nitida

Aucuba

Aucuba

A. japonica Japanese laurel: Japan. V striking shiny-lvd shrub. Type has rather pale lvs. Frs handsome waxy red, fls white. *A.j. variegata* (Gold-dust plant) v pop in southern gdns. *Ht, Spd:* 7 ft; *Fl:* 3–4; *Z:* 7

Azara

Azara

A. serrata: Chile. Rather tender. Lvs in 2s or 3s on downy shoots. Fls yellow, frs whitish, plant uprt. Hardier *A. microphylla* has mustard-yellow vanilla-scented fls in Mar. *Ht:* 10 ft; *Spd:* 5 ft; *Fl:* 7; *Z:* 9

Ballota

Ballota

B. pseudodictamnus: Med. Low scarcely woody sub-shrub with woolly white stems, rounded sage-green lvs and whorls of white purple-spotted ½ in fls that appear pink. Prop by cuttings. *Ht, Spd:* 2 ft; *Fl:* 7; *Z:* 7

Berberis

Barberry

A huge genus of wickedly prickly shrubs, evergreen and deciduous with masses of small yellow or orange flowers in spring.

B. darwinii: Chile. V popular evergreen. Spiny 3-pointed lvs, v many orange-yellow fls. Frs oval, glistening, bluish-black. *Ht:* 6 ft; *Spd:* 4 ft; *Fl:* 4–5; *Z:* 7

B. julianae Wintergreen barberry: China. V dense hardy evergreen. Lvs spiny to 3 in; twigs thorny. Yellow fls in clusters; frs blue-black. *Ht, Spd:* 6 ft; *Fl:* 5–6; *Z:* 6

B. × stenophylla: gdn origin. Graceful arching evergreen bush. Stems spiny, profuse yellow fls. *Ht, Spd:* 10 ft; *Fl:* 4–5; *Z:* 6

B. darwinii

B. thunbergii: Japan. Decid, densely prickly bush. Clustered yellow fls. Brilliant red aut col, small red frs. *B.t. atropurpurea* most reliable purple-lvd shrub. Lvs of 'Aurea' yellow; 'Rose Glow' purple, mottled silver and pink. *Ht:* 6 ft; *Spd:* 6 ft; *Fl:* 4–5; *Z:* 4

B. wilsoniae: China. Arching, decid. Frs. lvs soft coral in aut. *Ht:* 3 ft; *Spd:* 4 ft; *Fl:* 4–5; *Z:* 6

B. × stenophylla

Beschorneria

B. yuccoides: Mexico. Exotic grey-green lvd yucca-like plant. Lvs 18 in × 2 in in rosette. Fls nodding, vivid green with coral-red bracts. Needs shelter. Prop by div, seed. *Ht:* 4 ft; *Spd:* 3 ft; *Fl:* 5–6; *Z:* 10

Buddleia

Fast-growing soft-wooded shrubs making angular patterns with opposite branching. Honey-smelling flowers are a great attraction to butterflies. Most have flowers in stiff or soft spikes.

B. davidii Summer lilac: China. Stiff common shrub wildly popular with butterflies. Lvs long, pointed, soft green, white beneath. Sp has panicles to 20 in of mauve fls surpassed by sev good named cvs inc: 'Black Knight' (AGM) violet; 'Empire Blue' (AGM); 'Royal Red' (AGM). Prune hard in Mar. *Ht, Spd:* 9 ft+; *Fl:* 7–10; *Z:* 6

B. davidii

B. fallowiana*: China. Finer but less hardy with white woolly lvs and panicles of honey-scented lavender-blue fls to 10 in. 'Alba' is a white-flowered cv. Needs shelter. Prop by cuttings. *Ht:* 10 ft; *Spd:* 6 ft; *Fl:* 6; *Z:* 7

B. globosa Orange ball buddleia: Chile, Peru. More substantial semi-evergreen bush. Fls orange-yellow ball-shaped, 2–10 in a branched terminal head. Prop by cuttings. *Ht, Spd:* 10 ft; *Fl:* 5–6; *Z:* 7

B. globosa

Box

B. sempervirens Common box: Eur, W Asia, N Africa. Smells of ancient gdns. Lvs oval, close-packed, dark glossy green. Tiny fls look yellow but are green with prominent anthers. Rabbit-proof. *B.s.* 'Suffruticosa' (Edging box) neat, lighter green dwarf form to 5 ft usually clipped. *Ht:* to 20 ft; *Spd:* to 20 ft; *Fl:* 4; *Z:* 6

B. sempervirens 'Suffruticosa'

Beauty-berry

C. bodinieri: China. Uprt shrub grown for its small, round vivid bluish-lilac frs borne in bunches in Oct–Nov. Lvs slim, purplish in aut. Prop by seed, cuttings. *Ht:* 6 ft; *Spd:* 3 ft+; *Fl:* 7; *Z:* 7

C. japonica: Japan. Smaller; lvs oval, fls pink, frs shiny, lilac. Both spp fr more freely in gps. *Ht:* 4 ft; *Spd:* 3 ft; *Fl:* 8; *Z:* 7

C. japonica

Bottle brush

Graceful wavy shrubs with vivid bottle-brush flowers in summer. In this characteristically Australian flower design the "bristles" are the stamens.

C. citrinus: Aust. Tall shrub/ small tree. Lvs narrow, fls in cylindrical 4 in spikes, prominent red stamens and flattened oval woody frs. 'Splendens' (AGM) bright crimson. Prop by cuttings. *Ht:* to 15 ft; *Spd:* 10 ft; *Fl:* 6; *Z:* 9
C. salignus: Aust. Young growth silky, finely hry. Stamens creamy yellow, may be pale pink. One of the hardiest spp. Prop by cuttings. *Ht:* 15 ft+; *Spd:* 10 ft+; *Fl:* 6; *Z:* 9

C. citrinus

Calluna

Heather

C. vulgaris: Eur, Asia Minor, E N Amer. Densely bushy; lvs massed, tiny. V many white-purple fls. Some cvs have coloured fol, eg: 'Blazeaway' lvs red in wtr, fls lilac-mauve; other good cvs inc 'Peter Sparkes' (AGM) fls pale pink, double; 'Tib' fls rosy red, double. (See also pp 130, 132.) *Ht, Spd:* 30 in; *Fl:* 7–11; *Z:* 5

C. vulgaris 'Elsie Powell'

Camellia

Camellia

The most sumptuous of winter and spring flowers and remarkably hardy. Best in acid soil and light woodland shade.

C. japonica*: Japan, Korea. Fls single, semi-double, double, peony or anemone-like, red in sp. Cvs reds, pinks to white and striped. Rec (all AGM): 'Adolphe Audusson' blood red; 'Contessa Lavinia Maggi' double, white or pink striped cerise; 'Lady Clare' peach-pink semi-double. *Ht:* to 30 ft; *Fl:* 4–6; *Z:* 7

C. reticulata: China. Fls deep rose pink, single. Semi-double cvs inc 'Captain Rawes' (AM); 'Trewithen Pink' (AM). *Ht:* to 25 ft; *Spd:* 8 ft+; *Fl:* 2–4; *Z:* 8

C. japonica 'Magnolii flora'

C. sasanqua: Japan. Fls white or pale pink, frag, single. Cvs inc 'Crimson King' red; 'Narumi Gata' (AM) white tinged pink. *Ht:* 15 ft; *Spd:* 6 ft+; *Fl:* 10–4; *Z:* 7

C. × williamsii: gdn origin. Superb, free-flowering. Fls pink or white single, pink semi-double in 'Donation' (AGM). *Ht:* 10 ft; *Spd:* 6 ft; *Fl:* 11–5; *Z:* 7

C. reticulata

Pea tree

C. arborescens: Siberia, Manchuria. Pretty uprt shrub/small tree. Lvs small, compound, fls yellow, pea-like. 'Lorbergii' more elegant, narrow-lvd. Prop by seed, cuttings. *Ht:* to 15 ft; *Spd:* 6 ft+; *Fl:* 5; *Z:* 3

Carpenteria

Carpenteria

C. californica*: Cal. Handsome shrub for a warm spot. Lvs narrow, pointed. Frag fls 3 in wide, single, white, with prominent golden anthers. Prop by seed, layers, cuttings (slow). *Ht:* to 8 ft; *Spd:* 3 ft; *Fl:* 6–7; *Z:* 8

C. californica

Caryopteris

Caryopteris

C. × clandonensis 'Arthur Simmonds'*: gdn origin. Small rounded shrub, many greyish stems. Lvs dull grey in bud opening soft grey-green. Fls bright blue in 2 in clusters. *Ht:* 3 ft; *Spd:* 4 ft; *Fl:* 8–9; *Z:* 7

Cassia

Cassia

C. corymbosa: S Amer. Tender sp for sheltered place or cool greenhouse. Lvs have pairs of lflts. Fls in clusters rich yellow single, cup-shaped, 3 in wide. Prop by seed, cuttings. *Ht, Spd:* 6 ft; *Fl:* 8–9; *Z:* 8

Ceanothus

California lilac

Fast-growing shrubs from the dry hillsides of California, invaluable for their blue flowers, a rare color in shrubs.

C. 'Autumnal Blue'*: gdn origin. Probably the hardiest of the rather tender evergreen hyb ceanothus. Lvs blunt, oval, rich green. Fls fluffy, china blue. Fast growing, prop by cuttings. *Ht, Spd:* 11 ft; *Fl:* 7–9; *Z:* 8

C. dentatus: Cal. Fast-growing uprt evergreen. Lvs small, thick, dark green, pale below. Fls bright blue in thimble-shaped clusters 1½ in wide. Name often used for larger-lvd *C. × veitchianus*. *Ht:* 11 ft; *Spd:* 6 ft; *Fl:* 5; *Z:* 8

C. dentatus

C. 'Gloire de Versailles': gdn origin. Decid hyb. Lvs larger, young stems jade green. Masses of powder-blue fls in loose panicles to 8 in. *Ht, Spd:* 6 ft; *Fl:* 7–10; *Z:* 8

C. impressus*: Cal. Spreading small evergreen. Deeply furrowed lvs slightly hry. Fls deep blue in 1 in clusters. *Ht, Spd:* to 5 ft; *Fl:* 4–5; *Z:* 8

C. impressus 'Puget Blue'

Ceratostigma

Ceratostigma

C. willmottianum★: China. Low soft-wooded shrub with long late-smr season. Lvs light green, bristly, may redden in aut. Fls brilliant blue, open, tubular in groups 2½ in diam. *Ht, Spd:* 3 ft; *Fl:* 7–10; *Z:* 8

Cercis

Cercis

C. siliquastrum Judas tree: E Med. Small branchy tree; pale lvs almost round. Rich pink pea-fls from bare branches and even trunk. *C. canadensis* (American redbud) sim. *Ht:* 20 ft; *Spd:* 20 ft+; *Fl:* 5; *Z:* 6

Chaenomeles (=Cydonia)

Flowering quince

C. × superba 'Crimson and Gold'

C. speciosa (=*C. lagenaria*, *Pyrus japonica*): China. Rounded bush, can be wall-trained. Brs spiny, angular, lvs oval. Rose-like fls over a long season 2 in diam, single, semi-double or double with prominent anthers. Frs yellowish, round. Cvs inc 'Moerloosii' (AM) pale pink and white; 'Nivalis' (AM) white; 'Sanguinea Plena' double red. *Ht, Spd:* to 8 ft; *Fl:* 2–5; *Z:* 5

C. × superba: gdn origin. Smaller, equally vig. Fls Jan–Feb if sheltered and intermittently to Aug. Best cvs (all AGM) inc 'Crimson and Gold'; 'Knap Hill Scarlet'; 'Rowallane' crimson red. *Ht, Spd:* to 5 ft; *Z:* 5

Chimonanthus

Winter sweet

C. praecox (=*fragrans*)★: China. Deliciously frag fls on bare wtr brs. Waxy pale yellow fls 1 in wide with inner ring of short purple ptls. Good on lime soils and against walls. *Ht, Spd:* to 11 ft; *Fl:* 12–3; *Z:* 7

Chionanthus

Fringe-tree

C. virginicus: E N Amer. Tall shrub or bushy small tree grown for its abundant loose fluffy frag fls with fringe-like creamy white ptls. Prop by cuttings. *Ht:* 20 ft+; *Spd:* 15 ft; *Fl:* 6; *Z:* 5

Choisya

Mexican orange

C. ternata

C. ternata★: Mexico. Highly rec rounded shrub with glossy green 3-lobed lvs and heads of white star-shaped frag fls each to 1½ in wide in Apr–May and intermittently to Dec. Lvs unpleasantly pungent if crushed. Prop by cuttings. *Ht:* to 10 ft; *Spd:* to 8 ft; *Z:* 9

Rock rose

Aromatic, often gummy, Mediterranean evergreens with myriads of short-lived fragile flowers. For dry soil. Increase all types by cuttings.

C. × aguilari: Spain, Morocco. Natural hyb, plain white fls. 'Imaculatus' (AGM) better form bearing myriads of large white purple-blotched fls. Lvs sticky. *Ht:* 4 ft; *Spd:* 30 in; *Fl:* 6–7; *Z:* 8

C. × cyprius: gdn origin. One of the hardiest hybs. Lvs somber dark green. Fls white, 3 in wide, with crimson blotch at base of each ptl. Inclined to arch and build up solid mass of fol. *Ht:* to 8 ft; *Spd:* 5 ft; *Fl:* 6–7; *Z:* 7

C. laurifolius: Eur. Lvs hrlss, oval, pointed, sticky. Fls plain white 2 in wide in generous clusters. Sim size to above but more uprt. *Fl:* 6–8; *Z:* 8

C. populifolius: Eur. Slightly less hardy with larger, paler long-stkd poplar-shaped lvs. Fls white, conspic yellow base to each ptl. *Ht:* 6 ft; *Spd:* 4 ft; *Fl:* 6–7; *Z:* 8

C. × cyprius

C. laurifolius

Lemon

C. ichangense Ichang lemon: China. Nearly hardy lemon and decorative small shrub with single white frag fls and bright yellow edible lemon frs. Worth trying in correct zone. *Ht:* 10 ft; *Spd:* 5 ft; *Fl:* 5–6; *Z:* 10

Clerodendrum

C. trichotomum★: Japan. Large lfy dome-shaped bush grown for its lurid turquoise-blue frs. Lvs have fetid smell if crushed but fls v frag, star-like with persistent maroon spls. *Ht, Spd:* 18 ft; *Fl:* 7–9; *Z:* 7

Clethra

C. alnifolia Sweet pepper bush: N Amer. Uprt, twiggy. Wonderfully frag fls in 6 in spikes. Lvs oval, nearly smooth. 'Paniculata' (AGM) best cv. Prop by layers, suckers. *Ht, Spd:* 7 ft; *Fl:* 8; *Z:* 5
C. barbinervis: China, Japan. Sim to above but to 9 ft. Good aut col. Fls fluffier, young lvs downy. *Spd:* 9 ft; *Fl:* 7–9; *Z:* 6

C. alnifolia

Bladder senna

C. arborescens: S Eur. Amusing inflated pea-pod bladders (fun to pop) follow yellow pea-like ¾ in fls. Lvs grey-green, compound. Quick growing, good for new and seaside gdns. *Ht:* 6 ft; *Spd:* 5 ft; *Fl:* 6–9; *Z:* 6

Convolvulus

Convolvulus

Convolvulus

C. cneorum*: S Eur. Shining ever-grey shrublet. Fls funnel-shaped, 1 in wide, v pale pink. Best at foot of a warm wall or against a sunny rock. A plant to cherish. Prop by cuttings. *Ht:* 30 in; *Spd:* 3 ft; *Fl:* 5–9; *Z:* 9

Cordyline

Cordyline

C. australis: Aust, NZ. Palm-like with mop heads of 3 ft sword-shaped lvs. Fls frag, white, frs bead-like, cream, blue-tinged. *Ht:* to 40 ft; *Spd:* 8 ft; *Fl:* 5; *Z:* 9
C. indivisa Hawaiian T. plant: NZ. Sim but bigger lvs. Fls grey-white flushed purple in 4 ft plumes. Frs purplish. *Ht:* to 25 ft; *Spd:* 10 ft; *Fl:* 5; *Z:* 10

C. australis

Cornus

Dogwood, Cornel

Most valuable genus for flowers, autumn color, fruit, variegated foliage, interesting habit and bark color (not all, alas, on the same plant). Increase plants by cuttings.

C. alba Tatarian dogwood: Siberia. Clump-forming. Slim, uprt blood red stems best in wtr. Lvs col in aut. Fls in flat heads, fr white, tinged blue. Rec cvs 'Elegantissima' (AGM) lvs white margins; 'Spaethii' (AGM) lvs yellow varieg. *Ht, Spd:* 8 ft; *Fl:* 5–6; *Z:* 4
C. florida Flowering dogwood: E USA. Glorious with white pink or red ptl-like bracts. *Ht, Spd:* 20 ft; *Fl:* 5; *Z:* 4

C. alba 'Spaethii'

C. kousa Japanese dogwood: Japan, Korea. Big, bushy. Fls abundant, creamy-white bracts to 1½ in in 4s, frs like strawberries. *C.k. chinensis** taller, both superb aut col. *Ht, Spd:* to 20 ft; *Fl:* 5–6; *Z:* 4
C. mas Cornelian cherry: Eur. Excellent wtr-flowering twiggy shrub/small tree. Fl heads 1 in wide, acid-yellow with yellow-green bracts. Frs red, oval. Also a pretty white-varieg form*. *Ht, Spd:* to 25 ft; *Fl:* 2–3; *Z:* 4
C. nuttallii Pacific dogwood: W N Amer. Rare but superb: 6–8 creamy-white bracts round purplish-green central boss. Frs orange-red. Brilliant aut col. No lime. *Ht, Spd:* 20 ft; *Fl:* 5; *Z:* 8

C. mas

Corokia

Corokia

C. cotoneaster Zigzag bush: NZ. Tangled bush with small narrow dark green lvs like white suede below and dusting of bright yellow star-shaped fls. Frs small, round, red. *Ht:* 7 ft; *Spd:* 5 ft; *Fl:* 5; *Z:* 9

Corylopsis

C. pauciflora: Japan. Hazel-like lvs pink tinted when young and in aut. Fls frag, pale yellow in 2s or 3s, large pale bracts. *C. spicata* (AM) less pretty. *Ht:* 6 ft; *Spd:* 6 ft+; *Fl:* 3–4; *Z:* 7

Corylus

C. maxima 'Purpurea'* Purple filbert: S Eur (sp). Dark purple lvs broad oval to 5 in long, downy when young. Caterpillars can make them shabby in smr. Bears purple 4 in catkins in Feb–Mar. Fr typical hazelnut with long husk. Prop by suckers, layers. *Ht:* to 20 ft; *Spd:* to 10 ft; *Z:* 3

C. maxima 'Purpurea'

Smoke tree

C. coggyria (=Rhus cotinus)*: S Eur-China. Bushy, branchy. Lvs round/oval. Fl heads soft frothy masses to 8 in. 'Notcutt's Variety' (AGM) deep purple lvs, purple-pink fls; 'Royal Purple' (AGM) paler. Best aut col in poor soil. *Ht, Spd:* 10 ft; *Fl:* 7–8; *Z:* 6

Cotoneaster

Easy, hardy, immensely varied shrubs unremarkable in flower but useful for their varied habits and usually brilliant fruits.

C. conspicuus (=C.c. 'Decorus')*: Tibet. Small-lvd evergreen. Fls small, white; berries bright red. Good on banks. *Ht:* 4 ft; *Spd:* 8 ft; *Fl:* 5; *Z:* 6

C. dammeri (=humifusus): China. Prostrate evergreen, lvs oval, frs glistening red. Tolerates shade. 'Skogholm' pop ground cover. *Ht:* 9 in; *Spd:* 5 ft; *Fl:* 5–6; *Z:* 4

C. divaricata Spreading cotoneaster: China. Spreading, arching decid shrub for border or hedge. Lvs turn red in aut. Profuse small pink fls; frs red, egg-shaped. *Ht:* 6 ft; *Spd:* 9 ft; *Fl:* 5–6; *Z:* 6

C. horizontalis Rock spray: China. Spreading, decid, herringbone brs. V good varieg form*. *Ht:* to 5 ft; *Spd:* 8 ft; *Fl:* 5–6; *Z:* 6

C. microphyllus Small-leaved cotoneaster: Him, China. Tiny-lvd evergreen; young shoots woolly. Good on banks or in rock gdn. *Ht:* 3 ft; *Spd:* 4 ft+; *Fl:* 5–6; *Z:* 7

C. simonsii: Assam. Decid, stiff, uprt. Frs large, scarlet. Makes hedge with a little pruning. *Ht:* 8 ft; *Spd:* 6 ft; *Fl:* 5–6; *Z:* 6

C. conspicuus

C. horizontalis

Broom

The most varied of the three genera of "brooms" (the others are *Genista* and *Spartium*) includes colors other than yellow.

C. battanderi

C. × praecox

C. multiflorus (=albus) White Spanish broom: SW Eur, N Africa. Tough, uprt. Masses of pea-like white fls. *Ht:* 10 ft; *Spd:* 5 ft; *Fl:* 5–6; *Z:* 7

C. battandieri* Moroccan broom: Morocco. Silver-silky laburnum-like lvs; fls golden-yellow in uprt plumes, strong pineapple frag. *Ht, Spd:* 12 ft; *Fl:* 6–7; *Z:* 7

C. × praecox Warminster broom: gdn origin. V prolific creamy ½ in fls. 'Albus' is white; 'Gold Spear' and 'Allgold' smaller, fls deeper yellow. *Ht, Spd:* 5 ft; *Fl:* 5; *Z:* 7

C. scoparius Scotch broom: Eur. Brilliant yellow, free-flowering. Hybs in wide col and bicol range, eg × 'Andreanus' yellow/brownish-crimson; × 'Killiney Salmon' orange/pink. *Ht:* 12 ft; *Spd:* 5 ft; *Fl:* 5; *Z:* 5

Daboecia

Irish heath

D. cantabrica: St Dabeoc's heath, Connemara heath. Low-growing heath. Buds egg-shaped opening into bright, clear purple bells. 'Alba' (AGM) fls white, lighter green lvs; 'Atropurpurea' (AGM) deep purple; 'Praegerae' glowing pink. *Ht:* 2 ft+; *Spd:* 18 in; *Fl:* 6–11; *Z:* 6

Daphne

Daphne

Dignified small shrubs with intensely fragrant flowers. Even in cool, limy, well-drained soil they may be short-lived.

D. retusa

D. mezereum

D. blagayana: SE Eur. Deliciously frag creamy-ivory tubular fls in massed head. Lvs evergreen. Likes to run between stones. *Ht:* 2 ft; *Spd:* 3 ft; *Fl:* 3–4; *Z:* 6

D. cneorum Garland flower: Eur. Trailing stems, many short evergreen lvs. Fls pink or rosy red in dense gps 2 in wide with sweet frag. May fl in aut. *D. × burkwoodii* taller semi-evergreen hyb to 4 ft. 'Somerset' (AGM) better. *Ht:* 1 ft; *Spd:* 18 in; *Fl:* 4–5; *Z:* 6

D. mezereum* Mezereon: Eur. Pop wtr-flowering cottage-gdn plant; memorable cloying frag. Pinky-grey fls ½ in wide can be rich purple/red. Fr red, poisonous. White forms with amber fr to be treasured. *Ht:* 4 ft; *Spd:* 3 ft; *Fl:* 2–3; *Z:* 5

D. retusa: China. Dense evergreen shrublet. Fls rose-purple, pale throat, red fr. *Ht, Spd:* 3 ft; *Fl:* 5–6; *Z:* 7

Thorn apple

D. sanguinea: Peru. Tender, exotic. Fls pendulous, tubular, flared to 8 in, rusty orange-red. Lvs hry, oval. Prop by cuttings. *Ht, Spd:* to 10 ft; *Fl:* 5–6; *Z:* 10

D. suaveolens Angel's trumpet: Mexico. Sim in habit but lvs variable, often longer; fls frag, white. Both hardy in S Eur. *Ht, Spd:* to 15 ft; *Fl:* 6–8; *Z:* 10

D. suaveolens

Desfontainea

D. spinosa (=hookeri): S Amer. Usually small-medium bush but taller in warm regions. Lvs holly-like; fls scarlet, tubular to 1½ in, open yellow throat. Frs small, fleshy. *Ht:* 8 ft+; *Spd:* 5 ft+; *Fl:* 7–9; *Z:* 9

Deutzia

Deciduous early-summer shrubs of extreme pink-and-white charm but rarely making a landmark and sadly without scent.

D. × rosea (=gracilis rosea): gdn origin. Dainty; v many flared, bell-shaped pale pink fls, no frag. 'Carminea' (AGM) deeper col. *Ht, Spd:* 3 ft; *Fl:* 5–6; *Z:* 5

D. scabra (=crenata): China, Japan. To 10 ft, peeling bark. Doubles inc 'Pride of Rochester' and 'Candidissima' pure white. *Spd:* 4 ft; *Fl:* 6–7; *Z:* 6

D. scabra 'Candidissima'

Disanthus

D. cercidifolius*: Japan. Quietly attractive, lvs can be brightest of all reds in aut. Fls tiny, frs nut-like. *Ht, Spd:* 8 ft; *Fl:* 10; *Z:* 7

Dorycnium

D. hirsutum (=Lotus hirsutus)* Hairy Dorothy: S Eur. Hry silver-grey sub-shrub. Circular heads of pale pink-flushed pea-fls and chocolate brown seed pods. Prop by seed. *Ht, Spd:* 3 ft; *Fl:* 6–10; *Z:* 5

Drimys

D. winteri (=Wintera aromatica) Winter's bark: Andes. Handsome sp made famous by Sir Francis Drake's Captain William Winter. Lvs long, shining, glaucous below. Fls waxy white, sweetly frag in loose gps. Bark grey-brown aromatic. *D. w. andina* reaches 3 ft and will fl when small. *Ht:* 20 ft; *Spd:* 15 ft; *Fl:* 5; *Z:* 9

D. winteri

Elaeagnus

Elaeagnus

Most valuable vigorous hardy shrubs, evergreen and deciduous, with fragrant flowers and foliage ideal for screening.

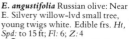

E. angustifolia Russian olive: Near E. Silvery willow-lvd small tree, young twigs white. Edible frs. *Ht, Spd:* to 15 ft; *Fl:* 6; *Z:* 4

E. pungens: Japan. Bushy evergreen. Varieg cvs inc: 'Dicksonii' wide, yellow margin; 'Maculata' central yellow dash; 'Aurea-variegata' (AGM) thin yellow margin. *E.* × *ebbingei* more vig. *Ht, Spd:* 15 ft; *Fl:* 10–11; *Z:* 7

E. pungens 'Maculata'

Embothrium

Fire bush

E. coccineum (=lanceolatum, longifolium): Chile. Tall, uprt, startling in fl with bottle-brushes of vivid orange-scarlet tubes. *E. c. lanceolatum* (AM) hardier, scarlet fls. *Ht:* 35 ft; *Spd:* 10 ft; *Fl:* 5–6; *Z:* 8

Enkianthus

Enkianthus

E. campanulatus: Japan. Enchanting uprt twiggy, decid bush. Fls waxy, bell-shaped, cream suffused and shot with reddish-brown. Superb aut col. *E. perulatus* white-fld. *Ht:* 8 ft; *Spd:* 5 ft; *Fl:* 5; *Z:* 5

Erica

Heath, Heather

The hardy European heaths range from dwarfs to small trees. One or another flowers almost every month. All have masses of minute evergreen leaves and prominent, often colored, petal tubes which die on the plant, remaining a good brown color. Both flower and foliage color seem infinitely variable. Most demand acid soil and all are best propagated by cuttings.

E. arborea★ Tree heath: Med, N Africa. Usually seen as 'Alba' with frag fls and soft fol. *Ht, Spd:* 10 ft; *Fl: 4; Z:* 8
E. carnea (=herbacea)★ Spring heath: Alps. Lvs pale green, fls white. or pink. Takes lime. *Ht:* 9 ft; *Spd:* 18 in; *Fl:* 11–5; *Z:* 6
E. ciliaris Fringed heath: SW Eur. Pitcher-shaped rose-pink fls. Lvs downy except in taller 'Mawaeana'. *Ht:* 1 ft; *Spd:* 18 in; *Fl:* 7–11; *Z:* 8

E. arborea

E. cinerea Twisted heather: W Eur. Dense mats of lvs. Some, eg 'Golden Hue' have golden fol. Cvs for wide col range inc 'Alba Minor' white; 'C.D.Eason' (AGM) and 'Rosea' (AGM) pink. *Ht:* 15 in; *Spd:* 18 in; *Fl:* 6–9; *Z:* 5

E. × *darleyensis:* gdn origin. Lime tolerant, bushy. 'A.T.Johnson' (AGM) rich rose-red; 'George Rendall' (AGM) deeper pink. *Ht, Spd:* 3 ft; *Fl:* 11–5; *Z:* 9

E. cinerea

Heath, Heather

E. erigena (= mediterranea):
SW Eur. Takes lime but not
dryness. Fls white, pink or deep red.
'W.T. Rackliff' white. *Ht, Spd:*
18 in; *Fl:* 3–5; *Z:* 6

E. lusitanica Spanish heath:
SW Eur. Spikes of frag white
fls pink in bud. *Ht, Spd:* to 10 ft; *Fl:*
1–4; *Z:* 6

E. tetralix Cross-leaved heath:
Eur. Fls pink, white or
crimson. 'Mollis' (AGM) white. *Ht,*
Spd: 18 in; *Fl:* 6–10; *Z:* 5

E. vagans Cornish heath: S
Eur. Long 9 in pokers of fl.
'Lyonesse' (AGM) creamy white.
Ht, Spd: 4 ft; *Fl:* 6–9; *Z:* 6

E. terminalis (= stricta) Corsican
heath: Eur. Rose-pink fls, hardy. *Ht,*
Spd: 4 ft; *Fl:* 6–9; *Z:* 8

E. erigena

E. tetralix 'Mollis'

Loquat

E. japonica★ Loquat: China, Japan. One of the biggest-lvd semi-hardy
evergreens. Lvs to 9 in, fls frag, yellowish-white. Frs soft orange, apricot-
like, delicious. *Ht:* to 30 ft; *Spd:* 10 ft; *Fl:* 11–4; *Z:* 9

Erythrina

E. crista-galli Common coral tree: Brazil. Usually wall-trained, often
cut back in frost. Waxy, pea-like 2 in fls in long gps. Lvs green,
divided into 3. Prop by cuttings. *Ht, Spd:* 8 ft; *Fl:* 5–6; *Z:* 9

Escallonia

E. 'Donard' hybs: gdn origin.
Among hardiest hybs; bell-
shaped fls in profusion. Lvs shiny,
often clammy. Fls in red-pink, e.g.
'Slieve Donard' apple-blossom pink.
E. 'Iveyi' with bigger lvs needs
protection, fls white. Prop by
cuttings. *Ht:* 8 ft; *Spd:* 6 ft; *Fl:* 6–9;
Z: 9

E. 'Donard Seedling'

Eucryphia

E. glutinosa (= pinnatifolia):
Chile. Lvs cut into 5 toothed
lflts. Fls white, 2½ in wide, boss of
golden stamens. Rich aut col. *Ht:*
15 ft; *Spd:* 10 ft+; *Fl:* 7–8; *Z:* 9

E. × nymansensis
'Nymansay'★: gdn origin.
Fast-growing lime tolerant noble
uprt evergreen hyb. Fls sim. *Ht:*
18 ft; *Spd:* 6 ft; *Fl:* 8–9; *Z:* 9

E. glutinosa

Spindle tree

Shrubs with bright seed capsules splitting to reveal even brighter seeds. Deciduous ones may color well in autumn.

E. japonicus

E. alatus

E. alatus Winged euonymus: China, Japan. Unique cerise to rose-red aut col. Flat branching habit, corky wings on stems; seeds orange. Good as a hedge. *Ht*: 8 ft; *Spd*: 8 ft+; *Fl*: 5–6; *Z*: 3

E. europaeus European spindle tree: Eur. Big bush; smooth soft lvs. Brilliant lf col, red frs and orange seeds in aut. 'Red Cascade' (AGM) rec. *Ht*: 12 ft+; *Spd*: 5 ft+; *Fl*: 5–6; *Z*: 4

E. fortunei Winter creeper: E Asia. Sprawling sometimes climbing evergreen smotherer. Fls and seeds inconspic except in *E. f. virgatus*, seeds orange. Good varieg cvs 'Silver Queen'; 'Emerald n' Gold'. *Ht*: 30 in; *Spd*: 4 ft; *Z*: 5
E. japonicus: Japan. Glossy evergreen. Best cv 'Duc d'Anjou'; the varieg 'Aureus' may revert. *Ht*: 6 ft; *Spd*: 5 ft; *Fl*: 6; *Z*: 7

E. planipes*: Japan. Splendid, decid. Lvs pointed, red-purple in aut, seeds red. Often offered as *E. sachalinensis*. *Ht*: 10 ft; *Spd*: 5 ft+; *Fl*: 6; *Z*: 7

E. yedoensis: Japan. Name debatable but not its aut beauty, pink frs, red seeds, pink lvs. *Ht*: 10 ft; *Spd*: 5 ft; *Fl*: 6; *Z*: 5

E. europaeus

Exochorda

Pearl bush

E. racemosa (=grandiflora): China. Almond-like milky-white fls on a pendulous bush. Lvs oval, sea-green. Will tolerate some lime but *E. korolkowii* (AM) v happy on lime. *Ht*: 12 ft; *Spd*: 8 ft; *Fl*: 5; *Z*: 5

Fatsia

Fatsia

F. (=Aralia) japonica*: Japan. Lustrous, jungly, deep-lobed lvs to 15 in wide on green stks. Fls off-white, ball-shaped, several to a 1½ in head. Lvs of 'Variegata' irregularly tipped green. Smaller-lvd × *Fatshedera lizei* probably hyb with common ivy. *Ht, Spd:* to 15 ft; *Fl:* 10–11; *Z:* 9

F. japonica

Feijoa

Feijoa

F. sellowiana Pineapple guava: S Amer. V pretty; small grey-green oval lvs, white felted below. Fls aromatic, ptls white, crimson at base, crimson stamens. Egg-shaped frs. *Ht, Spd:* 10 ft; *Fl:* 6; *Z:* 9

Fig

F. carica Common fig: Med, W
Asia. Decid shrub/small tree. Lvs
bold, 3–5 lobed, odd evocative
smell. Restrict rts, keep soil poor.
Reliable hardy cvs inc: 'Brown
Turkey'; 'White Marseilles'. *Ht:*
15 ft; *Spd:* 20 ft; *Fl:* 7; *Z:* 8
F. pumila: China, Japan. Evergreen
climber, bristling with aerial rts. *Ht:*
10 ft; *Spd:* 6 ft+; *Z:* 10

F. pumila

Forsythia

F. × intermedia: gdn origin.
Easy and loud in fl: a sheet of
striking yellow. 'Spectabilis' (AM)
golden yellow twisted ptls. *Ht, Spd:*
8 ft; *Fl:* 3–4; *Z:* 4
F. suspensa: China. More vig;
try 'Beatrix Farrand'; *F.s.
atrocaulis* (both AM). *Ht, Spd:* 10 ft;
Fl: 3–4; *Z:* 4

F. × intermedia

Fothergilla

F. gardenii: SE USA. Small shrub, fiery aut col. Long oval lvs on crooked
stems. Fls short, white, frag bottle-brushes. *F. major*★ and its clone *F.
monticola* (AM) larger, better. *Ht, Spd:* 4 ft; *Fl:* 4–5; *Z:* 6

Fuchsia

South American natives ideal for bedding or conservatories for
their long flowering season and ease of propagation (by cuttings).
Fancy sorts are mainly hybrids of *F. fulgens*.

F. magellanica: S Amer. The
hardiest sp. Woody bush to
6 ft, lvs thin, oval, toothed. Elegant
single pendulous fls to 2 in with
scarlet spls over purple ptls. There
are cream-varieg and dwarf forms
but best cv is 'Versicolor'★ (AM)
wrongly called *F.m. variegata* with
silvery grey-pink-tinted lvs and
dripping with fls. 'Molinae' has
dainty blush-pink to white fls and
pale green lvs. *Spd:* 4 ft; *Fl:* 7–10;
Z: 6

F. gdn hyb 'Mrs Popple'

F. gdn hybs: Selections for sun
and medium shade on most
soils. Shrubby in mild gdns,
herbaceous in cooler ones. Keep
moist in smr. Best are 'Chillerton
Beauty' (AM) blush-pink/violet;
'Mrs Popple' (AM) scarlet/purple,
crimson anthers; 'Madame
Cornelissen' (AM) semi-double,
scarlet/white; 'Margaret' carmine/
purple. *Ht:* to 5 ft; *Spd:* to 4 ft; *Fl:* 7–
10; *Z:* 9

F. gdn hyb 'Madame Cornelissen'

Garrya

Garrya

G. elliptica*: Cal, Oregon. Tough, rather dull lvs lighter below. Fls beautiful grey-green catkins to 9 in but to 15 in in cv 'James Roof'. Good wall-trained. Prop by cuttings. *Ht, Spd:* 10 ft; *Fl:* 1–2; *Z:* 8

Gaultheria

Gaultheria

G. shallon

G. procumbens Checkerberry green: E N Amer. Suckering shrub. Fls globular/pitcher-shaped, pale pink or white; frs round, bright red amongst oval fol. *Ht:* 6 in; *Spd:* 3 ft; *Fl:* 7–8; *Z:* 4

G. shallon Salal: W N Amer. Rampant, stoloniferous, lvs leathery. Fls bell-shaped, pinkish-white. Can be a pest in damp, acid soil. *Ht:* 6 ft; *Spd:* 6 ft; *Fl:* 5–6; *Z:* 6

Genista

Broom

Pea-flowered brooms, related to *Cytisus*, very varied in habit, but almost always yellow-flowered. They are excellent for dry, limy soil, needing no food.

G. aetnensis (=Spartium aetnense)* Mt Etna broom: Sicily. Rapidly makes small tree with near-lflss pendulous branchlets dripping with yellow fls. *Ht:* 18 ft; *Spd:* 10 ft+; *Fl:* 7–8; *Z:* 7

G. hispanica* Spanish broom: SW Eur. Dense, prickly; makes pouffe of rich green growth studded with yellow fls. Prop by seed, cuttings. *Ht, Spd:* 4 ft; *Fl:* 5–6; *Z:* 6

G. hispanica

Grevillea

Grevillea

G. rosmarinifolia

G. rosmarinifolia: Aust. Rosemary-like small shrub; lvs dark green needles, young shoots downy. Soft red fls in terminal bunches each narrow, tubular to 1 in, curved at ends. *Ht, Spd:* 4 ft; *Fl:* 5–6; *Z:* 10

G. sulphurea: Aust. Sim to above but lvs pale green, fls pale yellow with split, curled back ptl tube and protruding stigma. *Ht, Spd:* 4 ft; *Fl:* 5–6; *Z:* 10

Griselinia

Griselinia

G. (=Pukateria) littoralis: NZ. Tall, bushy, lvs glossy, spoon-shaped. Makes good hedge in mild areas esp nr sea. Fls inconspic. Young growth frost-tender. Prop by cuttings. *Ht:* 20 ft; *Spd:* 15 ft; *Z:* 9

Snowdrop tree, Silver bell

H. carolina: SE USA. Decid small tree/big shrub beautiful in May when dripping with $\frac{1}{2}$ in white bell-fls. Frs like small ribbed pears. *H. monticola* bigger esp in 'Vestita'* and perhaps better. *Ht:* 20 ft; *Spd:* 25 ft+; *Z:* 6

Halimium

Halimium

H. ocymoides: SW Eur. Grey-green lvs; sol rich yellow fls, each ptl blotched chocolate at base. Hyb × *Halimiocistus* 'Ingwersenii' with white fls in May–July also good but smaller. *Ht, Spd:* to 3 ft; *Fl:* 6; *Z:* 8

Hamamelis

Witch-hazel

H. × intermedia ("japollis"): gdn origin. Oval, hazel-like lvs col beautifully in aut. Fls to 1¼ in wide made up of strap-shaped ptls which are often wrinkled and have a slight fragrance. Prop by layers, grafting. *Ht, Spd:* 5 ft; *Fl:* 12–3; *Z:* 5

H. × intermedia

H. mollis* Chinese witch-hazel: China. Sim to above but wider ptls with persisting coppery-red spls, penetrating sweet frag. *Ht:* 8 ft; *Spd:* 6 ft; *Fl:* 12–3; *Z:* 5

H. vernalis Vernal witch-hazel: C USA. Sim to above, blooms in mid wtr. V frag yellow to reddish fls open fully on warm days, close on cold ones. *Ht, Spd:* 10 ft; *Fl:* 12–3; *Z:* 5

H. mollis

Hebe (=Veronica)

Hebe

Neat evergreens with small leaves in orderly ranks. Mostly tough and adaptable except in hard frost. Tiny flowers in spikes.

H. albicans: NZ. Hardy, glaucous lvs; fls 2 in compact white spikes. *Ht:* 18 in; *Spd:* 2 ft; *Fl:* 8–9; *Z:* 8

H. brachysiphon: NZ. Tidy dome of dense fol, remarkably hardy. White fls, brown anthers. *H. rakaiensis* smaller, bright green. *Ht, Spd:* 5 ft; *Fl:* 7–9; *Z:* 8

H. gdn hybs: V many good cvs inc: 'Autumn Glory', 'Carl Teschner' violet, dwarf; 'Great Orme' pink; 'Midsummer Beauty' lavender blue for months on end. *Ht, Spd:* to 3 ft; *Fl:* 7–10; *Z:* 8

H. brachysiphon

H. salicifolia Willow-leaved hebe: NZ. Wide willow-lvs. Fls white or pale lilac in tapering racemes. *H. s. variegata* less hardy. *Ht:* 4 ft; *Spd:* 5 ft; *Fl:* 7–9; *Z:* 8

H. speciosa: NZ. Thicker fls. Rec: 'Gauntletii' pink; 'La Seduisante' crimson; 'Veitchii' purple. *Ht, Spd:* 5 ft; *Fl:* 8–10; *Z:* 10

H. speciosa 'La Seduisante'

Helianthemum

Sun rose

H. gdn hybs*: Med (sp). Low, spreading shrubs producing profuse fresh crop of 1 in fls daily. Must have full sun. Rec sorts inc: 'Ben Ledi' rose-red, dark green lvs; 'Henfield Brilliant' orange-red, grey lvs; 'Wisley Pink' pale pink, orange anthers, grey lvs; 'Wisley Primrose' primrose yellow, grey lvs; 'Mrs C.W.Earle' double red. Prop by cuttings. *Ht:* 1 ft; *Spd:* 20 in; *Fl:* 5–7; *Z:* 6

H. gdn hybrid 'Wisley Pink'

Helichrysum

Everlasting, Straw flower

H. lanatum: S Africa. Sub-shrub; lvs long, narrow ever-grey. Flat heads small lemon-yellow fls. *Ht, Spd:* 18 in; *Fl:* 7; *Z:* 8
H. petiolatum*: S Africa. Tender. Lvs oval, woolly grey. Long brs form dome shape. *H. p. aureum* has soft yellow flannel-lvs; *H. p. variegatum* silver and deep green fol. *Ht:* 15 in; *Spd:* 30 in; *Z:* 10

H. petiolatum

Hibiscus

Hibiscus

Rich, expensive-looking late-summer feature with flowers in decadent colors. Late in leaf, rather slow-growing, will withstand hard pruning to shape.

H. rosa-sinensis Chinese hibiscus: China. Magnificent broadleaf evergreen. Single, semi-double and double fls to 8 in wide in many shades of white, pink, red, orange and yellow. Lvs glossy, oval. *Ht:* 15 ft; *Spd:* 12 ft; *Fl:* 4–9; *Z:* 9
H. syriacus Rose of Sharon: Syria. Uprt late-flowering shrubby mallow with oval lvs and shuttlecock-shaped fls to 3 in wide. *Ht:* 8 ft; *Spd:* 4 ft; *Fl:* 8–10; *Z:* 5

H. syriacus 'Dorothy Crane'

Hippophae

Hippophae

H. rhamnoides* Sea buckthorn: Eur–E Asia. Spiny bush, grey-green lvs silvery below. Fls inconspic but with both sexes present amber berries load branches in aut. Resists sea. *Ht:* 10 ft; *Spd:* 6 ft; *Fl:* 4; *Z:* 3

Hoheria

Hoheria

H. glabrata*: NZ. Tall evergreen with soft serrated lvs and translucent white, cherry-like frag fls 1½ in diam. Taller *H. lyallii** fls in June; semi-evergreen *H. sexstylosa* to 20 ft bears smaller more profuse fls in July–Aug. Prop by seed, cuttings. *Ht:* 15 ft; *Spd:* 10 ft; *Fl:* 6–7; *Z:* 9

Hydrangea

Most garden sorts are varieties of *H. macrophylla*; divided into mop-headed Hortensias and flat-headed Lacecaps, which have open sterile florets around a mass of smaller fertile ones.

H. aspera★: E Asia. Magnificent shrub. Lvs softly bristly; pink-mauve inner florets, pale blue outer ones. *H. villosa* v sim. *Ht, Spd:* 8 ft; *Fl:* 6–8; *Z:* 7

H. gdn hybs: Vig, bushy. Best Hortensias inc 'Altona' (AM) rosy-pink; 'Madame Emile Mouillière' (AM) white, blue eye; 'Générale Vicomtesse de Vibraye' (AM) pure blue. Best Lacecaps inc: 'Blue Wave' (AM); 'Sea Foam' blue edged white; 'Veitchii' white in shade, pink in sun. Blue fls turn pink on akaline soil. *Ht, Spd:* to 6 ft; *Fl:* 7–9; *Z:* 6

H. aspera

H. macrophylla: Japan. Rounded fl heads to 10 in across pink if soil is alkaline, blue on acid soil. Lvs coarse, bright green, decid. *Ht:* 12 ft; *Spd:* 10 ft; *Fl:* 8–9; *Z:* 6

H. paniculata: China, Japan. Uprt with lilac-like 8 in white fl plumes. 'Vera' is excellent. *Ht, Spd:* 6 ft; *Fl:* 6–7; *Z:* 4

H. quercifolia Oak-leaved hydrangea: N Amer. Vig, spreading, grown for its splendid lobed lvs to 8 in with rich aut col. *Ht:* 4 ft; *Spd:* 6 ft; *Fl:* 6–9; *Z:* 5

H. 'Générale Vicomtesse de Vibraye'

H. quercifolia

St John's wort

Adaptable long-flowering shrubs and ground cover with buttercup-like shining yellow flowers. Useful but easily overused.

H. androsaemum Tutsan: Eur, N Africa. Neat bush; fls small, frs berries. *Ht, Spd:* 3 ft; *Fl:* 6–9; *Z:* 6

H. calycinum Aaron's beard: Eur, Asia Minor. Semi-evergreen, vig ground cover. Fls to 4 in wide, central boss of anthers. *Ht:* 1 ft; *Spd:* 2 ft+; *Fl:* 6–9; *Z:* 6

H. 'Hidcote'★: gdn origin. Semi-evergreen. Fls to 3 in diam, orange anthers. *Ht:* 5 ft; *Spd:* 6 ft+; *Fl:* 6–10; *Z:* 6

H. forrestii: Asia. Fls saucer-shaped, rust-col frs persist in aut with crimson fol. *Ht:* 5 ft; *Spd:* 4 ft; *Fl:* 7–10; *Z:* 6

H. × inodorum: Canary Is. Best in cv 'Elstead' with long red-orange frs and sev fls in flat head. *Ht, Spd:* 3 ft; *Fl:* 6–9; *Z:* 7

H. × moseranum: gdn origin. Dwarf; fls 2½ in wide, ptls overlapping. Prop all by cuttings. *Ht:* 18 in; *Spd:* 2½ ft; *Fl:* 7–10; *Z:* 7

H. calycinum

H. × moseranum 'Tricolor'

Ilex

Holly

England's native holly is shiny-leaved and cheerful in berry but slightly tender. N America's is hardy but dull-leaved. Asia provides many other leaf forms of a most valuable, varied shrub.

I. aquifolium 'Silver Queen'

I. cornuta

I. aquifolium English holly: Eur, N Africa, W Asia. Spiny sparkling-lvd dense bushy evergreen. Dozens of good cvs, many varieg, inc: 'Argentea Marginata' (AM) broad lvs, silver-edged, frs freely; 'J.C. van Tol' pyramidal, lvs almost spineless, frs freely; 'Madame Briot' lvs edged and mottled gold. *Ht:* 30 ft; *Spd:* 10 ft; *Z:* 6

I. cornuta Chinese holly: China, Korea. Dense bushy evergreen; lvs almost rectangular, spines at top and corners. Frs big, red, sparse. *Ht, Spd:* 8 ft; *Z:* 6

I. crenata: Japan, Korea. Slow-growing. Lvs small, narrow, evergreen. Use 'Mariesii' in rock gdn. *Ht:* 8 ft; *Spd:* 3 ft; *Z:* 6

I. opaca American holly: E USA. V like *I. aquifolium* but lvs dull green, frs smaller, usually red, sometimes orange or yellow. Hardier, more widely grown. Many excellent cvs. *Ht:* 45 ft; *Spd:* 12 ft; *Z:* 5

I. pernyi: China. Lvs triangular, spiny, paler green. Berries red in 2s or 3s. *Ht:* 10 ft; *Spd:* 6 ft+; *Z:* 6

Indigofera

Indigo

I. heterantha (=gerardiana): Him. Fine-textured bushy shrub, late coming into growth. Lvs vetch-like, fls pea-like, bright purplish-pink in 5 in spikes. Frs long, thin pods. *Ht:* to 4 ft; *Spd:* 4 ft+; *Fl:* 6–10; *Z:* 6

Itea

Itea

I. ilicifolia

I. ilicifolia: China. Evergreen holly-like shrub. Lvs glossy, dark green. Fls catkin-like, greenish-white, lightly frag to 1 ft long in late smr. Prop by cuttings. *Ht:* to 12 ft; *Spd:* 5 ft+; *Fl:* 8; *Z:* 7

Jasminum

Jasmine

J. humile Italian jasmine: SE Eur, China–Him. Bushy dark-green-lvd; yellow flared tubular fls; glossy black round frs. Cv 'Revolutum' better and more frag. Prop by cuttings. *Ht:* 6 ft; *Spd:* 5 ft; *Fl:* 6–7; *Z:* 8

Juniper

This genus of conifers provides the most shrubs (apart from dwarfs) widely varied in habit, texture and color, easy to grow and therefore of great interest. Two leaf forms, juvenile (spiky) and adult (scale-like), may appear on the same branch.

J. chinensis Chinese juniper: E Asia. Bushy, often pyramidal, aromatic. Innumerable cvs, eg 'Kaizuka' bright bottle-green, gesticulating branches. Smaller hyb *J. × c.* 'Pfitzerana (AGM) sturdy, spreading; golden-lvd 'Pfitzerana Aurea' and glaucous *J. × c.* 'Hetzii' all first class. *Ht:* to 40ft; *Spd:* 8 ft+; *Z:* 5

J. chinensis

J. conferta★ Shore juniper: Japan. Prostrate, lvs large, prickly, pale green. *Ht:* 8 in; *Spd:* 4 ft; *Z:* 6

J. communis Common juniper: N Hem. Narrow columnar sorts inc 'Compressa' dwarf, spire-like, 1 ft; 'Hibernica'★ uprt, 12 ft; 'Horni-brookii' prostrate, 4 in. *Z:* 2

J. horizontalis Creeping juniper: N Amer. Pop blue-green, prostrate. 'Bar Harbour' is glaucous. *Ht:* 8 in; *Spd:* 4 ft; *Z:* 2

J. squamata 'Meyeri': China. Lurid steel-blue forward-pointing lvs, long brs. *Ht:* 15 ft; *Spd:* 7 ft; *Z:* 5

J. squamata 'Meyeri'

Kalmia

A close relation of the rhododendron with small but stylish pink/white flowers and good glossy foliage. Among the hardiest of all broadleaved evergreens.

K. angustifolia Sheep's laurel: E N Amer. Narrow lvs; rosy-red saucer-shaped fls up-facing in round heads 2 in wide. 'Rubra' has redder fls. *Ht, Spd:* 3 ft; *Fl:* 6; *Z:* 2

K. latifolia★ Mountain laurel: E N Amer. More common. Fls like upturned Victorian lamp-shades in larger gps white to pink deeper col in bud and along pleats. *Ht, Spd:* 6 ft; *Fl:* 6; *Z:* 5

K. latifolia

Jew's mallow

K. japonica: China, Japan. Uprt, bamboo-like shrub with bright green stems and light green lvs hry on underside. Fls orange-yellow to 1½ in diam. More elegant than commoner form 'Pleniflora' (Bachelor's buttons, AM). Dwarf 'Variegata' (='Picta') creamy-white varieg lvs but is inclined to revert to type. Prop by veg means. *Ht:* 6 ft; *Spd:* 3 ft+; *Fl:* 4–5; *Z:* 5

K. japonica

Kolkwitzia

Kolkwitzia

K. amabilis★ Beauty bush: China. Stems stiff but soon arch over to form dense bush. Lvs small, pointed, matte green. Fls foxglove-like, 2½ in, pale pink with yellow throat and freely produced. Alas no scent. 'Pink Cloud' (AGM) is clear pink. Prop by cuttings, suckers. *Ht:* 6 ft+; *Spd:* 8 ft+; *Fl:* 5–6; *Z:* 5

K. amabilis

Laurus

Laurel, Sweet bay

L. nobilis★ *Bay:* Med. Shiny-lvd wide pyramidal bush, can be trained to mop-head or conical shape. Lvs narrow oval, used for flavoring. Fls inconspic, frs round, black. *Ht:* 18 ft; *Spd:* 5 ft+; *Fl:* 4; *Z:* 8

Lavandula

Lavender

L. angustifolius (=officinalis)★: Med. Grown as a bush or clipped as a hedge. Narrow 2 in grey flat lvs, fls in 2½ in spikes on long stems. Cvs inc 'Alba' white 'Hidcote' (AM) purple; 'Munstead' (AM) lavender-blue; 'Twickel Purple' deep blue/purple, spreading; 'Vera' wider lvs, fls lavender-blue. *Ht, Spd:* 3 ft; *Fl:* 6–7; *Z:* 6

L. angustifolius 'Munstead'

Lavatera

Mallow

L. olbia Tree mallow: Med. Usually planted in form 'Rosea'★ which has rosy-pink mallow fls 4 in wide over a long period and 3–5 lobed softly hry lvs. Sp is pink/purplish. *Ht:* 6 ft; *Spd:* 5 ft; *Fl:* 6–10; *Z:* 8

Leptospermum

Leptospermum

L. scoparium Manuka: Aust, NZ. Liberal clothing of tiny oval pointed lvs. Fls ¾ in wide, 5 white ptls, followed by woody, persistent seed capsules. Cvs inc 'Nichollsii' (AM) crimson ptls, darker center, lvs bronze–purple; 'Red Damask' (AM) deep double red. Prop by seed (sp), cuttings. *Ht:* 15 ft; *Spd:* 10 ft; *Fl:* 5–6; *Z:* 9

L. scoparium

Lespedeza (=Desmodium)

Lespedeza

L. thunbergii: China, Japan. Woody plant that dies down annually. Long, lax stems, pale green, silky lvs. Fls pea-like, rosy purple in loose poker-like heads. Prop by div. *Ht:* to 8 ft; *Spd:* 5 ft; *Fl:* 9–10; *Z:* 5

Leucothoe

L. (=Andromeda) fontanesiana: SE USA. Suckering; ideal ground cover. Fls pitcher-shaped, white in dense spikes on stem undersides. 'Rainbow' has lvs splashed cream. *Ht:* 5 ft; *Spd:* 4 ft; *Fl:* 5; *Z:* 4

Leycesteria

L. formosa: Him. Bright eau de nil green hollow stems useful in wtr; lvs heart-shaped, fls pale pink, becoming white, alternating with pale crimson bracts. Frs round, reddish-purple. Seeds itself. *L. crocothyrsos* (AM) rarer and less hardy has golden-yellow fls, green bracts. *Ht, Spd:* 6 ft; *Fl:* 6–9; *Z:* 7

L. formosa

Privet

L. japonicum Japanese privet: E Asia. Bushy evergreen, lvs deep green. Fls white, small in 6 in pyramidal heads with heavy scent. *Ht, Spd:* 10 ft; *Fl:* 7–9; *Z:* 7
   L. lucidum★: China. May make a small tree. Lvs glossy to 4 in, fl heads to 8 in. Frs like small grapes. Varieg cvs inc 'Excelsum Superbum'★ and 'Tricolor'. *Ht:* 18 ft; *Spd:* 10 ft; *Fl:* 8–9; *Z:* 8
L. ovalifolium California privet: Japan. Ubiquitous hedging, nasty smell. 'Aureum' gold varieg. *Ht, Spd:* 10 ft; *Fl:* 7; *Z:* 6

L. ovalifolium 'Aureum'

Honeysuckle

L. nitida: China. Fast-growing densely bushy; lvs tiny, oval, evergreen, often used for hedging; inconspic, tubular ½ in frag fls. Berries (if any) purple. Cv 'Baggesen's Gold'★ yellow-lvd. *Ht:* 6 ft; *Spd:* 5 ft+; *Fl:* 5; *Z:* 7
   L. pileata Privet honeysuckle: China. For full or part shade. Semi-evergreen, densely twiggy, excellent ground cover. Fls frag, yellowish-white, frs round, violet, translucent. *Ht:* 3 ft; *Spd:* 4 ft; *Fl:* 5; *Z:* 5
L. × purpusii★: gdn origin. Twiggy, round bush. Lvs broadly oval; fls on bare wood in wtr creamy-white, intensely scented. *Ht, Spd:* 6 ft; *Fl:* 12–2; *Z:* 6
L. tatarica Tartarian honeysuckle. USSR. Narrower lvs and pink fls, red berries. Cvs 'Hack's Red' and 'Arnold Red' have red fls. *Ht, Spd:* 12 ft; *Fl:* 5–6; *Z:* 3

L. nitida 'Baggesen's Gold'

L. tatarica

Lupinus

Lupine

L. arboreus Tree lupine: Cal. Bushy evergreen with typically lupine-like lvs and creamy-white or yellow fls. Short-lived but v attractive and useful esp by the sea. Seeds freely. Hybs with pink or mauve fls sometimes seen by roadsides and are worth taking cuttings from. *Ht:* 6 ft+; *Spd:* 5 ft; *Fl:* 6–7; *Z:* 7

L. arboreus

Magnolia

Magnolia

A genus including the finest of all flowering trees. Those chosen here are the most popular and adaptable smaller ones, of superlative beauty in their tulip-textured flowers and great quality in leaf and even in bud, twig and branch.

M. × soulangiana*: gdn origin. Best basic sp. Fls on bare brs, 6 in ptls white, purple backs, reflexed. Best (AGM) cvs: 'Alba Superba'; 'Brozzonii' and 'Lennei' purple and white. *Ht, Spd:* 25 ft; *Fl:* 4–5; *Z:* 5

M. stellata*: Japan. Fls before lvs; many (to 18) strap-shaped ptls turn pink with age. Best (AM) cvs 'Rosea' pink buds, paler in ptl; 'Rubra' deeper col. *Ht:* 10 ft; *Spd:* 20 ft; *Fl:* 3–4; *Z:* 6

M. stellata

Mahonia

Mahonia

Like a larger-leaved evergreen *Berberis* without the vicious prickles. All yellow-flowered, starting in the depths of winter.

M. aquifolium Oregon grape: W N Amer. Suckering, clump-forming. Lvs have glossy prickly lflts reddish in aut. Fls bell-shaped in 5 in spikes, black frs have bluish bloom. V tough and useful. Prop by seed, suckers, div. *Ht:* 3 ft; *Spd:* 3 ft+; *Fl:* 4–5; *Z:* 6
M. bealei: China. More uprt, lvs 3× as large, fl spikes 6 in. Often wrongly called *M. japonica. Ht, Spd:* 6 ft; *Fl:* 10–3; *Z:* 6

M. aquifolium

M. japonica*: origin unknown. Sprawling, lvs darker green. Fls larger, frag. *Ht:* 6 ft; *Spd:* 8 ft+; *Fl:* 11–3; *Z:* 7
M. × media 'Charity'*: gdn origin. Superb uprt hyb; plumes of fl to 1 ft, frs violet, tinted grey. Prop by cuttings *Ht:* 10 ft; *Spd:* 8 ft+; *Fl:* 11–3; *Z:* 8
M. lomariifolia: China, Burma. The finest lvs; but may be so leggy it looks like a palm. *Ht:* to 12 ft; *Spd:* 5 ft; *Fl:* 11–1; *Z:* 9

M. japonica

Melianthus

M. major*: S Africa, India. Huge pale sea-green v decorative lvs divided into toothed lflts. Fls woolly plumes of soft crimson-red in July–Sept. Only hardy in a sheltered corner of a warm gdn. Prop by div, cuttings. *Ht, Spd:* 4 ft; *Z:* 9

M. major

Metrosideros

M. lucida: NZ. Bottle-brush shrub/small tree. Lvs small, elliptic, pointed, burnished hue when young. Fls terminal, fluffy bright crimson stamens. Tolerates a little lime. *Ht, Spd:* 10 ft; *Fl:* 8; *Z:* 10

Michelia

M. doltsopa (=excelsa): Him, China. Rounded bush related to magnolia. Lvs leathery, shimmering, paler below. Fls waxy white, heavily frag, may be tinged yellow in aut. *Ht:* 30 ft; *Spd:* 25 ft; *Fl:* 4; *Z:* 8

Myrtle

M. communis* Common myrtle: S Eur–W Asia. Densely bushy; pointed lvs aromatic, esp when crushed. Rose-like white fls 1 in wide have delightful central boss of stamens. Frs purple-black berries. *M.c. tarentina* (Tarentum myrtle) less hardy, smaller lvs, yellowish-white berries. Prop by cuttings. *Ht, Spd:* 5 ft; *Fl:* 7–8; *Z:* 8

M. communis

Chinese sacred bamboo, Heavenly bamboo

N. domestica*: China. Little uprt plant. Long lvs divided into thin lflts reddish when young, purple-tinted in aut. Fls creamy-white in pyramidal terminal plumes to 15 in wide followed, in warm gdns, by bright red berries. Universal in Japanese gdns. 'Nana Purpurea' dwarf, purplish lvs. *Ht:* 6 ft; *Spd:* 4 ft+; *Fl:* 6–7; *Z:* 7

N. domestica

Neillia

N. thibetica (=longiracemosa): China. Tall bushy; dense uprt stems arch towards tips. Lvs small, oval, toothed. Fls rose-pink, tubular in terminal groups, long spls. *Ht:* to 6 ft; *Spd:* 4 ft; *Fl:* 5–6; *Z:* 6

Nerium

N. oleander Common oleander, Rose-bay: Med, Asia. Leathery-lvd shrub of Med streets and gdns. Fls open periwinkle-like to 1½ in diam, several in a head, are usually pink or white although yellow and double-flowered sorts are obtainable. Will take some lime. Good in tubs with protection in wtr. Prop by cuttings. *Ht:* 12 ft; *Spd:* 15 ft+; *Fl:* 6–10; *Z:* 8

N. oleander

Olearia

Daisy bush

An entirely Australasian genus of evergreen shrubs, mainly easy and fast-growing in full sun but none hardy against extreme frost. Daisy-like flowers are mainly white or off-white.

O. × haastii: NZ. Densely bushy. Grey-green lvs rounded, white felt beneath. Fls profuse, ½ in wide, yellow centers. One of the hardiest. Prop all spp by cuttings. *Ht:* 8 ft; *Spd:* 4 ft; *Fl:* 7–8; *Z:* 8

O. macrodonta: NZ. Lvs larger, holly-like, leaden green, silver-white beneath. Fls tiny in round heads to 6 in diam. Extreme frost can kill. *Ht:* 10 ft; *Spd:* to 20 ft; *Fl:* 7; *Z:* 8

O. phlogopappa: Aust. Branching, uprt, lvs and young stems felted. Fls in loose clusters sometimes blue or pink. *Ht:* 6 ft; *Spd:* 4 ft; *Fl:* 5; *Z:* 8

O. × scilloniensis: gdn origin. Grey-green lvs and white fls in profusion in May. *Ht:* to 8 ft; *Spd:* to 5 ft; *Z:* 8

O. stellulata: Aust. Larger lvs than O. phlogopappa, yellowish felt. 'Splendens' has larger fls. Selected forms blue or pink. *Ht:* 6 ft; *Spd:* 5 ft; *Fl:* 5; *Z:* 8

O. × haastii

O. macrodonta

Osmanthus

Osmanthus

Relations of the olive: in appearance somewhere between olive and holly. Fragrant fillers rather than the focus of a garden.

O. (=Siphonosmanthus) delavayi*: China. Lvs smaller, more toothed and pointed. Fls sim to above earlier, more frag. *Ht, Spd:* 8 ft+; *Fl:* 4; *Z:* 7

O. heterophyllus (=ilicifolius) Holly osmanthus: Japan. Lustrous evergreen v like holly but with opposite lvs and frag yellow-green fls. Frs blue-black. *Ht, Spd:* 18 ft; *Fl:* 6–7; *Z:* 6

O. delavayi

Pachysandra

P. terminalis: Japan. Creeping. Lvs diamond-shaped, pale green, toothed near tip. Fls 2 in terminal spikes, pale green or whitish, purple tinge. 'Variegata' white varieg lvs. *Ht:* 1 ft; *Spd:* 20 ft; *Fl:* 2–3; *Z:* 6

Peony

"Tree" peonies are not greatly different from herbaceous ones in action, merely keeping woody stems, but their young growth can be nipped by spring frosts. Well worth growing.

P. delavayi: China. Fls 2 in wide, single, crimson-red, gold stamens. Frs big, dark seeds. *Ht:* 4 ft; *Spd:* 3 ft; *Fl:* 5; *Z:* 6

P. lutea ludlowii*: Tibet. Larger all over, striking lvs. Fls single, yellow, 2½ in diam. *Ht, Spd:* 6 ft; *Fl:* 5–6; *Z:* 6

P. suffruticosa* Tree peony: China, Tibet. Bushy sp of incomparable beauty. Fls to 1 ft wide, ptls white or palest pink, maroon blotch at base. Cvs inc fuller and double sorts from scarlet to wine coloured. Plant in cool spot to delay flowering until after frost. *Ht, Spd:* 6 ft; *Fl:* 5–6; *Z:* 6

P. suffruticosa

Parahebe

P. (=Veronica) catarractae: NZ. Shrublet; lvs coarsely toothed on wiry trailing stems. Fls speedwell-like in slim 8 in spires may have crimson/purple lines. Also pink/purple/blue forms. *Ht, Spd:* 1 ft; *Fl:* 8–9; *Z:* 8

Parrotia

P. (=Hamamelis) persica* Iron tree: Iran, Caucasus. Large bush with long branches often at 45°. Lvs green, hazelnut-like, turning fiery red, orange, crimson and yellow in aut. Fls little tufts of red stamens on the bare branches in early spr. *Ht:* 20 ft; *Spd:* to 40 ft; *Fl:* 3; *Z:* 5

P. persica

Pernettya

P. mucronata: S Amer. Suckering shrub, little leathery lvs. Fls white, bell-like, ¼ in long, frs white, pink or purple berries. Plant in gps with ♂ plant to ensure fruiting. Cvs inc 'Davis's Hybrids' (AGM), frs large; 'Bell's Seedling' (AGM), frs dark red; 'Pink Pearl' frs soft pink. *Ht:* 3 ft; *Spd:* 3 ft+; *Fl:* 5–6; *Z:* 7

P. mucronata

Philadelphus

Mock orange, "Syringa"

Easy, profligate with white flowers famous for their far-carrying scent. Otherwise a dull bush. Prune hard after flowering.

P. 'Belle Etoile'*: gdn origin. White fls 2 in wide, soft crimson stain at ptl base. 'Beauclerk' (AM) pure white. Prop by cuttings. *Ht:* 6 ft; *Spd:* 8 ft; *Fl:* 6–7; *Z:* 5

P. coronarius (=pallidus): Eur, Asia Minor. Creamy-white fls. 'Aureus'* is one of best golden-lvd shrubs but less free in fl. *Ht, Spd:* 10 ft; *Fl:* 6–7; *Z:* 4

P. microphyllus: W N Amer. Dwarf twiggy bush. Free-flowering, strongly frag. 'Manteau d'Hermine' cream, double. *Ht:* 3 ft; *Spd:* 4 ft; *Fl:* 6–7; *Z:* 5

P. 'Belle Etoile'

Phillyrea

Phillyrea

P. latifolia*: SE Eur, Asia Minor. Lvs glittering, dark green ovals. Fls small, greenish-white, frag may be followed by black berries. *P. (=Osmanthus) decora* larger lvd. *Ht:* to 15 ft; *Spd:* 10 ft; *Fl:* 4–5; *Z:* 7

Phlomis

Phlomis

P. fruticosa Jerusalem sage: Med. Low, soft hry shrub of character for hot, dry places. Fls soft yellow, nettle-like in whorls to 1½ in on spikes. *P. chrysophylla* sim but yellow-green lvs. Prop by seed, cuttings. *Ht:* 3 ft; *Spd:* 4 ft; *Fl:* 6–9; *Z:* 7

P. fruticosa

Photinia

Photinia

P. × fraseri*: gdn origin. Young shoots coppery-red, lvs sim turning rich green. Replaces *Pieris* on lime. Try 'Birmingham'; 'Red Robin'; 'Robusta' (AM, hardy). *Ht:* 6 ft; *Spd:* 8 ft; *Fl:* 4–5; *Z:* F

P. serrulata Chinese photinia: China. Often leggy. Worthy for early flush of red new lvs. Fls white, frs haw-like if present. *Ht:* 18 ft; *Spd:* 12 ft; *Fl:* 4–5; *Z:* 7

P. serrulata

Physocarpus

Ninebark

P. opulifolius Eastern ninebark: E N Amer. Coarse but valuable because of extreme hardiness. Tiny white fls in dense clusters; bark peeling. Cv 'Nanus' to 2 ft. *Ht:* 9 ft; *Spd:* 6 ft; *Fl:* 5–6; *Z:* 2

Pieris

Of many virtues but demand acid soil and shelter from late frosts for their beautiful new growth. *P. floribunda* hardier but less striking than *P. japonica*. Plant only selected forms.

P. floribunda Mountain andromeda: E USA. V like following but tiny white fls in uprt slightly nodding pyramidal gps. Fl buds prominent all wtr. *Ht, Spd:* 6 ft; *Fl:* 4–5; *Z:* 5

P. formosa Himalayan andromeda: Asia. Bushy; lvs narrow. Young stems pale green, young fol bronze; fls closed bells. *Ht, Spd:* 8 ft; *Fl:* 4–5; *Z:* 8

P. japonica Japanese andromeda: Japan. Lvs v shiny, tinted red-bronze when young. *Ht:* to 10 ft; *Spd:* 8 ft; *Fl:* 3–4; *Z:* 6

P. formosa

Pittosporum

Pittosporum

P. eugenioides Tarata: NZ. Dark stems; wavy-edged lvs pale beneath. Fls yellowish bell-shaped, sweet frag. 'Variegatum' excellent. *Ht:* 20 ft; *Spd:* 8 ft; *Fl:* 4–5; *Z:* 9

P. tenuifolium: NZ. Paler lvs on black stems. Fls chocolate-purple, frs contain glistening black seeds. *Ht:* to 30 ft; *Spd:* 8 ft+; *Fl:* 4–5; *Z:* 9

P. tenuifolium

Polygala

Milkwort

P. chamaebuxus Bastard box. Dwarf creeping evergreen. Lvs box-like, fls white and yellow, pea-like; frs flat. *P.c. grandiflora* (='Purpurea', AM) magenta/yellow fls. *Ht, Spd:* 1 ft; *Fl:* 4–6; *Z:* 7

Potentilla

Cinquefoil

Among the longest-flowering shrubs, rarely covered in flowers but cheerful in summer and pleasantly twiggy in winter.

P. arbuscula: Him, China. Fls single, bright yellow, 1 in diam. *Ht, Spd:* 4 ft; *Fl:* 6–10; *Z:* 3

P. 'Manchu': gdn origin. Dwarf shrub, white fls. *Ht:* 8 in; *Spd:* 30 in; *Fl:* 6–9; *Z:* 3

P. fruticosa Shrubby cinqefoil: N Hem. Yellow fls. Cvs inc 'Abbotswood' white, 'Elizabeth' rich yellow; 'Longacre'* pale yellow; 'Red Ace' brick red. *Ht:* 3 ft; *Spd:* 4 ft; *Fl:* 6–9; *Z:* 3

P. × 'Vilmoriniana'*: gdn origin. Uprt hyb; lvs silvery-green, fls pale primrose yellow. *Ht:* 4 ft; *Spd:* 30 in; *Fl:* 6–10; *Z:* 3

P. fruticosa

Prunus

The genus that includes cherries, plums, peaches and almonds also furnishes two important evergreen "laurels".

P. laurocerasus

P. laurocerasus Cherry laurel: E Eur, Asia Minor. Common, much maligned evergreen useful for deep shade. Fls white in short spikes, frs black. Narrow-lvd cvs inc 'Otto Luyken' (AM); 'Schipkaensis' (AM, v hardy); 'Zabeliana' (AGM) lvs willow-like. *Ht*: 30 ft; *Spd*: 40 ft; *Fl*: 4; *Z*: 7

P. lusitanica★ Portuguese laurel: SW Eur. Hardier, more handsome and adaptable than above; less good in shade, better for clipping. Fls white; frs round, red, ripening black. *Ht*, *Spd*: 18 ft; *Fl*: 6; *Z*: 8

P. mume★ Japanese apricot, Mei: E Asia. Shrub/small tree. Young stems green, fls frag, single, pink. 'Beni-shi-dori' (AM) soft crimson double. *Ht*: to 18 ft; *Spd*: 6 ft+; *Fl*: 3; *Z*: 6

P. mume

Punica

Pomegranate

P. granatum

P. granatum: Afghanistan, Iran. Tall; needs protection in cool zones. Dwarf 'Nana' hardier and more useful; easy in a well-drained spot. Lvs narrow, light green. Fls bright scarlet, tubular to 2 in, ruff at mouth. Edible fr ripens only in warmth. *Ht*: 12 ft; *Spd*: 8 ft; *Fl*: 6–9; *Z*: 8

Pyracantha

Firethorn

P. atalantioides

P. atalantioides: China. Tall, vig, narrow lvs. Fls white in flat clusters 2 in wide, long-lasting red berries delicacies to birds. 'Aurea' (AM) yellow frs. *Ht*: 15 ft; *Spd*: 8 ft+; *Fl*: 5–6; *Z*: 7

P. coccinea Scarlet firethorn: S Eur, Asia. Less vig, wider lvs. Frs red-orange. 'Lalandei' (AGM) more pop with larger lvs. *Ht*, *Spd*: 15 ft; *Fl*: 6; *Z*: 6

P. koidzumii: Japan. Best southern sp. Frs dark red to orange. *Ht*, *Spd*: 10 ft; *Fl*: 5; *Z*: 8

Raphiolepis

Raphiolepis

R. × delacourii: gdn origin. Neat round bush, young growth pale green, hry, lvs dark green. Fls pale pink, 5 ptls. Shelter from severe frost. *R. indica* less hardy, paler fls. *Ht*, *Spd*: 5 ft; *Fl*: 1–10; *Z*: 8

Buckthorn

R. alaternus: Med. Vig, densely glossy evergreen; lvs oval to 2 in. Fls tiny, yellowish green, frs red berries. 'Argenteovariegata'* greyish-green-lvd, irregular white edge. *Ht:* 8 ft; *Spd:* 6 ft; *Fl:* 4; *Z:* 8

Rhododendron, Azalea

A thousand species right round the Northern Hemisphere make this the single most important shrubby genus. In gardening (but not botany) it divides into azaleas, thin branched, mainly deciduous shrubs, and rhododendrons which are generally evergreen with flowers often in a single raceme or spike. All prefer and most need acid soil. Being shallow-rooted they move well.

Decid Azaleas: gdn origin: Sev series of hybs in fl from early May to late June. Many are frag. Often fine aut col. *Z:* 3

R. calendulaceum: E USA. Yellow or orange to scarlet fls in early June last 2 weeks. *Z:* 7

Exbury: Gdn origin. Mostly single fls to 4 in wide in big, round clusters. Cols white, pink, red, yellow or orange. *Z:* 6

Ghent★:* Tall, late-flowering. Try 'Daviesii' white, creamy-yellow throat, fls long, tubular, flared; 'Narcissiflorum' (AGM) light yellow, deeper throat, frag.

Mollis★:* Usually to 6 ft, less twiggy, earlier, bigger fls in hotter cols (LF) 'Spek's Orange' (AGM) dark orange in bud opening to bright orange with greenish flare.

Knap Hill: Young growth may be bronze. 'Exbury' strain best. Plants reach 5–8 ft, eg 'Hotspur' (AM) glowing flame red, yellow flare in throat; 'Strawberry Ice' (AGM) flesh pink, deeper pink markings and yellow flare. Dense round fl truss.

Evergreen Azaleas: gdn origin. Hybs of Japanese spp. Cooler cols; less hardy. *Ht:* to 4 ft; *Spd:* to 6 ft; *Fl:* 4–5; *Z:* PF

Glenn Dale: USA. Medium size. Best is 'Elizabeth' old rose-pink.

Kurume: Japan. Densely bushy with layers of small lvs. Can reach 5 ft. Named sorts inc 'Blaauw's Pink' salmon pink fls one inside another; 'Hinamoyo' (=Hinomayo, AM) fierce magenta, needs careful placing.

Vuyk hybs: Holland. Large funnel-shaped fls on small bushes. Good clean cols, fl May–early June. Try 'Blue Danube' piercing violet-blue; 'Palestrina' fls white with pale green stripe; 'Vuyk's Scarlet' (AGM) brilliant light crimson.

Azalea Knap Hill 'Hotspur Orange'

Azalea Knap Hill 'Persil'

Azalea Knap Hill 'Fireglow'

Azalea Kurume 'Blue Danube'

Rhododendron

R. × 'Praecox'

R. racemosum

R. williamsianum

R. hybrid 'Pink Pearl'

R. hybrid 'Sappho'

R. carolinianum: E USA. Compact, rounded, early blooming. Narrow elliptical lvs to 3 in brown below. Fls pale rosy-purple. 'Album' has white fls. *Ht, Spd:* 6 ft; *Fl:* 5; *Z:* 6

R. catawbiense: E USA. V vig, hardy spreading evergreen. Profuse lilac-purple fls but most noted for its gorgeous hybs, inc: 'Roseum Elegans' fuschia-purple, green markings; 'Albert' white to pale lilac, brown markings; 'Mrs C.S. Sargent' rose, yellow-green markings. *Ht:* 6 ft; *Spd:* 8 ft; *Fl:* 6; *Z:* 6

R. keiskei: Japan. One of the rare evergreen rhododendrons with pale yellow fls. Lvs to 2¼ in. *Ht, Spd:* 8 ft; *Fl:* 5; *Z:* 6

R. × 'Praecox': gdn origin. Early and worth planting in sheltered spot. Semi-evergreen, twiggy; fls wide open, funnel-shaped, light purple with pink tinge. *Ht:* 4 ft; *Spd:* 3 ft; *Fl:* 2–3; *Z:* 6

R. racemosum: China. Slender shrub, stems reddish; fls small, clustered, pale or deep pink. *Ht:* 4 ft; *Spd:* 3 ft; *Fl:* 3–4; *Z:* 6

R. (=Azalea) schlippenbachii*: Korea, China, USSR. Outstanding decid; lvs light green, oblong, pointed usually in whorls of 5, often purplish when young. Fls wide open, funnel-shaped, pale rosy pink soft brown spots on top 3 ptls, long stamens. Rich yellow/orange and crimson aut col. Protect from spr frost. *Ht:* to 10 ft; *Spd:* 6 ft+; *Fl:* 4–5; *Z:* 5

R. smirnowii: Caucasus. Evergreen lvs white and woolly on undersides; many big fls white to rosy red, ptls may have wavy margins. *Ht, Spd:* 9 ft; *Fl:* 5; *Z:* 5

R. williamsianum*: China. Hummock-forming evergreen; lvs nearly round, notched at base, glaucous beneath. Young growth bronze. Fls bell-like, 2½ in wide, rose-pink. *Ht, Spd:* 5 ft; *Fl:* 4; *Z:* 7

R. hybs: Gdn origin. "Hardy hybs" combine best features of sev spp. Among the best are 'Boule de Neige' early white; 'Sunset' pale yellow shaded pink; 'Wissahickon' bright red; 'Ben Mosley' pink; 'Mars' deep red; 'Coombe Royal' delicate pink; 'Moonstone' changes from pale pink to creamy yellow; 'Stella Maris' pink and yellow; 'Bow Bells' bell-shaped, bright pink; 'Pink Pearl' pale pink; 'Sappho'* white, purple-black blotch in each fl. *Fl:* 5–6; *Z:* 6

Sumac

⚙ ⚘ **R. typhina** Stag's horn sumac: E N Amer. Gaunt bush/small tree. Stout pithy stems, many slim lflts. Distinctive woolly crimson fr. Glorious aut col. 'Dissecta' (AM) smaller. *Ht, Spd:* 12 ft; *Fl:* 4–5; *Z:* 3

Currant

Fruit-bush relations grown for their dangling single or tassel-grouped flowers including some of the earliest spring blooms.

R. odoratum (=aureum) Clove or Golden currant: W N Amer. Open, uprt bush, shiny pale green deep-lobed small lvs. Fls frag, bright yellow in 2 in tassels; frs black. *Ht, Spd:* 6 ft; *Fl:* 4; *Z:* 5

⚙ ⚘ **R. sanguineum** Flowering currant: W N Amer. Erect, bushy, typical currant lvs and smell. Fls in 4 in tassels white, pink or crimson according to cv. Frs black. Rec (both AM) 'King Edward VII' less tall, fls rich crimson; 'Pulborough Scarlet' soft light red. *Ht, Spd:* 6 ft; *Fl:* 4; *Z:* 5

R. sanguineum

⚙ ⚘ **R. speciosum★:** Cal. Like a gooseberry with spiny stems. Fls bright red, pendulous, fuchsia-like to 1½ in. Good against a wall. *Ht, Spd:* 6 ft; *Fl:* 4–5; *Z:* 6

R. speciosum

Rose or False acacia

⚙ ⚘ **R. hispida:** SE USA. Awkward but beautiful suckering sprawler. Young stems bristly; pale, oval lflts. Fls rose-pink, pea-like, frs bristly pods to 2 in. Prop by seed. *Ht, Spd:* to 8 ft; *Fl:* 5–6; *Z:* 6

Rubus

R. cockburnianus★: China. Like an elegant blackberry, stems ghostly white. V effective in wtr. Fls inconspic, frs black. *Ht:* 8 ft; *Spd:* to 30 ft; *Z:* 6

R. tricolor: China. Vig, trailing semi-evergreen, stems bristly. Fls white, rose-like, frs red. *Ht:* 1 ft; *Spd:* 5 ft; *Fl:* 7; *Z:* 6

⚙ ⚘ **R. 'Tridel':** gdn origin. Stems soft grey-brown, flaking. Fls white, 2 in wide, golden stamens. Look for 'Benenden'. *Ht, Spd:* 8 ft; *Fl:* 5; *Z:* 6

R. 'Tridel'

Ruscus

R. aculeatus Butcher's broom: Eur–Iran. Sturdy, vig, savagely prickly. Lf-like stems have tiny greenish-white fls in center. Frs glossy red berries if ♂ and ♀ plants are grown together. *Ht:* 3 ft; *Spd:* 18 in+; *Fl:* 3–4; *Z:* 8

Salix

Willow

S. hastata 'Wehrhahnii'*: gdn origin. V many 2 in soft catkins yellowing with pollen. *Ht, Spd:* 4 ft; *Z:* 4

S. purpurea Purple osier: Eur. Dense, decid shrub. Catkins to 1 in before lvs; twigs purple in wtr. *Ht:* 9 ft; *Spd:* 6 ft; *Fl:* 3–4; *Z:* 5

S. repens Creeping willow: Eur. V pretty but not dense ground cover. Lvs oval or spoon-shaped, young catkins silvery. *Ht:* 1 ft; *Spd:* 3 ft+; *Fl:* 4–5; *Z:* 4

S. repens

Salvia

Sage

S. microphylla (=grahamii) Graham's sage: Mexico. Thin-stemmed small-lvd sub-shrub; needs warmth. Lvs oval, pointed, irregularly toothed in pairs. Fls slim, salvia-like to 2 in, bright red becoming bluish-purple with age. Young growth has purplish tinge. *Ht, Spd:* 4 ft; *Fl:* 6–10; *Z:* 9

S. microphylla

Sambucus

Elder

S. nigra 'Aurea' Golden elder: Eur (sp). Bright yellow-lvd cv. White frag fls in flat heads; glistening black berries. Also varieg, lacy-lvd and purple-lvd cvs. *Ht, Spd:* 8 ft; *Fl:* 6; *Z:* 5

S. racemosa 'Plumosa Aurea'* Red-berried elder: Eur (sp). Lvs deeply toothed. Fls white, frs bright red. Prune hard. *Ht:* 8 ft; *Spd:* 5 ft; *Fl:* 4–5; *Z:* 4

S. nigra

Santolina

Lavender-cotton

Mediterranean dwarf daisy-bushes with aromatic very fine-textured evergreen foliage forming dense low hummocks. For sharp-drained soil.

S. chamaecyparissus: S Eur. Grey-white dense fol composed of tiny lflts. Yellow fls in domed heads to ¾ in wide. *S.c. corsica** (='Nana', AGM) 2 ft tall is dense with shorter lvs and good for edging or dwarf hedges. *Ht, Spd:* 30 in; *Fl:* 7–8; *Z:* 7

S. virens (=viridis) Holy flax: S Eur. Shrublet to 2 ft forming low hummock. Lvs deep green. Fls pale yellow. Prop both spp by cuttings. *Spd:* 2 ft; *Fl:* 7; *Z:* 7

S. chamaecyparissus

Sarcococca

S. humilis (=hookerana humilis)★:
China. Dwarf slow-growing
suckering shrub. Lvs narrowly oval,
pointed, glossy. Tiny white fls in
mid-wtr, in little bunches in lf axils
are sweetly frag and followed by
shiny black berries. Prop by div,
cuttings. *Ht, Spd:* 18 in; *Fl:* 1–3; *Z:* 6

S. humilis

Sassafras

S. albidum (=officinale): N Amer.
Fascinating aromatic tree (but can be
used as a large shrub) with variable
lvs, sometimes with 1 lobe,
sometimes more. Fls pale greenish-
yellow usually borne before lvs are
fully developed. Good aut col. Prop
by seed. *Ht:* 30 ft; *Spd:* 10 ft; *Fl:* 5;
Z: 4

S. albidum

Senecio

S. monroi: NZ. Rounded evergreen. Lvs pewter-grey, oval, 1½ in long,
white felt beneath; fls daisy-like in flat round heads to 6 in wide. The
Dunedin hybs of *S. laxifolius (=greyi)*, notably 'Sunshine' are larger in all
their parts reaching 4 ft to 8 ft and flower from July–Aug. Prop all sorts by
cuttings. *Ht:* 30 in; *Spd:* 4 ft; *Fl:* 7; *Z:* 8

Skimmia

Glossy evergreens grown chiefly for the pleasure of their sealing-
wax-red berries nestling among rich green leaves: a non-berrying
male plant is usually needed to achieve this.

S. japonica★: Japan. Dense
round shrub, lvs narrowly
oval, pointed, leathery, often
yellowish-green. Frag fls white in
pyramidal heads to 3 in. Berries
waxy red, persistent. Cv 'Rubella'★
(=reevesiana 'Rubella', AM) selected
male clone with dull reddish stks
and more compact form. Prop by
cuttings. *Ht:* to 5 ft; *Spd:* 5 ft+; *Fl:*
4–5; *Z:* 8
S. reevesiana: China. Slow-
growing and smaller, both sexes on
same plant; has white fls and red frs.
Will not tolerate limestone. *Ht:* 2 ft;
Spd: 30 in; *Fl:* 5; *Z:* 8

S. japonica

Sorbaria (=Spiraea)

Sorbaria

S. sorbifolia False spirea: N Asia. Suckering, decid. Big compound lvs appear earlier than on most plants. Large, terminal clusters of creamy-white spirea-like fls. Spreads quickly. *Ht, Spd:* 6 ft; *Fl:* 6–7; *Z:* 6

Sparmannia

Sparmannia

S. africana* African hemp: Africa. Fast-growing, tender; good indoors in tubs. Lvs huge maple-like, soft green. Fls white, red and yellow stamens Dec–April indoors. *Ht:* 8 ft; *Spd:* 6 ft; *Fl:* 5–6; *Z:* 10

Spartium

Spanish broom

S. junceum: Med, Canary Is. Quick-growing, uprt. Stems rush-like, deep green with occasional tiny lvs. Fls pea-like, ¾ in wide, rich yellow, pleasantly frag. Seed pods black. Best if last year's wood pruned hard in March. Plant v small (before rts have coiled round inside fl pot). *Ht:* 10 ft; *Spd:* 5 ft; *Fl:* 7–9; *Z:* 8

S. junceum

Spiraea

Spirea

Twiggy relations of roses with myriads of very small flowers. Often gracefully arching but need intelligent pruning to look their best: cut away old wood on early-flowering sorts; shorten last year's growth in spring on later-flowering ones.

S × arguta: Gdn origin. Froth of tiny white fls on young brs. Lvs small, light green. Prop all spp by cuttings. *Ht, Spd:* 6 ft; *Fl:* 4–5; *Z:* 5

S. × bumalda 'Anthony Waterer': gdn origin. Dense dwarf shrub. Lvs narrow, toothed, pointed, occasionally splashed cream with a little pink. Fls in flat round heads to 5 in wide, brilliant carmine fading to soft raspberry. *Ht, Spd:* 30 in; *Fl:* 6–9; *Z:* 5

S. × bumalda 'Anthony Waterer'

S. prunifolia Bridal wreath: Japan. Arching bush; lvs often bright orange-yellow in aut. Fls individually displayed on last year's wood, neat, fully double white. *Ht:* 5 ft; *Spd:* 4 ft; *Fl:* 4–5; *Z:* 4

S. thunbergii: China, Japan. Soft, twiggy. Lvs short, tapering. Fls white in clusters 1 in wide before lvs appear. V useful. *Ht, Spd:* to 5 ft; *Fl:* 3–4; *Z:* 5

S. × vanhouttei: gdn origin. Tall uprt stems make thicket. Lvs glaucous beneath, toothed, spade or diamond-shaped. Fls white in clusters along stems. *Ht, Spd:* 6 ft; *Fl:* 6; *Z:* 5

S. × vanhouttei

Stachyurus

 S. praecox★: Japan. Wtr-flowering vase-shaped bush with stiff 4 in tassels of primrose-yellow fls. Buds formed in previous yr are catkin-like on lfless reddish branches. *Ht:* to 10 ft; *Spd:* 8 ft; *Fl:* 2–3; *Z:* 7 , LF

Bladder-nut

S. colchica: Caucasus. Strong-growing, uprt. Lvs of 3–5 toothed lflts matte green above, shining beneath. White hyacinth-like fls have collar of greenish spls. V pretty but rare. *S. holocarpa* (AM) has trifoliate lvs and fls pink in bud opening white and inflated 2 in seed pods. Prop by cuttings. *Ht:* 10 ft; *Spd:* 6 ft; *Fl:* 5; *Z:* 5

Stephanandra

Quietly elegant shrubs not showy in flower but with pretty leaves, good autumn color and unusual habit and stem color.

S. incisa (=flexuosa): Japan, Korea. Twiggy shrub; lvs pale, triangular, rounded corners, deeply toothed. Fls tiny, whitish. 'Crispa' is also good ground cover. *Ht, Spd:* to 8 ft; *Fl:* 6; *Z:* 6
S. tanakae: Japan. Graceful, uprt. Lvs 3× above. Fl sprays looser, more showy. Orange aut col; striking brown stems. *Ht, Spd:* 6 ft; *Fl:* 6–7; *Z:* 6

S. tanakae

Stewartia

S. malacodendron★: SE USA. Distinguished shrub/small tree. Likes cool soil. Lvs softly downy on edges and undersides. Exquisite white fls, ptls just indented, 2 in wide; purple stamens, bluish anthers. Bark flakes in shades of blue and brown. *Ht:* 15 ft; *Spd:* 10 ft; *Fl:* 7–8; *Z:* 7
S. pseudocamellia★: Japan. Lvs not hry. Fls sim, white stamens, orange anthers. Good aut col. *Ht:* 30 ft; *Spd:* 10 ft; *Fl:* 7–8; *Z:* 6

S. pseudocamellia

Stranvaesia

S. davidiana: China. Stems tall, uprt, rather sparsely lfy. Lvs long, narrow, rich shining green, pale when young and on underside, older lvs often redden in aut. Fls small, white, 5-petaled, in loose heads to 3 in wide followed by glistening crimson berries. Prop by cuttings. *Ht:* 16 ft; *Spd:* 6 ft; *Fl:* 6; *Z:* 8

S. davidiana

Styrax

Styrax

S. hemsleyana: China. Tall shrub/small tree. Lvs tapered at base. White fls like half-open stars on downy 6 in spikes, yellow anthers in prominent tuft. *S. obassia* taller, slower-growing, fl spikes terminal, drooping. Prop both by seed. *Ht:* 18 ft; *Spd:* 15 ft; *Fl:* 6; *Z:* 6

Sycopsis

Sycopsis

S. sinensis: China. Evergreen cousin of witch-hazel less fussy about soil. Fls have no ptls but tuft of yellow stamens and red-brown anthers cupped in dark brown bracts. *Ht:* 12 ft; *Spd:* 6 ft; *Fl:* 2–3; *Z:* 5

Symphoricarpos

Snowberry

Obliging and original genus easy to grow and offering unique white (or pink) marble-like berries. Good ground cover.

S. albus: E N Amer. Invasive, suckering. Lvs oval; frs white. *Ht:* 4 ft; *Spd:* 16 ft; *Z:* 6
S. × chenaultii: gdn origin. Cv 'Hancock' excellent ground cover; frs reddish, purple or pink. *Ht:* 18 in; *Spd:* 3 ft; *Fl:* 6–7; *Z:* 6
S. × doorenbosii (=hybrida): gdn origin. Non-suckering, uprt. Try 'Magic Berry' frs rich pink; 'Mother of Pearl' (AM) frs white; 'White Hedge' frs small. *Ht:* 5 ft; *Spd:* 4 ft; *Fl:* 6–7; *Z:* 6

S. albus 'Laevigatus'

Syringa

Lilac

Fancy-flowered forms of lilac are splendid and richly scented in late May or early June but for the rest of the year there is scarcely a more tedious bush. Increase by cuttings.

S. microphylla Small-leaved lilac: China. Dainty; buds deep rose-pink opening to lilac. With 'Superba'★ fls over long period. *Ht:* 6 ft; *Spd:* 4 ft; *Fl:* 6, 9; *Z:* 6
S. persica★ Persian lilac: Iran–N China. More rounded, fls frag in plump bunches. 'Alba' white. *Ht, Spd:* 6 ft; *Fl:* 5; *Z:* 6
S. × prestoniae: gdn origin. Vig; fls in drooping pointed 9 in plumes. Try 'Bellicent' (AGM) rose-pink; 'Fountain' soft pink; 'Isabella' purple. *Ht:* 13 ft; *Spd:* 10 ft; *Fl:* 5–6; *Z:* 3

S. microphylla

S. vulgaris Common lilac: Eur. Sp dull but gloriously frag; many good cvs inc: Singles: 'Maud Notcutt' (AM) white; 'Primrose'; 'Firmament' blue; 'Buffon' pink; 'Congo' deep red; 'Massena' purple. Doubles: 'Madame Lemoine' (AM) white; 'Michael Buchner' (AM) lilac-blue. *Ht:* 18 ft; *Spd:* 10 ft; *Fl:* 5–6; *Z:* 3

S. vulgaris 'Alba'

Tamarix

Tamarisk

T. pentandra (= hispida aestivalis): Eur. Feathery bush. Lvs tiny stem-hugging, young growth purple. Fls frag, tiny in 3 in plumes of pale pink. *Ht:* 12 ft; *Spd:* 8 ft; *Fl:* 8–9; *Z:* 3

T. tetrandra: SE Eur, Asia. Sim but fls on previous yr's growth in spr when pale pink fls are uncommon, esp on alkaline soil. *Ht:* 12 ft; *Spd:* 8 ft; *Fl:* 5–6; *Z:* 3

T. pentandra

Taxus

Yew

T. baccata★ English yew: Eur, Asia. Dark green needle-lvs. Frs cup-shaped, fleshy, bright red, seeds v poisonous. Invaluable for hedges and topiary, excellent as a bush. *Ht:* to 40 ft; *Spd:* 15 ft; *Z:* 6

T. cuspidata Japanese yew: Japan. Most widely planted yew in USA. V sim to above. Sev good smaller cvs. *Ht:* 25 ft; *Spd:* 20 ft; *Z:* 5

T. baccata

Teucrium

Germander

T. fruticans: S Eur. Quick-growing, dense evergreen bush. Lvs white felted beneath, aromatic when bruised. Fls lobelia-like to ¾ in, pale blue with large lower lip. *Ht:* 5 ft; *Spd:* 4 ft+; *Fl:* 6–10; *Z:* 9

Tibouchina

Tibouchina

T. urvilliana (=semidecandra)★: Brazil. Frost tender but highly desirable conservatory plant. Fls single, saucer-shaped to 4 in wide with 5 overlapping glowing purple ptls with reddish tinge. Lvs oval, pointed, silky with 5 deep parallel veins. Prop by cuttings. *Ht:* 6 ft; *Spd:* 5 ft; *Fl:* 6–10; *Z:* 9

T. urvilliana

Ulex

Gorse

U. europaeus: Eur. This and *U. gallii* 2 most common spp, mainly fl in Mar–May and Aug–Sept resp but odd fls seen at any time. Spiny stems; yellow pea-like fls. 'Plenus' (AGM) double. *Ht, Spd:* 8 ft; *Z:* 6

Umbellularia

Californian bay or laurel

U. californica: Cal, Oregon. Large bush/small tree. Lvs tough, oval, tapering, giving off pungent "headachy" aroma when crushed. Fls greeny-yellow in clusters, ripe frs purple. *Ht, Spd:* 20 ft; *Fl:* 4; *Z:* 8

Vaccinium

The genus of blueberries, cranberries and whortleberries, sub-shrubs only at home in gardens of very acid nature.

V. corymbosum Highbush blueberry: E USA. Most beautiful and important sp. Uprt plant with dense branches and twigs reddish in wtr. Lvs to 3 in, elliptical, scarlet in aut. Clusters of little white to pinkish bell-shaped fls followed by delicious blue or blue-black frs. Many cvs give succession of fr throughout smr. *Ht, Spd:* 12 ft; *Fl:* 5–6; *Z:* 5

V. vitis-idaea Cowberry: N Temp mts. Creeping dwarf evergreen. Lvs tiny; fls pale pink or white, frs deep red. *Ht:* 6 in; *Spd:* 2 ft; *Fl:* 5–6; *Z:* 6

V. vitis-idaea

Viburnum

Viburnum

One of the 3 or 4 most important genera of garden shrubs, offering white or pink flowers from mid-winter to summer, evergreens, striking shapes, sweet scent and rich autumn colors. Most are easy to grow and to propagate by cuttings.

V. × burkwoodii: gdn origin. Evergreen; buds pink, fls white, frag, in heads to 3½ in wide. *Ht:* 5 ft; *Spd:* 6 ft; *Fl:* 4–5; *Z:* 5

V. carlesii: Korea. Rounded shrub. Fls heads dome-shaped, fls white, tubular, v frag. *V. × juddii* (AGM) v sim but taller, less hardy. *Ht, Spd:* 5 ft; *Fl:* 4–5; *Z:* 4

V. davidii: China. Lvs long, 3 parallel veins. Fls small, white in flat heads 3 in wide. Frs oval, turquoise if sev planted. *Ht:* 4 ft; *Spd:* 5 ft; *Fl:* 6; *Z:* 7

V. opulus Guelder rose: Eur. Decid, lvs maple-like. Fl heads hydrangea-like, frs red. *Ht:* 15 ft; *Spd:* 8 ft; *Fl:* 6–7; *Z:* 5

V. plicatum (=fomentosum) Japanese snowball: Japan, China. Vig uprt. Fl heads white balls. *Ht:* 8 ft; *Spd:* 10 ft; *Fl:* 5–6; *Z:* 4

V. carlesii

V. plicatum

V. rhytidophyllum Leather leaf viburnum: China. Bold evergreen. Fls tiny, yellowish-white in heads 4 in wide. Frs red, profuse if sev planted. *Ht:* 8 ft; *Spd:* 12 ft; *Fl:* 5; *Z:* 6

V. sieboldii: Japan. Glossy dark green 6 in lvs turn red in aut. Fls white in flat clusters. Red frs on red stks turn black when ripe. *Ht, Spd:* 30 ft; *Fl:* 5; *Z:* 5

V. tinus Laurustinus: Eur. Bushy evergreen. Buds pink, fls tiny in flat heads to 4 in wide; frs dull blue ripening black. *Ht:* 15 ft; *Spd:* 10 ft; *Fl:* 12–4; *Z:* 8

V. tinus

Periwinkle

V. major Greater periwinkle: Eur. Adventurous evergreen. Lvs heart-shaped; fls bright blue, 1 in diam. 'Variegata' white varieg; 'Maculata' gold varieg. *Ht:* 1 ft; *Spd:* 4 ft; *Fl:* 4–5(–9); *Z:* 7

V. minor Myrtle: Eur. Smaller, better ground cover. Cvs white, burgundy or pale blue fls, also varieg and double forms. *Ht:* 6 in; *Spd:* 3 ft; *Fl:* 4–5(–9); *Z:* 4

V. major

 Vitex

Vitex

V. agnus-castus Chaste tree: S Eur. Grey-green shrub; needs wall protection in cool zones. Lvs horsechestnut-like. Frag violet fls in slim branched spikes. 'Alba' white fld. *Ht, Spd:* 10 ft; *Fl:* 9–10; *Z:* 7

 Weigela (=Diervilla)

Weigela

W. florida (=amabilis): China. Sp undistinguished with oblong soft green lvs, tubular pink or red fls, but try 'Foliis purpureis' smaller, purple lvs, pink fls; taller 'Variegata' (AM) fls pink, lvs edged creamy yellow; 'Abel Carrière' (AGM) fls rose-carmine, yellow throat; 'Bristol Ruby' deep pink. *Ht, Spd:* 6 ft; *Fl:* 5–6; *Z:* 5

W. florida 'Bristol Ruby'

Yucca

Yucca

Spiky, attention-getting with a sub-tropical air. Rosettes of tapering leaves and spectacular spikes of flower.

Y. filamentosa*: SE USA. Suckering shrub. Thread-like filaments at lf edges. Plume of bell fls to 6 ft. 'Variegata' creamy-yellow varieg. *Y. flaccida* sim, taller, lvs wider; best cv 'Ivory'★ (AM). *Ht, Spd:* 3 ft; *Fl:* 7–8; *Z:* 5

Y. gloriosa* Spanish dagger: SE USA. Woody palm-like trunks; lvs stiff sharp points; fls creamy-white. *Ht, Spd:* 4 ft; *Fl:* 7–9; *Z:* 6

Y. recurvifolia: SE USA. Lf ends curved back; fls as above. *Ht, Spd:* 4 ft; *Fl:* 7–9; *Z:* 5

Y. filamentosa

Zenobia (=Andromeda)

Zenobia

Z. pulverulenta (=speciosa pulverulenta)*: SE USA. Enchantingly pretty; lvs oval, young fol glaucous, young stems whitish. Fls richly frag white bells. Frs like flattened balls. *Ht, Spd:* 6 ft; *Fl:* 6–7; *Z:* 6

Subtropical plants

Gardeners in the subtropical regions of the world, including southern California, Florida, Arizona and parts of southern Texas, have a different range of possibilities from those in other areas—and also of problems. Where frosts are rare or non-existent a whole new catalog of garden plants is opened up, yet many plants such as apples that rely on regular periods of dormancy induced by the cold of winter are unhappy and fail to perform. Lawn grass becomes a serious problem, pests as well as plants flourish in the luxury of a frost-free environment, while in urban areas a lethal smog may descend on the garden.

In this section of the book we are concerned with the good garden plants that are usually impracticable in other areas of regular, even slight frost but are highly desirable in the sub-tropics—and in addition plants whose good behavior under extreme conditions makes them popular where gardening is a constant battle with heat and drought.

Defining exactly where these subtropics are located is not so simple as it sounds. The complications are best expressed in the climate zone system for the western United States developed by *Sunset Magazine* of Menlo Park, California. On the Sunset scheme there are no less than 24 zones of significantly different climate—differences brought about by such influences as latitude and altitude, the cold Pacific and the intervening Coast Range, the Sierra and the desert. In this book we have translated the 24 zones into the 10 standard zones of the US Department of Agriculture. But to understand and take full advantage of the climate, and to save choosing your plants merely by copying the successes of your neighbors, some further reading is essential. We recommend without reservation the *Sunset New Western Garden Book* which explains the 24-zone system in full, whose information is good for all climate zones and whose editors have generously contributed their experience of subtropical gardening to the list of plants that follows.

Herbaceous perennials

Aeonium

A. arboreum: Morocco. V useful decorative succ for outdoors or in pots. Branched stems to 3 ft each topped with rosette of lightly fringed pale green fleshy lvs. Fls yellow in long clusters. Rosettes of 'Atropurpureum' dark purple, of 'Zwartkop' nearly black. Many sim spp. *Spd:* 3 ft; *Fl:* 1–3; *Z:* 10

A. arboreum

Aloe

Aloe

A. arborescens* Tree aloe: S Africa. Biggest of a showy, drought-tolerant genus. Big clumps of grey-green lvs on branching stems. Fls bright vermillion to clear yellow in spiky gps. *Ht, Spd:* 15 ft; *Fl:* 12–2; *Z:* 10

Alpinia

Ginger

A. speciosa (= zermbet, nutans)* Shell ginger: Trop Asia. Most handsome of all the gingers. Stems, maroon when mature, bear shiny 2 ft lvs with distinct parallel veins. Fls shell-like, waxy, frag, pink or white marked red or brown, in drooping clusters on branched stems. Protect from wind. *A. purpurata* sim, stems deeper col. Prop by div of rhizomes. *Ht:* 10 ft; *Spd:* 3 ft; *Fl:* 7–9; *Z:* 10

A. purpurata

Arctotheca

Cape weed

A. calendula: S Africa. Good but invasive ground cover. Lvs grey-green, deeply cut; yellow daisy fls 2 in wide for most of year but best in Mar–June. Prop by seed, runners. *Ht:* 8 in; *Spd:* 10 ft; *Z:* 10

Aspidistra

Cast iron plant

A. elatior (= lurida): China. V useful for its love of deep shade and pop houseplant. Lvs tough, glossy dark green to 30 in long on grooved 8 in stks. Fls brown, inconspic. 'Variegata' has lvs striped white but reverts to type if soil too rich. Hose or dust lvs regularly to keep them glossy. Prop by div. *Ht, Spd:* to 4 ft; *Z:* 10

A. elatior

Billbergia

Billbergia

B. nutans Queen's tears: Brazil. Normally grows on trees (an epiphyte). Spiny-toothed clustered lvs and drooping spikes of rosy-red bracts round green, blue-edged ptls. Prop by suckers. *Ht, Spd:* 18 in; *Fl:* 4–5; *Z:* 10

Calocephalus

Cushion bush

C. brownii*: Aust. Unusual mound-forming shrubby per. Tiny thread-like lvs pressed on branching stems give silvery-white effect. Clustered button-like fl heads. Good ground cover. *Ht, Spd:* 3 ft; *Fl:* 8–10; *Z:* 9

Carpobrotus

Ice plant, Sea fig, Hottentot fig

C. edulis (= Mesembryanthemum edule): S Africa. Trailing coarse-lvd succ per for covering sunny banks. Fls daisy-like, pale yellow to rose pink. Fr edible, tasteless. Smog-resistant. *Ht:* 6 in; *Spd:* 2 ft; *Fl:* 6–7; *Z:* 10

Chlorophytum

Chlorophytum

C. comosum Spider plant: Africa. Ubiquitous house plant; good ground cover in warmest zones. Clumps of grass-like lvs to 3 ft interspersed with curved stems bearing mini-plants at their ends which can be used for propagation. Lvs of pop 'Variegatum' and 'Vittatum' white striped. Fls white. *Ht, Spd:* 3 ft; *Fl:* 11–12; *Z:* 10

C. comosum 'Variegatum'

Chrysanthemum

Chrysanthemum

C. frutescens* Marguerite, Paris daisy: Canary Is. Quick-growing, v branched. Lvs bright green, coarse cut. Daisy fls to 2½ in wide in white, yellow or pink. Best cvs inc 'Silver Leaf' lvs grey-green, masses of white fls; 'June Bride' fls rose pink, cushion-centered; 'Spring Fever' fls white, heavy yellow center. *Ht:* 3 ft; *Spd:* 4 ft; *Fl:* 6–8; *Z:* 10

C. frutescens

Coreopsis

Coreopsis

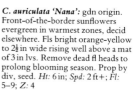

C. auriculata 'Nana': gdn origin. Front-of-the-border sunflowers evergreen in warmest zones, decid elsewhere. Fls bright orange-yellow to 2½ in wide rising well above a mat of 3 in lvs. Remove dead fl heads to prolong blooming season. Prop by div, seed. *Ht:* 6 in; *Spd:* 2 ft+; *Fl:* 5–9; *Z:* 4

C. auriculata 'Nana'

Cotyledon

C. orbiculata*: S Africa. Compact
succ, first rate container plant. Lvs
fleshy, nearly white, narrow red
margins. Orange bell-shaped fls
drooping, clustered. *Ht, Spd:* 3 ft;
Fl: 6–8; *Z:* 10
C. undulata: S Africa. Sim to above
but wavy-edged lvs have heavy
dusting of white powder. *Ht, Spd:*
18 in; *Fl:* 4–6; *Z:* 10

C. undulata

Crassula

C. falcata: S Africa. Succ only flowering reliably outdoors in full sun. Lvs
sickle-shaped, fleshy. Dense spherical clusters of scarlet star-shaped fls in
Aug–Sept. Many sim spp. Prop by div. *Ht, Spd:* 4 ft; *Z:* 10

Cybidium

C. hybs*: gdn origin (sp SE Asia).
Delightful orchids for outdoors in
frost-free zones, indoors elsewhere.
Lvs grass-like. Catalogs list a wide
variety of pink, white, bronze,
yellow or green dark-throated fls.
The biggest-flowered forms have 12
or more 5 in fls to a stem. Dwarf
forms also available. *Ht:* 3 ft; *Spd:*
1 ft; *Fl:* 2–5; *Z:* 10

C. hybrid

Ice plant

D. floribundum Rosea ice plant: S Africa. Trailing succ; lvs smothered with
glistening dots like tiny ice crystals. Stunning sheets of pale pink fls in
May–June attractive to bees. *Ht:* 6 in; *Spd:* 2 ft+; *Z:* 10

Echeveria

Rosette-forming frost-tender succulents with leaves often over-
laid in a second color. Outdoors they spread to form a thick
carpet. All are excellent pot plants.

E. elegans: Mexico. Grey-white lvs
in tight rosette. Pink fls yellow-lined
in 8 in gps. Many offsets. Can burn
in hot sun. *Ht:* 4 in; *Spd:* 8 in; *Fl:*
12–2; *Z:* 10
E. gibbiflora*: Mexico. Bigger sp
grown for its broad grey-green lvs.
Lvs of 'Metallica' purplish lilac to
bronze. Other cvs wavy-lvd. *Ht:*
3 ft; *Spd:* 30 in; *Fl:* 12–2; *Z:* 10
E. imbricata: Mexico. Saucer-
shaped grey-green lvs and bell-
shaped orange-red fls in loose
clusters. Prop by freely produced
offsets. *Ht:* 4 in; *Spd:* 6 in; *Fl:* 12–2;
Z: 10

E. elegans

Euryops

Euryops

E. pectinatus: S Africa. Windproof daisies with finely cut grey-green lvs. Yellow fls to 2 in wide produced all yr but esp in Feb–June. Dead-head frequently. Prop by seed. *Ht:* to 3 ft; *Spd:* 2 ft; *Z:* 10

Felicia

Felicia

F. amelloides

F. amelloides (= Agathaea coelestis) Blue marguerite: S Africa. Wandering aromatic per with sky-blue fls almost all yr. Fls of 'Midnight', 'George Lewis' dark blue; 'Santa Anna' extra-large fls; 'Astrid Thomas' fls open at night. Prune hard to keep under control. *Ht:* 18 in; *Spd:* 5 ft; *Fl:* 1–12; *Z:* 7

Gazania

Gazania

G. rigens leucolaena

G. rigens leucolaena (= uniflora)* Trailing gazania: S Africa. Long trailing stems spread quickly. Lvs clear silver-grey; dazzling display of white, yellow or bronze daisy fls. Try 'Sunburst' fls orange, black eye; 'Sunrise Yellow' fls yellow, black eye, lvs green. *Ht:* 1 ft; *Spd:* 5 ft; *Fl:* 5–6; *Z:* 7

Kalanchoe

Kalanchoe

K. beharensis Felt plant: Madagascar. Succ making a houseplant anywhere, survives outdoors in v warmest zones. Triangular v hry felted lvs in 6–8 pairs strikingly waved and crimped. Fls inconspic. *Ht:* 5 ft; *Spd:* 2 ft; *Z:* 10

Lampranthus (= Mesambryanthemum)

Ice plant

L. spectabilis

L. aurantiacus: S Africa. Grey-green 3-sided lvs and bright orange fls. Try 'Glaucus' bright yellow; 'Sunman' gold. *Ht, Spd:* 18 in; *Fl:* 2–5; *Z:* 10
L. productus: S Africa. Lvs bronze-tipped. Fls purple. *Ht:* 15 in; *Spd:* 2 ft; *Fl:* 1–4; *Z:* 10
L. spectabilis Trailing ice plant: S Africa. Gleaming carpets of fol and v many pink, red or purple fls. *Ht:* to 1 ft; *Spd:* to 2 ft; *Fl:* 3–5; *Z:* 9–10

Limonium

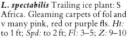

Statice, Sea lavender

L. perezii: Canary Is. Rich green, often fire-resistant fol and long flowering season. Fls good for drying have striking purple spls, tiny white ptls. Outstanding beach plant. *Ht:* 3 ft; *Spd:* 2 ft; *Fl:* 6–9; *Z:* 9

Neoregelia

N. spectabilis Painted fingernail plant: Tropics. Water-holding rosette of leathery olive green, scarlet-tipped lvs that turn bronze in strong light. Fls inconspic. *Ht, Spd:* 1 ft; *Z:* 10

 Oenothera

Evening primrose

O. berlandieri (= speciosa childsii) Mexican evening primrose: Mexico. Creates pink profusion of 1½ in fls in smr. Invasive if not controlled but good ground cover on dry slopes. *Ht:* 1 ft; *Spd:* 4 ft+; *Fl:* 6–7; *Z:* 4

 Osteospermum (= Dimorphotheca)

African daisy

O. fruticosum Freeway daisy, Trailing African daisy: S Africa. Rampant invader, spreads 4 ft per yr. Fls to 2 in wide, pale lilac above fading to nearly white, deeper col below. *Ht:* 1 ft; *Fl:* 11–3; *Z:* 9

 Pennisetum

Pennisetum

P. setaceum (= ruppelii) Fountain grass: N Africa. Makes dense clump of narrow arching lvs to 2 ft from which long, fuzzy, coppery-pink or purplish fl plumes emerge. 'Cupreum' has reddish-brown lvs, dark fl plumes. A menace if not controlled. Prop by cuttings. *Ht:* to 4 ft; *Spd:* 4 ft; *Fl:* 5–8; *Z:* 6

P. setaceum

Sedum

Stonecrop

S. confusum: Mexico. Spreading, branching; one of v many useful spp. Lvs pale green, shining, succ in rosettes. Fls yellow, star-shaped in dense groups. Prop by div. *Ht:* 9 in; *Spd:* 4 ft; *Fl:* 3–4; *Z:* 10

Verbena

Verbena

V. peruviana (= chamaedryfolia)★: S Amer. Per often grown as ann. Quickly makes mat of close-set fol. Fl clusters flat-topped on slim stems; fls have white center tube surrounded by flared red ptls. Many tidier cvs inc 'Starfire' red; 'Princess Gloria' rose red. *Ht:* 4 in; *Spd:* 10 ft; *Fl:* 6–8; *Z:* 10

V. peruviana

 *Viola*

Violet, Pansy

V. hederacea Australian violet: Aust. Tufted stoloniferous per. Lvs kidney-shaped; fls to ⅔ in wide v short spurred, white or blue fading to white at ptl tips. *Ht:* 4 in; *Spd:* 5 ft; *Fl:* 6–8; *Z:* 9

Alpines, rock garden plants

Achillea

Yarrow

A. tomentosa Woolly yarrow: Eur, Orient. Makes pretty flat mats of fern-like deep green hry fol. Flat heads of brilliant golden fls. 'Primrose Beauty' pale yellow; 'King George' cream. Remove dead heads. Prop by seed. *Ht:* 1 ft; *Spd:* 2 ft; *Fl:* 6–8; *Z:* 3

A. tomentosa

Artemisia

Artemisia

A. caucasica Silver spreader: Caucasus. Well described by its name. Silvery, evergreen v pretty ground cover. Fls small, yellow. Fire resistant, needs no smr water. Prop by div. *Ht:* 6 in; *Spd:* 2 ft; *Z:* 4

Campanula

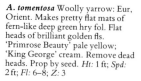

Bellflower

C. isophylla

C. portenschlagiana

C. isophylla* Italian bellflower: Eur. Enchanting wall cover with trailing 2 ft stems, heart-shaped pale green lvs and light blue starry fls. Larger white-fld 'Alba' pop; 'Mayi' lvs grey, softly hry, fls big, lavender blue. *Ht:* 4 in; *Fl:* 8–9; *Z:* 8
C. portenschlagiana (= muralis)* Dalmatian bellflower: S Eur. Fls flared 1 in violet bells. Not invasive. Prop by div. *Ht:* 7 in; *Spd:* 1 ft; *Fl:* 5–8 (– 10); *Z:* 4
C. poscharskyana Serbian bellflower: SE Eur. V vig, branched lfy per with semi-uprt fl stems to 1 ft+. Star-shaped fls to 1 in wide, blue, lilac or lavender. Best in shade. *Spd:* to 5½ ft; *Fl:* 4–5; *Z:* 9–10

Dichondra

Dichondra

D. micrantha (= carolinensis): USA. Ground-hugging cover fol plant spreading by underground runners. Small round lvs like miniature water lily pads. Can be used as a lawn. *Ht:* to 6 in; *Spd:* 1 ft; *Z:* 9

Laurentia (= Isotoma)

Laurentia

L. fluviatilis Blue star creeper: S Africa. Delicate-looking, creeping, spreading ground cover attractive round single rocks. Pale blue star-like fls all year but in profusion in May–June. Prop by div, seed. *Ht:* 3 in; *Spd:* 5 ft; *Z:* 8

L. fluviatilis

Ophiopogon

Lily turf

O. japonicus Mondo grass: Japan. Grass-like, clump-forming with pale lilac spike-like fls followed by blue frs. Best among rock groupings. Lvs dark green. 'Vittatus' has white striped lvs. *Ht, Spd:* 1 ft; *Fl:* 6; *Z:* 6

Polygonum

Knotweed

P. capitatum: India. Invasive evergreen trailer, needs rock surround to keep it in check. Lvs dark green turning pink with age; stems and small round fl heads also pink. Takes deep shade. Seeds itself freely. Treat as ann in cool zones. *Ht:* 6 in; *Spd:* 3 ft; *Fl:* 1–12; *Z:* 6

P. capitatum

Potentilla

Cinquefoil

P. tabernaemontani (= verna) Spring cinquefoil: Eur. Dainty tufted creeper. Bright green lvs have 5 lflts. Butter-yellow fls ¼ in wide in groups of 3–5. Can make a lawn. *Ht:* 4 in; *Spd:* 2 ft; *Fl:* 4–7; *Z:* 5

Sagina

Sagina

S. subulata Pearlwort, Irish or Scotch moss: Eur. Moss-like per sold in 2 forms: green (Irish) and golden-green (Scotch). Masses of tiny lvs on slim stems. Fls white, scattered, 4-ptld. Useful filler; becomes "humpy" in deep shade. Prop by seed. *Ht:* 1 in; *Spd:* 1 ft; *Fl:* 5–8; *Z:* 5

S. subulata

Ferns

Adiantum

Maidenhair fern

A. capillus-veneris Southern maidenhair: N Amer. Finely cut fronds twice divided but not forked as in other spp. Needs leaf mold or peat moss at roots. Prop by div, spores. *Ht, Spd:* 15 in; *Z:* 9

Asplenium

Asplenium

A. bulbiferum Mother fern: NZ. Graceful fern with delicately cut pale green fronds that give rise to plantlets that can be removed and used for propagation. Good as a houseplant in cool zones. *Ht:* 4 ft; *Spd:* 2 ft; *Z:* 9

A. bulbiferum

Cyrtomium

Hollyfern

C. falcatum*: Asia. Handsome coarse-textured fern to 3 ft with big, dark green, leathery fronds cut into lflts. An indoor or greenhouse plant in cooler zones. Prop by div, spores. *Spd:* 3 ft; *Z:* 9

C. falcatum

Davallia

Squirrel's foot fern

D. trichomanoides: Malaya. Ideal hanging-basket fern with v finely cut fronds arising from reddish-brown furry rhizomes (hence its name). Also good small-scale ground cover in partial shade. *Ht, Spd:* 1 ft; *Z:* 10

Humata

Bear's foot fern

H. tyermannii: China. Like *Davallia* in uses and looks but with dark brown furry rhizomes. Slower growing and less fussy about soil. Prop by div, spores. *Ht, Spd:* 10 ft; *Z:* 10

Microlepia

Microlepia

M. strigosa: Trop Asia. Robust fern with delicate, finely-cut triangular fronds. Useful for landscaping shaded areas of the gdn in frost-free zones. Sometimes sold as *M. speluncea*. *Ht, Spd:* 3 ft; *Z:* 10

Nephrolepis

Sword fern

N. cordifolia* Southern sword fern: Tropics, NZ. Tough, easy fern for indoors or out. Fronds narrow, uprt in tufts have close-packed fine-toothed lflts. Spreads quickly with fuzzy runners and needs keeping in check. Tolerates moving. Prop by div. *Ht:* 3 ft; *Spd:* 5 ft; *Z:* 10

N. cordifolia

Platycerium

Staghorn fern

P. bifurcatum: Aust. New Guinea. Odd fern that grows naturally on trees. In gdns best planted on bark slabs, tree fern stems or in hanging baskets. Fronds are of 2 kinds—flat, pale green sterile fronds ageing to tan and brown and clustered grey-green fertile fronds. Produces many offsets useful for propagation. *Ht, Spd:* 3 ft; *Z:* 7

P. bifurcatum

Polystichum

P. munitum★ Sword fern: N Amer.
V easy popular fern with leathery,
shiny, dark green once-cut fronds.
Old plants may have as many as 100
fronds. Use for large-scale ground
cover or around the base of a wall.
Ht, Spd: 4 ft; *Z:* 8

P. munitum

Leatherleaf fern

R. adiantiformis (= Asplenium capense): Tropics. Triangular, finely
divided fronds a deep glossy green are firm-textured and long-lasting when
cut. Will take full sun. Prop by div, spores. *Ht, Spd:* 3 ft; *Z:* 8

Tree fern

S. (= Cyathea, Alsophila) cooperi Australian tree fern: Aust. Fast-growing
tree fern with a scaly trunk topped by a tuft of bright green finely cut fronds
to 12 ft. Needs shelter. *Ht:* to 20 ft; *Spd:* 12 ft; *Z:* 9

Chain fern

W. fimbriata★ Giant chain fern: W
USA-Mexico. Moisture-loving fern
best in woodland or at water's edge.
Coarse-textured twice-cut fronds
make tall spreading shape. Prop by
spores. *Ht, Spd:* 8 ft; *Z:* 8

W. fimbriata

Bulbs

Ground orchid

B. striata Chinese ground orchid: China. Pale green plaited lvs and up to 12
lavender orchid-fls on a 2 ft stem for about 6 weeks in May–June. 'Alba' a
good white form. Prop by tubers. *Ht:* 2 ft; *Spd:* 1 ft; *Z:* 5

Iris

I. douglasiana★: W USA. Big
clump of evergreen lvs and 2, 3 or
more white, cream, yellow, blue or
deep purple fls. Will take full sun.
Ht, Spd: 2 ft; *Fl:* 5–6; *Z:* 8
I. innominata★: W USA. Smaller
with narrower lvs. Fls in shades of
red, orange, yellow, blue or lavender; best cvs gold, striped brown.
Ht: 9 in; *Spd:* 15 in; *Fl:* 5–6; *Z:* 8

I. innominata

Climbers

Antigonon

Antigonon

A. leptopus

A. leptopus* Rosa de Montana, Queen's wreath, Coral vine: Mexico. Fast-growing tendriled vine evergreen in warmest zones. Dark green heart-shaped pointed lvs and small rose pink fls to 1½ in long in drooping sprays. Excellent in low deserts. *Ht:* to 40 ft; *Spd:* 15 ft; *Fl:* 6–10; *Z:* 8

Asparagus

Asparagus

A. falcatus Sickle thorn asparagus: S Africa. Climbs to 40 ft using the curved thorns along its stem. Clusters of 3–5 tiny white fls. Frs brown berries. *A. setaceous* (Fern asparagus, Emerald feather) spiny-stemmed but aut flowering with fine-cut fol beloved of flower arrangers. *A.s.* 'Pyramidalis' has unusual windblown look. *Spd:* 10 ft; *FL:* 6; *Z:* 10

Bauhinia

Bauhinia

B. punctata

B. punctata (= galpinii)* Red bauhinia: Trop Africa. Evergreen to semi-decid half-climbing sprawler. Lvs deeply cut into 2 lobes. Brick red/orange fls as stunning as bougainvillea. Ideal espalier plant. *Ht, Spd:* 15 ft; *Fl:* 6–8; *Z:* 10

Beaumontia

Beaumontia

B. grandiflora Herald's trumpet, Easter lily vine: India. Wonderfully frag green-veined lily-like fls on arching, semi-twining branches. Lvs dark green. Best on a warm wall. *Ht, Spd:* 30 ft; *Fl:* 4–9; *Z:* 10

Cissus

Cissus

Relations of Boston ivy and Virginia creeper prized for their foliage and not fussy about sun or soil.

C. rhombifolia

C. antarctica Kangaroo treebine: Aust. Graceful shiny-lvd vine, v vig once established. Lvs oval, pointed, toothed. Good tumbling down a trellis or wall. *Ht, Spd:* to 10 ft; *Z:* 10
C. rhombifolia Grape ivy: S Amer. Beautiful dark green lvs with diamond-shaped lflts with bronze tint given by reddish hrs on underside. *Ht, Spd:* 20 ft; *Z:* 10
C. striata: S Amer. Like mini Virginia creeper with reddish stems. *Ht, Spd:* 19 ft; *Z:* 10

Glorybower

C. thomsoniae (= balfouri)★
Bleeding heart glorybower: W
Africa. Shrubby evergreen. Lvs
oval, dark green, shiny. Fls 1 in
scarlet tubes surrounded by white
spls each ¾ in long in flattish clusters
5 in wide. Good in tubs; only hardy
outdoors in protected places. *Ht:*
6 ft; *Spd:* 3 ft; *Fl:* 8–10; *Z:* 10

C. thomsoniae

Trumpet vine

**C. callistegioides (= Bignonia
violacea)** Violet trumpet vine: S
Amer. Striking violet or pale purple
3 in trumpet fls among glossy
evergreen fol. Likely to tangle so
needs hard pruning. Good among
other vines. *Ht, Spd:* 15 ft; *Fl:* 5–9;
Z: 10

C. callistegioides

Trumpet vine

**D. buccinatoria (= Phaedranthus
buccinatorius)★** Blood red trumpet
vine: Santa Cruz. Orange-red,
yellow-throated 4 in fl trumpets
fading to bluish red in bursts all year
as weather warms. Fls stand out well
from glossy lvs with oblong to oval
lflts. Feed young plants well. Prop
by cuttings. *Ht:* 25 ft; *Spd:* 10 ft;
Z: 10

D. buccinatoria

Jessamine

G. sempervirens Carolina
jessamine: Carolina. Cascades on a
trellis or makes neat curtain on a
wall. Stems twining; lvs shiny, pale
green in pairs on streamer-like
branches. Fls frag, tubular, yellow
to 1½ in. Prune severely if it gets top
heavy. Can be cut back to 3 ft for use
as ground cover. Prop by cuttings.
Ht: 15 ft; *Spd:* 10 ft; *Fl:* 12–2; *Z:* 8

G. sempervirens

Hardenbergia

H. comptoniana (= Comptonia peregrina) Lilac vine: Aust. Delicate fol
pattern contrasts well with long clusters of ½ in violet-blue pea fls. Needs
support. Prop by cuttings. *Ht:* 10 ft; *Spd:* 8 ft; *Fl:* 12–2; *Z:* 9

Hibbertia

Hibbertia

H. scandens Guinea gold vine: Aust. Luxuriant waxy dark green lvs and a long season of clear bright yellow fls like single roses on a fast-growing, invaluable twiner. *Ht:* 8 ft; *Spd:* 5 ft; *Fl:* 5–10; *Z:* 10

Hoya

Wax flower, Wax plant

H. carnosa: Aust. Not fully hardy but worthwhile for its big round clusters of waxy creamy-white frag fls each with perfect 5-pointed center star. Lvs red when young, maturing to rich green. 'Variegata' has lvs edged in whitish pink, but is even more tender: 'Krinkle Kurl' lvs wavy-edged. *Ht, Spd:* 10 ft; *Fl:* 6–8; *Z:* 10

H. carnosa

Lonicera

Honeysuckle

L. hildebrandiana★ Giant Burmese honeysuckle: Burma. Big, fast-growing with rope-like stems and dark evergreen lvs. Fls sweetly frag, long-lasting white, fading to yellow, tubular, to 7 in long. Pop with hummingbirds. Frs berry-like. Needs occasional thinning. Prop by cuttings. *Ht:* 8 ft; *Spd:* 5 ft; *Fl:* 6–8; *Z:* 9

L. hildebrandiana

Macfadeyana

Macfadeyana

M. unguis-cati Cat's claw. Yellow trumpet vine: Trop Amer. Semi-evergreen clambering anywhere with hooked, forked tendrils. Yellow trumpet fls to 2 in among glossy lflts. *Ht:* to 40 ft; *Spd:* 20 ft; *Fl:* 2–4; *Z:* 9

Pandorea

Pandorea

P. jasminoides Bower vine: Aust. Lvs with 5–9 egg-shaped lflts on slim fast-twining stems. Fls white, pink-throated, hibiscus-like, drop soon after blooming. 'Rosea' pink/rose. *Ht, Spd:* 25 ft; *Fl:* 6–10; *Z:* 9

Pyrostegia (= Bignonia)

Pyrostegia

P. venusta Flame vine: Brazil. Fast-growing evergreen quickly reaching 20 ft or more using its tendrils. Spectacular tubular orange fls in clusters of 15–20 contrast well with the glossy divided lvs. Good against a W wall. *Spd:* 15 ft; *Fl:* 9–11; *Z:* 10

P. venusta

Solandra

S. maxima (= **guttata**)★ Cup-of-gold vine: Mexico. Resistant to wind, smog and salt spray and a rampant grower that needs tying for support. Lvs broad, oval; buds balloon-like, fls bowl-shaped, golden yellow, striped in brownish purple, to 8 in wide. Best on a high wall or bank. *Ht, Spd:* to 40 ft; *Fl:* 3–5 (−9); *Z:* 10

S. maxima

Nightshade

S. rantonnetii: S Amer. Decid or evergreen informal fast-growing vine; can be staked into tree form. Lvs oval, bright green; fls violet-blue, yellow centers nearly all year. *Ht:* 15 ft; *Spd:* 10 ft; *Fl:* 2–11; *Z:* 10

Bluebell creeper

S. heterophylla★ Australian bluebell creeper: Aust. Clusters of brilliant blue bell-shaped ½ in fls and pale green fol attractive over a low wall. Needs training and support. *Ht, Spd:* to 8 ft; *Fl:* 6–9; *Z:* 9

Shrubs

Acacia, Wattle

Mainly Australian natives that adapt beautifully to West Coast conditions. There are hundreds of species to choose from, varying widely in habit and flowering season.

A. cyanophylla★ Blue-leaf wattle: Aust. Unusual long, bluish lvs; fls orange bells in profuse clusters. Prop by seed. *Ht:* 25 ft; *Spd:* 18 ft; *Fl:* 3–4; *Z:* 9

A. cyclops: Aust. Lvs dark green; fls bright yellow, lvs black, red-ringed frs. Good hedging. *Ht:* 12 ft; *Spd:* 18 ft; *Fl:* 3–4; *Z:* 9

A. podalyriifolia Pearl acacia: Aust. Satiny silvery-grey roundish lvs and pale yellow fluffy fls. *Ht:* 15 ft; *Spd:* 14 ft; *Fl:* 11–3; *Z:* 9

A. redolens (= **ongerup**); Aust. Narrow leathery grey-green lvs; fls puffy yellow balls. *Ht:* 2 ft; *Spd:* 15 ft; *Fl:* 3–4; *Z:* 9

A. verticillata: Aust. Conifer-like. Pale yellow fls in spikes. *Ht, Spd:* to 15 ft; *Fl:* 4–5; *Z:* 9

A. cyanophylla

A. verticillata

Acalypha

A. wilkesiana (= **tricolor**) Copper leaf: S Pacific Is. Wonderfully colorful. Bronzy green fol mottled red and purple or fol red, marked crimson and bronze, or green lvs edged crimson, stippled orange. *Ht, Spd:* 6 ft; *Z:* 10

Azara

Azara

A. microphylla* Boxleaf azara: Chile. Flat-branching spreading shrub/small tree. Lvs roundish, shining, dark green. Sweetly frag yellow fls in short clusters. *Ht:* 20 ft; *Spd:* 12 ft; *Fl:* 2–3; *Z:* 9

Baccharis

Baccharis

B. pilularis

B. pilularis Coyote bush, Dwarf chaparral broom: W USA. Remarkably adaptable bush surviving in all conditions from swamp to drought. Makes dense billowy mat covered with bright green toothed lvs. Fls inconspic; frs on ♀ plants cottony. Best cvs 'Twin Peaks' lvs dark green; 'Pigeon Point' larger lvs. *Ht:* 2 ft; *Spd:* 6 ft; *Z:* 8

Bambusa

Bamboo

B. oldamii

B. glaucescens (= multiplex, argentea): Asia. Dense giant grass, branching from base. Best cvs inc 'Alphonse Kerr' stems striped green on yellow, new stems pinkish and green; 'Fernleaf' lvs close packed. *Ht, Spd:* to 10 ft; *Z:* 9
B. oldhamii Oldham bamboo: Asia. Dense fol on erect plant. Good for screening or as a specimen. *Ht:* 20 ft; *Spd:* 30 ft; *Z:* 10

Bauhinia

Bauhinia

B. forficata

B. blakeana Hong Kong orchid tree: China. Huge orchid-like fls in tropical cols from maroon through purple to pink. Lvs grey-green. *Ht, Spd:* 15 ft; *Fl:* 9–11; *Z:* 10
B. forficata: Brazil. Large shrub/small tree. Spectacular creamy white fls with narrow ptls; lvs deep green. Short sharp thorns at branch joints on stems. *Ht:* to 20 ft; *Spd:* 15 ft; *Fl:* 4–7; *Z:* 9

Beaucarnea

Beaucarnea

B. recurvata Ponytail, Bottle palm: Mexico. Odd-looking succ with v swollen onion-like base above soil level and topknot of arched, drooping lvs. Fls inconspic, rare. Good houseplants. *Ht, Spd:* 10 ft; *Z:* 10

Brunfelsia

Brunfelsia

B. pauciflora 'Floribunda' Yesterday-today-and-tomorrow: gdn origin. Named from quick col change of fls from purple ("yesterday") to lavender ("today") to white ("tomorrow"). Lvs oval. *Ht, Spd:* 10 ft; *Fl:* 4–6; *Z:* 10

Calliandra

C. haematocephala (= inaequilatera) Pink powder puff: Bolivia. Quick-growing, showy, with big pink powder puffs of silky stamens. Lvs glossy copper turning to metallic green. *Ht, Spd:* 10 ft; *Fl:* 10–3; *Z:* 10

 Carissa

Carissa

C. grandiflora Natal palm: S Africa. Spiny shrub with lustrous leathery lvs and white, headily frag star-shaped fls occurring with green and ripe, red, plum-like edible frs. *Ht, Spd:* to 7 ft; *Fl:* 3–6; *Z:* 10

 *Cassia*

Cassia, Senna

C. alata Candle bush: Trop Amer. Decid, spreading. Golden-yellow spikes of pea fls 1 in wide. Lvs have 12–28 lflts. *Ht:* 10 ft; *Spd:* 15 ft; *Fl:* 11–1; *Z:* 9

C. artemisioides Feathery cassia: Aust. Light airy look given by lvs with 6–8 needle-like lflts. Fls sulfur yellow. *Ht, Spd:* 4 ft; *Fl:* 1–4 (–6); *Z:* 10

C. alata

Cestrum

Cestrum

C. nocturnum Night jessamine: W Indies. Creamy-white showy tubular fls have almost overpowering scent at night. Fls and white berries attract birds. Fast growing, needs pruning. *Ht, Spd:* 12 ft; *Fl:* 6–8; *Z:* 9

Citrus

Citrus

The glossy-leaved, fragrant-flowered genus of oranges, lemons, limes and grapefruit has been bred to produce many shrubs useful for landscaping and containers as well as for their fruit.

Grapefruit: To 15 ft on dwarf rtstock. Try 'Ruby' with pink flesh on fr. *Spd:* 10 ft; *Fl:* 5–6; *Z:* 9

Lemons: To 10 ft on dwarf rtstock. Cvs inc 'Improved Mayer' frs orange-like, tangy; 'Lisbon' free-fruiting; 'Ponderosa' huge coarse-skinned mild-tasting frs. *Spd:* 10 ft; *Fl:* 5–6; *Z:* 10

Limes: To 10 ft on dwarf rtstock; dense crown. Best cv 'Bearss' v thorny, fr v juicy. *Spd:* 8 ft; *Fl:* 5–6; *Z:* 10

Grapefruit

Mandarins: Best cvs to 12 ft. Try 'Clementine' lvs willowy, frs near-seedless, sweet; 'Owari' dwarf; 'Kinnow' columnar. *Spd:* 10 ft; *Fl:* 5–6; *Z:* 9

Oranges: Many cvs grown on dwarf stocks for use as shrubs. Try 'Washington' frs Dec–Feb; 'Skagg's Bonanza' earlier frs; 'Marrs' low acid frs, natural semi-dwarf. *Ht, Spd:* to 12 ft; *Fl:* 5–6; *Z:* 10

Orange

Cleyera

C. japonica (= Eurya ochnacea)*: SE Asia. New lvs beautiful deep
brownish red turning to glossy dark green. Creamy white frag fls followed
by dark red puffy frs lasting through wtr. *Ht:* 15 ft; *Spd:* 20 ft; *Fl:* 9–10; *Z:* 9

Cocculus

C. laurifolius: Him. Many-stemmed shrub with arching spreading
branches. Lvs leathery, shiny, prominent veins. Fls inconspic. Useful
screen or background. Prop by cuttings. *Ht, Spd:* to 25 ft; *Z:* 8

Coleonema (= Diosma)

Breath of heaven

C. album: White breath of heaven: S
Africa. Delicate filmy shrub. Lvs
heather-like. Tiny white fls over a
long period in wtr and spr. Clip
over after flowering. *Ht, Spd:* 5 ft;
Fl: 11–3; *Z:* 9
C. pulchrum Pink breath of heaven:
S Africa. Sim to above but pink fls.
Prop both spp by seed, cuttings. *Ht,
Spd:* 5 ft; *Fl:* 11–3; *Z:* 9

C. album

Coprosma

Coprosma

C. krikii: NZ. Spreading fol shrub
to 3 ft but may be nearly prostrate.
Lvs yellow-green, close set.
Tolerates beach conditions, helps
erosion control. *Spd:* 5 ft; *Z:* 9
C. repens (= baueri) Mirror plant:
NZ. Wonderfully glossy lvs.
Inconspic fls but frs yellow or
orange. Lvs of 'Argentea' blotched
white; of 'Variegata' yellow varieg.
Ht: 8 ft; *Spd:* 5 ft; *Z:* 8

C. repens

Crassula

Crassula

C. argentea Jade plant: S Africa. Succ landscaping shrub in mildest zones.
Thick pad-like lvs bright green, sometimes red-edged. Clustered pink star-
shaped fls in profusion. *Ht:* to 9 ft; *Spd:* 5 ft; *Fl:* 11–5; *Z:* 10

Cuphea

Cuphea

C. hyssopifolia False heather:
Mexico. Dwarf evergreen to 2 ft;
tiny pink purple or white slim bell-
shaped fls give interesting smr col.
Lvs long, narrow. *Spd:* 2 ft; *Fl:* 6–8;
Z: 10
C. ignea (= platycentra) Cigar
plant: Mexico. More lfy and
compact. Tubular ¾ in fls glowing
red with dark ring at end and white
tip. *Ht, Spd:* 1 ft; *Fl:* 7–10; *Z:* 10

C. ignea

Dizygotheca

False aralia

D. elegantissima Threadleaf false aralia: New Hebrides. Juvenile lvs fan-like with narrow fine-toothed lflts becoming broader and more coarsely toothed with age. Makes pretty lacy pattern against a wall but never blooms. Good houseplant in juvenile stage. Prop by cuttings. *Ht:* to 12 ft; *Spd:* 8 ft; *Z:* 10

D. elegantissima

Dodonaea

Hop bush, Hopseed bush

D. viscosa: gdn origin. Most pop form of a fast-growing bush. Lvs rich bronzy green, willow-like, becoming deeper col and purplish in wtr. Fls inconspic but attractive winged frs. *Ht:* 15 ft; *Spd:* 5 ft; *Z:* 9

Erica

Heath, Heather

E. canaliculata (= melanthera)★ Christmas heather: S Africa. Lvs dark green above, white below. Fls pink in 'Rosea', purple in 'Rubra'. Cv 'Boscaweniana' to 18 ft, v pale lilac-pink fls in Dec–Mar. *Ht, Spd:* 5 ft; *Fl:* 10–2; *Z:* 10
E. mammosa: S Africa. Stiff, uprt. Lvs bright green; bell fls in a variety of pink shades. *Ht, Spd:* 3 ft; *Fl:* 2–3 (−9); *Z:* 9

E. mammosa

Eriobotrya

Loquat

E. deflexa Bronze loquat: China. Oval pointed lvs keep bright coppery col a long time before turning green. Garlands of creamy white fls. Fr inedible. Prop by cuttings. *Ht:* 15 ft; *Spd:* 10 ft; *Fl:* 3–4; *Z:* 9

E. deflexa

Eriogonum

Wild buckwheat

E. giganteum St Catherine's lace: Cal. Free-branching shrub. Lvs greyish-white, broadly oval. Clustered pink or white fls in dome-like clusters over a long period. Prop by seed. *Ht, Spd:* 3 ft; *Fl:* 3–10; *Z:* 9

Erythrina

Coral tree

E. humeana Natal coral tree: S Africa. Remarkable for its long tassel-like clusters of long-stkd bright orange-red fls held well above dark green lvs. *E.h. raja* less tree-like. *Ht:* 25 ft; *Spd:* 20 ft; *Fl:* 8–11; *Z:* 9

Gardenia

G. jasminoides*: China. Glossy green pointed lvs and double white fls of intoxicating scent. Try 'August Beauty' to 6 ft, big fls May–Oct; 'Golden Magic' to 3 ft, fls Apr–Sept turning gold with age; 'Radicans' to 1 ft, lvs often streaked white, smaller fls in smr; 'Veitchii' to 4 ft, prolific fls May–Nov. *Spd:* to 6 ft; *Z:* 8

G. jasminoides

Grewia

Starflower

G. occidentalis (= caffra) Lavender starflower: S Africa. Quick-growing sprawler. Deep green, oblong fine-toothed lvs; fls star-shaped, lavender-pink, yellow centers. Prop by cuttings. *Ht, Spd:* 10 ft; *Fl:* 4–9; *Z:* 9

Heteromeles (= Photinia)

Heteromeles

H. arbutifolia Toyon, Christmas berry, California holly: Cal. Dense shrub; lvs glossy, leathery, bristly-toothed. Small white fls in flat clusters; frs red berries. *Ht, Spd:* 10 ft+; *Fl:* 6–7; *Z:* 9

Ilex

Holly

I. vomitoria Yaupon: SE USA. Narrow 1 in dark green lvs and a profusion of scarlet berries. Takes v alkaline soil. Try dwarf 'Nana' and free-branching 'Pride of Houston'. *Ht:* to 20 ft; *Spd:* 10 ft; *Z:* 6

Jasminum

Jasmine

J. mesnyi (= primulinum)* Primrose jasmine: China. Arching evergreen; lvs dark green, 3 lflts. Pretty but not frag lemon-yellow semi-double or double fls scattered singly all over. Can be clipped as a hedge. *Ht, Spd:* 8 ft; *Fl:* 11–4; *Z:* 8
J. sambac Arabian jasmine: India. Powerfully frag clustered white fls; evergreen undivided lvs. *Ht, Spd:* 5 ft; *Fl:* 1–12; *Z:* 10

J. mesnyi

Justica

Justica

J. brandegeana (= Beloperone guttata) Shrimp plant: Mexico. Makes a 3 ft × 4 ft mound. Tubular fls in drooping spikes in white, striped purple, surrounded by bronze bracts. Lvs apple green, egg-shaped. Bracts of cv 'Chartreuse' yellow. *Fl:* 4–5; *Z:* 10

J. brandegeana

Lantana

Quick-growing upright shrubs invaluable for all-year color, not fussy about soil and blooming best in poor soil. The leaves have a strong pungent odor when crushed.

L. camara: W Indies. Coarse, uprt. Lvs rough, dark green; fls tubular, yellow, orange or red in clusters. *Ht, Spd:* 5 ft; *Fl:* 1–12; *Z:* 10

L. montevidensis★: W Indies. Good ground cover, hardier than above. Lvs often tinged red or purplish in zone 9. Fls rosy lilac, tubular. Many cvs inc 'Dwarf White'; 'Yellow and Pink' to 4 ft; 'Sunburst' to 3 ft, fls shining gold; *Ht, Spd:* 6 ft; *Fl:* 1–12; *Z:* 9

L. camara

Tea tree

L. laevigatum Australian tea tree: Aust. Soft, informal shrub/small tree. Lvs dull grey-green, oval; ptls white, pink or red round hard central cone. Frs woody, long-lasting. *Ht:* 25 ft; *Spd:* 15 ft; *Fl:* 3–4; *Z:* 9

Melaleuca

M. nesophila Pink melaleuca: Aust. Unusual gnarled branches and thick spongy bark. Lvs thick, roundish. Brushes of mauve fls fading to white, tipped yellow. Woody frs last sev yrs. *Ht, Spd:* 25 ft; *Fl:* 3–11; *Z:* 9

Michelia

M. figo (= fuscata)★ Banana shrub: China. Dense, slow-growing, magnolia-like. Lvs glossy, mid-green; fls creamy-yellow shaded brownish purple, banana-like scent. Prop by cuttings. *Ht, Spd:* 8 ft; *Fl:* 3–5; *Z:* 10

Murraya

M. paniculata (= exotica)★ Orange jessamine: India. Graceful open shrub; glossy divided lvs and bell-shaped white fls with jasmine frag followed by small red frs. Also a dwarf form. *Ht, Spd:* 10 ft; *Fl:* 8–10; *Z:* 10

Myoporum

M. laetum: NZ. V fast growing to 30 ft. Fol dense. Fls white, marked purple, in clusters of 2–6. Small reddish-purple frs. One of the best seaside shrubs. *Spd:* to 20 ft; *Fl:* 6–8; *Z:* 9

M. parviflorum: Aust. Low, spreading, good ground cover. Dense, bright green fol; fls sim to above but all white. Frs purple. *Ht:* 3 in; *Spd:* 9 ft; *Fl:* 6–8; *Z:* 9

M. parviflorum

Philodendron

Philodendron

P. selloum

P. selloum: S Amer. "Jungly" tree-like sp to 8 ft grown for its fol. Lvs to 3 ft, deeply cut. The hardiest big-leaved sp grown outdoors, many others are pop houseplants. Cv 'Lundii' more compact. *Spd:* to 8 ft; *Z:* 10

Phyllostachys

Bamboo

P. nigra

P. aurea Golden bamboo: China, Japan. "Running" bamboo; stems below ground run quickly away from parent. Stems stiff, uprt with crowded joints at base; dense fol. *Ht:* 10 ft; *Spd:* 20 ft; *Z:* 7
P. nigra Black bamboo: China, Japan. Sim to above but smaller, new stems turn black in 2nd yr. *Ht:* 8 ft; *Spd:* 15 ft; *Z:* 7

Picea

Spruce

P. glauca 'Conica' Dwarf Alberta spruce: gdn origin. Dwarf form of tree native to N USA and Canada. Short fine soft needles grass-green, greying with age. Good pruned to a pyramid shape. *Ht:* 6 ft; *Spd:* 3 ft; *Z:* 3

Pittosporum

Pittosporum

P. tobira 'Variegatum'

P. phyllyraeoides: Aust. Weeping sp. Lvs v narrow; fls tiny yellow bells. Frs deep yellow. *Ht:* to 20 ft; *Spd:* 15 ft; *Fl:* 1–3; *Z:* 9
P. tobira*: China, Japan. Dense shrub. Sweetly frag fls creamy white. Round green frs split to reveal orange seeds. Many good cvs. *Ht:* 15 ft; *Spd:* 10 ft; *Fl:* 2–3; *Z:* 9
P. undulatum Victorian box: Aust. Lvs glossy, wavy-edged; fls white, frag; frs yellow, seeds orange-gold. *Ht, Spd:* to 40 ft; *Fl:* 2–3; *Z:* 10

Podocarpus

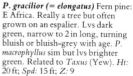

Podocarpus

P. macrophyllus

P. gracilior (= elongatus) Fern pine: E Africa. Really a tree but often grown on an espalier. Lvs dark green, narrow to 2 in long, turning bluish or bluish-grey with age. *P. macrophyllus* sim but lvs brighter green. Related to *Taxus* (Yew). *Ht:* 20 ft; *Spd:* 15 ft; *Z:* 9

Poinciana

P. pulcherrima Dwarf poinciana, Barbados pine: Tropics. Mound-forming quick growing, decid. Lvs dark green, many lflts. Clustered orange-red pea fls have protruding stamens. *Ht, Spd:* 10 ft; *Fl:* 4–9; *Z:* 10

 Portulacaria

Portulacaria

P. afra Elephant's food, Purslane tree, Spekboom: S Africa. Thick, juicy-stemmed shrub to 12 ft, loosely branched with small oval ½ in lvs. Seldom fls. Good screening, ground cover. *Spd:* 10 ft; *Z:* 10

Prunus

Prunus

P. caroliniana Carolina laurel cherry: N Carolina–Texas. Dense evergreen shrub/small tree. Fol glossy green; fls small creamy-white spikes. Frs black. *Ht:* 15 ft; *Spd:* 10 ft; *Fl:* 2–4; *Z:* 8
P. lyonii (= integrifolia) Catalina cherry: Cal. Sim to above but lvs toothed; frs black cherries. *Ht, Spd:* 20 ft; *Fl:* 4–5; *Z:* 9

P. lyonii

Sarcococca

Sarcococca

S. ruscifolia*: Him, China. Invaluable for shaded areas, with a polished look even in deepest shade. Lvs small, wavy-edged; v frag but nearly hidden white fls followed by red frs. *S. confusa* sim but frs jet black. Prop by div or cuttings. *Ht:* 5 ft; *Spd:* 6 ft; *Fl:* 3–4; *Z:* 7

Schefflera

Schefflera

S. (= Brassaia) actinophylla
Octopus tree: Trop Amer. Giant lvs each with 7–16 1 ft lflts held like an umbrella. Fls octopus-like, greenish yellow, turning pink then crimson. Frs dark purple. *Ht:* to 20 ft; *Spd:* 10 ft; *Fl:* 11–2; *Z:* 10
S. arboricola: Trop Asia. Lflts to 3 in; fls in flattened spheres yellow turning bronze. *Ht:* to 20 ft; *Spd:* 10 ft; *Fl:* 11–2; *Z:* 10

S. actinophylla

Strelitzia

Bird of paradise flower

S. reginae: S Africa. Grown for its spectacular long-lasting fls shaped like tropical birds colored in blue, orange and white. Dramatic blue-green banana-like lvs to 18 in on a clump-forming plant. Official city fl of Los Angeles. Prop by cuttings, seed. *Ht, Spd:* 5 ft; *Fl:* 10–3; *Z:* 10

S. reginae

Syzygium (= Eugenia)

Syzygium

S. paniculatum 'Compacta' Brush cherry: gdn origin. V pop hedging.
Young fol reddish turning coppery green. Fls white or cream with feathery,
tufty stamens. Frs rose-purple, edible, insipid. *Ht, Spd:* 15 ft; *Fl:* 6–8; *Z:* 10

Tecomaria

Tecomaria

T. capensis Cape honeysuckle: S
Africa. Scrambling evergreen; lvs
cut into many glistening lflts.
Brilliant orange-red tubular fls in
compact clusters. 'Aurea' has paler
fol and yellow fls and needs more
heat. Can be climber-like if tied to a
support. *Ht:* to 25 ft; *Spd:* to 20 ft;
Fl: 10–2; *Z:* 9

T. capensis

Ternstroemia

Ternstroemia

T. gymnanthera (= japonica):
Japan. Rounded shrub grown for its
gleaming, leathery red-stkd lvs
which are bronzy-red when young
ageing to deep bronze or purplish
red. Fls frag but not showy; frs
round, yellow or red, splitting to
show black seeds. *Ht:* 4 ft; *Spd:* 5 ft;
Fl: 6–7; *Z:* 8

T. gymnanthera

Tetrapanax (= Aralia)

Tetrapanax

T. papyriferus Rice paper plant:
China. Furry tropical evergreen
quickly reaching 15 ft. Big, lustrous,
long-stkd lvs white felted below. Fls
creamy white on long tan-colored
furry stems in Dec. Fuzzy hrs from
young growth can cause severe
irritation. *Spd:* 15 ft; *Z:* 9

T. papyriferus

Tupidanthus

Tupidanthus

T. calyptratus: India. Like *Schefflera* (p 183) but branches from the base to
form a broader, denser shrub. Lvs fan-like to 20 in wide, each lflt to 7 in.
Excellent container plant. *Ht:* to 20 ft; *Spd:* 10 ft; *Z:* 10

Ugni

Ugni

U. molinae (= Myrtus ugni) Chilean guava: Chile. Straggly when young
with dark-green bronze-tinted lvs. Fls white, rose-tinted, brush like. Fr red
or purple, apple fragrance, edible *Ht, Spd:* 6 ft; *Fl:* 5–7; *Z:* 9

Index

For easy reference, where plants appear in more than one section of the book those sections are marked with a letter in brackets as follows: annuals (A); herbaceous perennials (P); alpines and rock garden plants (R); bog, waterside and pond plants (W); herbs (H); ferns (F); bulbs, corms and tubers (B); climbers (C); shrubs (S); subtropicals (T).

Aaron's beard 139
Abelia 120
Abutilon 120
Acacia 120(S), 175(T)
Acacia, False 153
    Pearl 175
    Rose 153
Acaena 59
Acalypha 175
Acanthus 19
Acer 120
Achillea 19(P), 59(R)
Achillea 19(P), 168(T)
    Alpine 59
Achimenes 83
Acidanthera 83
Aconite, Winter 90
Aconitum 19(P), 112(C)
Acorus 71
Actinidia 112
Adiantum 82(F), 169(T)
Aeonium 163
Aesculus 120
Aethionema 59
Afrikander, Yellow
    marsh 93
Agapanthus 19
Agathaea 166
Agave 20
Ageratum 7
Ajuga 20
Akebia 112
Alchemilla 20(P), 59(R)
Alisma 71
Allamanda 112
All heal 56
Allium 59(R), 77(H),
    83(B)
Aloe 20(P), 163(T)
Aloe, Tree 163
Alpinia 163
Alsophila 171
Alstroemeria 20
Althaea 7
Alyssum 14(A), 60(R)
Amaranthus 7
Amaryllis 84
"Amaryllis" 93
Amelanchier 121
Anagallis 7
Anaphalis 21
Anchusa 21, 24
Andromeda 143, 149,
    161
Androsace 60
Anemone 21(P), 67(R),
    84(B)
Anethum 77
Angelica 77
Angelica tree 121
Angel's trumpet 131
Antennaria 60
Anthemis 77
Anthericum 84

Antigonon 172
Antirrhinum 7
Antholyza 84
Anthriscus 77
Aponogeton 71
Apricot, Japanese 150
Aquilega 21
Arabis 60
Aralia 121, 134(S),
    184(T)
Aralia, False 179
Arbutus 121
Archangel 38
Arctostaphylos 121
Arctotheca 163
Arctotis 8(A), 21(P)
Arenaria 60
Arisaema 84
Arisarum 60
Aristolochia 112
Armeria 21(P), 61(R),
    77(H), 121(S)
Artemisia 22(P), 61(R),
    77(H), 121(S),
    168(T)
Arum 85
Arum, Bog 73
    Dragon 90
    Italian 85
    Water 71
Aruncus 22
Arundinaria 122
Asarina 61
Asclepias 22
Asparagus 172
Asperula 61
Aspidistra 163
Asplenium 169, 171
Aster 22(P), 61(R)
Aster, Alpine 61
    China 8
    Stoke's 54
× *Asterago* 54
Astilbe 23
Astrantia 23
Atriplex 8
Aubrieta 62
Aucuba 122
Aunt Eliza 84
Avena 34
Avens, Mountain 64
Azalea 151–2
Azara 122(S), 176(T)
Azara, Boxleaf 176

Babiana 85
Baboon root 85
Baccharis 176
Baby blue eyes 15
Baby's breath 33(P),
    65(R)
Bachelor's buttons
    9(A), 51(P)
Balloon flower 48

Ballota 122
Balm, Bee 43
    Lemon 42
Balsam 13
Bamboo 122(S), 176,
    182(T)
    Black 182
    Chinese sacred 145
    Golden 182(T)
    Heavenly 145(S)
    Oldham 176(T)
Bambusa 122(S), 176(T)
Banana shrub 181
Baptisia 23
Barberry 122
Barrenwort 29
Basil 80
Basket of gold 60
Bauhinia 172, 176
Bay, Californian 159
    Sweet 142
Bearberry 121
Bear's breeches 19
Beaucarnea 176
Beaumontia 172
Beauty bush 123, 142
Begonia 85
Bellbind, Baby 63
Bellflower 9(A), 24(P),
    62(R), 168(T)
    Chilean 117
    Chimney 9
    Chinese 48
    Dalmatian 168
    Great 24
    Italian 168
    Peach-leaved 24
    Serbian 168
Bellis 62
Bells of Ireland 15
Beloperone 85
Benthamidia see
    Cornus (S)
Berberidopsis 113
Berberis 122
Bergamot 43
Bergenia 23
Beschorneria 123
Betonica 54
Bignonia 173, 174
Billbergia 164
Bindweed 10(A),
    63(P), 128(S)
Bird of paradise flower
    183
Birth root 101
Bittersweet 113
Black-eyed Susan
    52(P), 119(C)
Bladder-nut 157
Bladder senna 127
Blazing star 102
Bleeding heart 28
Bletilla 171

Blood flower 93
Bloodroot 68
Bluebell creeper 175
Bluebell, Spanish 94
   Virginia 42
Blueberry, Highbush
   160
Blue-eyed grass 70
Bocconia 41
Borago 62(R), 78(H)
Borage 78
   Baby 62
Bottle brush 124
Bougainvillea 113
Bouncing Bet 52
Bower vine 174
Box 123
   Bastard 149
   Victorian 182
Brassaia 183
Brassica 8
Breath of heaven 178
Briar, Sweet 105
Bridal wreath 31(P),
   156(S)
Brodiaea 85, 90, 94
Bromelia 24
Bromeliad 24, 30
Broom 63(R), 130, 136
   (S)
   Dwarf 63
   Moroccan 130
   Mt Etna 136
   Scotch 136
   Spanish 130
   Warminster 130
   White Spanish 130
Brunfelsia 176
Brunnera 24
Buckthorn 151
   Sea 138
Buckwheat, Wild 179
Buddleia 123
Bugbane 26
Bugle 20
Bugloss, Viper's 11
Bunchberry 63
Burnet 52
Burning bush 28
Burr-weed, New
   Zealand 59
Butcher's broom 153
Butomus 71
Buttercup 100
Butterfly weed 22
Buxus 123

Cabbage, Ornamental
   8
Caesalpinia 183
Caladium 85
Calceolaria 8
Calendula 8
Calla 71, 76
Calliandra 177
Callicarpa 123
Callistemon 124
Callistephus 8
Calluna 124
Calocephalus 164
Calochortus 86

Caltha 72
Camassia 86
Camellia 124
Campanula 9(A), 24(P),
   62(R), 168(T)
Campion 40(P), 69(R)
   Rose 40
Campsis 113
Canary nasturtium 119
Candle bush 177
Candytuft 13(A), 66(R)
Canna 24(P), 86(B)
Canterbury bells 9
Cape weed 163
Caragana 125
Caraway 78
Cardinal flower 73
Cardiocrinum 86
Carpenteria 125
Carpobrotus 164
Carum 78
Caryopteris 125
Cassia 125(S), 177(T)
Cast iron plant 163
Catananche 24
Catmint 43
Catchfly 40, 58(P),
   69(R)
Cat's claw 174
Catsear 60
Ceanothus 125
Celandine, Lesser 51
Celastrus 113
Celosia 9
Centaurea 9(A), 25(P)
Centranthus 25
Century plant 20
Cephalaria 25
Cerastium 62
Ceratostigma 63(R),
   126(S)
Cercis 126
Cestrum 177
Chaenomeles 126
Chamomile 77
Chaste tree 161
Checkerberry 136
Cheiranthus 9
Chelone 25
Cherry, Brush 184
   Cornelian 128
Cherry pie 34
Chervil 77
Chimonanthus 126
Chinese lantern 48
Chives 77
Chlorophytum 164
Choisya 126
Christmas berry 180
Christmas rose 34
Chrysanthemum 9(A),
   26(P), 164(T)
Chrysanthemum,
   Florist's 26
   Tricolored 9
Cicely, Sweet 79

Cigar plant 178
Cimicifuga 26
Cineraria 18(A), 26(P)
Cinquefoil 50(P),
   68(R), 149(S),
   169(T)
   Shrubby 149
   Spring 169
Cissus 172
Cistus 127
Citrus 127(S), 177(T)
Clarkia 10
Clematis 26(P), 114(C)
Cleome 10
Clerodendrum 127(S),
   173(T)
Clethra 127
Cleyera 178
Clianthus 114
Clivia 86
Clytostoma 173
Cobaea 115
Cocculus 178
Cockscomb 9
Colchicum 87
Coleonema 178
Coleus 10
Columbine 21
Colutea 127
Comfrey 54(P), 81(H)
Comptonia 179
Coneflower 17(A), 29,
   52(P)
   Hedgehog 29
   Purple 29
Convallaria 87
Convolvulus 10(A),
   63(R), 128(S)
   Dwarf 10
Copper leaf 175
Coprosma 178
Coral bells 35
Coral flower 35
Coral plant 113
Coral tree 133(S),
   179(T)
   Natal 179
Cordyline 128
Coreopsis 10(A), 27(P),
   164(T)
Coriander 78
Coriandrum 78
Cornel 128
Cornflower 9
Corn, Indian 18
Cornus 63(R), 128(S)
Corokia 128
Cortaderia 27
Corydalis 63(R), 87(B)
Corylopsis 129
Corylus 129
Cosmos 10
Cotinus 129
Cotoneaster 129
Cotyledon 165
Cowberry 160
Cowslip, 72
   Blue 51
   Cape 96
Coyote bush 176
Crambe 27

Cranesbill 32(P), 65(R)
  Meadow 32
Crassula 165, 178
Creeping Jenny 67
Cress, Rock 60
  Wall 60
Crinum 87
Crocosmia 87
Crocus 78(H), 88(B)
Crocus 88(B)
  Autumn 87
Crown Imperial 91
Cucurbita 115
Cup-and-saucer-vine
  115
Cuphea 178
Cupid's dart 24
Cup-of-gold vine 175
Cumin 78
Cuminum 78
Currant, Buffalo 153
  Flowering 153
  Golden 153
Curtonus 84
Cushion bush 164
Cyathea 171
Cyclamen 88
Cydonia 126
Cymbidium 165
Cynoxylon see
  Cornus (S)
Cyperus 72
Cypress, Summer 13
Cyrtomium 170
Cytisus 63(R), 130(S)

Daboecia 130
Dactylorrhiza 27
Daffodil 98–9
Dahlia 89
Daisy, African 8,
  11(A), 44(P),
  167(T)
  Barberton 33
  Crown 9
  English 62
  Freeway 167
  "Hen and Chicken" 62
  Pan's 164
  Shasta 26
  Transvaal 33
Daisy bush 146
Daphne 63(R), 130(S)
Datura 131
Davallia 170
Deadnettle 38
  Dwarf 38
Delphinium 11(A),
  27(P)
Desfontainea 131
Desmodium 142
Deutzia 131
Dianthus 11(A), 28(P),
  64(R)
Dicentra 28
Dichelostemma 90
Dichondra 168
Dictamnus 28
Dierama 90
Diervilla 161
Digitalis 11(A), 28(P)

Dill 77
Dimorphotheca 11(A),
  44(P), 167(T)
Diosma 178
Diplacus 42
Disanthus 131
Distictis 173
Dittany 28
Dizygotheca 179
Dogwood 63(R),
  128(S)
Dodecatheon 64
Dodonaea 179
Dogwood 63(R),
  128(S)
Doronicum 29
Dorycnium 131
Dracunculus 90
Drimys 131
Dropwort 31
Drosanthemum 165
Dryas 64
Dryopteris 82
Dutchman's breeches
  28
Dutchman's pipe 112

Eccremocarpus 115
Echeveria 165
Echinacea 29
Echinops 29
Echium 11
Edelweiss 66
Eglantine 105
Eichhornia 72
Elaeagnus 132
Elder, Golden 154
  Red-berried 154
Elecampane 36
Elephant's food 183
Embothrium 132
Endymion 94
Enkianthus 132
Epimedium 29
Eranthis 90
Eremurus 90
Erica 132–3(S), 179(T)
Erigeron 30
Erinus 64
Eriobotrya 133(S),
  179(T)
Eriogonum 179
Eryngium 30
Erysimum 11
Erythrina 133(S),
  179(T)
Erythronium 91
Escallonia 133
Eschscholzia 12
Eucryphia 133
Eugenia 184
Euonymus 134
Eupatorium 30
Euphorbia 12(A), 30(P),
  64(R)
Eurya 178
Euryops 166
Evening primrose 44
Everlasting 13(A), 34,
  65(P), 138(S),
  168(T)
Exochorda 134

Fascicularia 30
× *Fatshedera* 134
Fatsia 134
Feijoa 134
Felicia 166
Felt plant 166
Fennel 78
Fenugreek 81
  Classical 81
Fern, Australian tree
  171
  Bear's foot 170
  Chain 171
  Giant chain 171
  Leatherleaf 171
  Maidenhair 82, 169
  Male 82
  Mother 169, 170
  Ostrich plume 82
  Sensitive 82
  Southern sword 170
  Squirrel's foot 170
  Staghorn 170
  Sword 171
  Tree 171
Fescue, Sheep's 31
Festuca 31
Ficus 135
Fig 135
  Hottentot 164
  Sea 164
Figwort 51, 53
  Cape 48(P), 148(S)
Filbert, Purple 129
Filipendula 31
Fire bush 132
Firecracker,
  Californian 90
Firethorn 150
Flag, Crimson 100
Flame flower 119
Flame vine 174
Flax 14(A), 39(P)
  Holy 154
Fleabane 30
Flower of Jove 40
Flower of the West
  Wind 103
Foam flower 55
Foeniculum 78
Forget-me-not 15(A),
  74(W)
Forsythia 135
Fothergilla 135
Fountain grass 167
Four o'clock 42
Foxglove 11(A), 28(P)
Francoa 31
Fraxinella 28
Freesia 91
Fringe-tree 126
Fritillaria 91
Fritillary 91
Fuchsia 135
Fumitory 63
Funkia 36

Gaillardia 31
Galanthus 91

Galax 31
Galega 31
Galeobdolon 38
Galingale 72
Galtonia 92
Gardener's garters 46
Gardenia 180
Garland flower 63(R),
    130(S)
Garlic, Clove 77
Garrya 136
Gas plant 28
Gaultheria 136
Gayfeather 38
    Spiked 38
Gazania 32(P), 166(T)
Gelsemium 173
Genista 136
Gentian 32(P), 65(R)
    Trumpet 65
    Willow 32
Gentiana 32(P), 65(R)
Gentian root 32
Geranium 32(P), 65(R)
Geranium 16
Gerbera 33
Germander 70(R),
    159(S)
    Wall 55(P), 70(R)
Geum 33
Ginger 163
Gladiolus 92–3
Glaucium 12
Globe flower 56(P),
    76(W)
Gloriosa 93
Glorybower 173
    Bleeding heart 173
Glory flower, Chilean
    115
Glory of the snow 86
Glory vine 119
Gloxinia 101
Glyceria 72
Goat's beard 22
Goat's rue 31
Godetia 12
Gold-dust plant 122
Golden rod 54
Gooseberry, Chinese
    112
Gorse 159
Gourd, Ornamental 115
Grapefruit 177
Grape vine 119
Grevillea 136
Grewia 180
Griselina 136
Guava, Chilean 184
    Pineapple 134
Guinea gold vine 174
Guinea-hen flower 91
Gum tree, Chilean
    see Escallonia
Gunnera 72
Gypsophila 12(A),
    33(P), 65(R)

Haberlea 65
Haemanthus 93
Hairy Dorothy 131

Halesia 137
× Halimiocistus 137
Halimium 137
Hamamelis 137, 147
Hardenbergia 173
Harlequin flower 101
Hawaiian T. plant 128
Hawkweed 66
Hawthorn, Chinese
    148
    Water 71
Heartsease 58
Heath 179(T)
    Cornish 133
    Corsican 133
    Cross-leaved 133
    Irish 130
    St Dabeoc's 130
    Spanish 133
    Spring 133
    Tree 132
Heather 124, 132–3(S),
    179(T)
    Bell 132
    Christmas 179
    False 178
Hebe 137
Hedera 115
Hedychium 33
Helenium 33
Helianthemum 138
Helianthus 12(A), 33(P)
Helichrysum 13(A),
    34(P), 65(R), 138(S)
Helictotrichon 34
Heliopsis 34
Heliotrope 34
Heliotropium 34
Helipterum 13
Hellebore 34
    False 57
    Stinking 34
    White 57
Helleborus 34
Hemerocallis 35
Hemp, African 156
Hepatica 65
Herald's trumpet 172
Hermodactylus 95
Hesperis 35
Heuchera 35
Hibbertia 174
Hibiscus 36(P), 138(S)
Hieracium 66
Hippeastrum 93
Hippophae 138
Hoheria 138
Holboellia 116
Holly 140
    California 180
    Chinese 140
Hollyhock 7
Honesty 14(A), 40(P)
Honeysuckle 117(C),
    143(S), 174(T)
    Cape 184
    Giant Burmese 174
    Privet 143
    Tartarian 143
Hop Bush 179
Hopseed bush 179

Horsechestnut 120
Hosta 36
Houseleek 69
Houttuynia 72
Hoya 174
Humata 170
Humming bird's
    trumpet 58
Hyacinth, Grape 97
    Japanese see
        Ophiopogon
    Roman 94
    Summer 92
    Water 72
Hyacinthoides 94
Hyacinthus 94
Hydrangea 116(C),
    139(S)
Hymenocallis 94
Hypericum 66(R),
    139(S)
Hyssop 79
Hyssopus 79

Iberis 13(A), 66(R)
Ice plant 53(P), 164,
    165, 166(T)
    Rosea 165
    Trailing 166
Ilex 140(S), 180(T)
Impatiens 13
Incarvillea 36
Indian shot plant 86
Indigo, Blue 23
    False 23
Indigofera 140
Inula 36
Ipheion 94
Ipomoea 116
Iris 37(P), 66(R),
    73(W), 94–5(B),
    171(T)
    Bearded German 37
    Bulbous 94–5
    Clematis-flowered 73
    Crested 66
    German 37
    Gladwyn 37
    Siberian 73
    Snake's head 95
    Winter-flowering 37
Isotoma 168
Itea 140
Ivy 115
    Boston 117
    Canary Island 115
    Grape 172
    Persian 115
Ixia 96

Jacob's ladder 49
Jade plant 178
Jasmine 116(C), 140(S),
    180(T)
    Arabian 180
    Chilean 117
    Italian 140
    Primrose 180
    Rock 60
    Star 119
    Winter 116

Jasminum 116(C),
140(S), 180(T)
Jessamine 173
  Carolina 173
  Night 177
  Orange 181
Joe-pye weed 30
Jonquil 98
Joseph's coat 7
Judas tree 126
Juncus 73
Juniper 141
Juniperus 141
Justica 180

Kalanchoe 166
Kale, Ornamental 8
Kalmia 141
Kentranthus 25
Kerria 141
Kirengeshoma 37
Kochia 13
Knapweed 9(A), 25(P)
  Mountain 25
Kniphofia 37
Knotweed 49(P),
  68(R), 118(C),
  169(T)
Kolkwitzia 142

Lachenalia 96
Lady's mantle 20(P),
  59(R)
Lady's parasol 49
Lady's seal 49
Lamb's ears 54
Lamb's tongue 54
Lamiastrum 38
Lamium 38
Lampranthus 166
Lantana 181
Lapageria 117
Larkspur 11
Lathyrus 13(A), 38(P),
  117(C)
Laurel 142
  Californian 159
  Cherry 150
  Mountain 141
  Portuguese 150
  Sheep's 141
  Spotted 122
Laurentia 168
Laurus 142
Laurustinus 160
Lavatera 14(A), 142(S)
Lavender 142
  Sea 39(P), 166(T)
Lavender-cotton 154
Lavendula 142
Leadwort 63(R),
  118(C)
Lemon 177(T)
  Inchang 127(S)
Lenten rose 34
Leonitis 38
Leontopodium 66
Leopard's bane 29
Leptandra 57
Leptospermum 142(S),
  181(T)

Lespedeza 142
Leucojum 96
Leucothoe 143
Levisticum 79
Lewisia 66
Leycesteria 143
Liatris 38
Libertia 38
Ligularia 39(P), 73(W)
Ligusticum 79
Ligustrum 143
Lilac 158
  California 125
  Summer 123
Lilac vine 173
Lilium 96–7
Lily 96–7
  African blue 19(P)
  Arum 76(W)
  Belladonna 84(B)
  Blood 93(B)
  Climbing 93(B)
  Corn 96(B)
  Creeping 93(B)
  Cuban 100(B)
  Day 35(P)
  Foxtail 90(B)
  Giant Himalayan
    86(B)
  Ginger 33(P)
  Goldband 96(B)
  Kaffir 100(B)
  Lemon 35(P)
  Madonna 96(B)
  Mahogany fawn
    91(B)
  Mariposa 86(B)
  Martagon 97(B)
  New Zealand flax
    47(P)
  Peruvian 20(P)
  Plantain 36(P)
  St Bernard's 84(B)
  Scarborough 103 (B)
  Sea 99(B)
  Tiger 97(B)
  Toad 56(P)
  Trout 37(P)
  Turk's cap 97(B)
Lily of the Nile 76
Lily of the valley 87
Lily turf 39(P), 169(T)
  Blue 39
Lime 177
Limonium 39(P), 166(T)
Linaria 14
Ling 124
Linseed 14
Linum 14(A), 39(P)
Lion's tail 38
Lippia 79
Liriope 39
Lithodora see
  Lithospermum
Lithospermum 67
Lobelia 14(A), 73(W)
Lobster's claw 114
Lobularia 14
London pride 52
Lonicera 117(C),
  143(S), 174(T)

Loosestrife 40, 41(P),
  67(R)
  Purple 41
Loquat 133(S), 179(T)
  Bronze 179
Lotus 131
Lotus, East Indian 74
Lovage 79
Love-in-a-mist 16
Love-lies-bleeding 7
Lupine 40
  False 55
  Tree 144
Lupinus 40(P), 144(S)
Lungwort 51
Lychnis 40
Lysichitum 73
Lysimachia 40(P),
  67(R), 73(W)
Lythrum 41

Macfadeyana 174
Macleaya 41
Madrona 121
Magnolia 144
Mahonia 144
Maize 18
Majorana 80
Mallow 14(A), 41(P)
  False 53
  Jew's 141(S)
  Musk 41(P)
  Rose see *Hibiscus*
  Tree 142(S), see
    also *Abutilon*
Malva 41
Mandarin 177
Mandevilla 117
Manna grass 72
Manuka 142
Manzanita 121
Maple, Fullmoon 120
Marguerite 164
  Blue 166
Marigold 18(A)
  African 18
  Cape 11
  French 18
  Marsh 72(W)
  Pot 8
Marjoram 80
Marvel of Peru 42
Masterwort 23
Matteuccia 82
Matthiola 15
May apple 49
Meadow rue 55
Meadowsweet 31
Mealies 18
Meconopsis 41
Melaleuca 181
Melianthus 145
Melissa 42
Mentha 74(W), 79(H)
Mertensia 42
Mesembryanthemum
  164, 165, 166
Metrosideros 145
Mezereon 130
Michaelmas daisy 22

Michelia 145(S), 181(T)
Microlepia 170
Mignonette 17
Milfoil 19
Milkweed 22
Milkwort 149
Milla 94
Mimulus 42(P), 74(W)
Mint 79(H)
  Water 74(W)
Mirabilis 42
Mirror plant 178
Miscanthus 42
Mock orange 148
Molinia 43
Molucella 15
Monarda 43
Mondo grass 169
Money plant 14
Moneywort 67
Monkey flower 42(P),
  74(W)
Monkey musk 74
Monkshood 19(P),
  112(C)
Montbretia 87
Morina 43
Morning glory 116
Moss, Irish 169
  Scotch 169
Mouse-tail plant 60
Mullein 57
Murrya 181
Muscari 97
Myoporum 181
Myosotis 15(A), 74(W)
Myrrhis 79
Myrtle 145(S), 161(T)
Myrtus 145(S), 184(T)

Nandina 145
Narcissus 98–9
Nasturtium 18(A),
  80(H), 119(C)
Navelwort 44
Neillia 145
Nelumbo 74
Nemesia 15
Nemophila 15
Neoregelia 167
Nepeta 43
Nephrolepis 170
Nerine 99
Nerium 146
Nicotiana 15(A), 44(P)
Nigella 16
Nightshade 175
Ninebark 148
Nordmannia 56
Nuphar 74
Nymphaea 75

Obedient plant 48
Ocimum 80
Octopus tree 183
Oenothera 44(P), 167(T)
Old woman 61
Oleander, Common
  146

Olearia 146
Olive, Russian 132
  Wild see *Elaeagnus*
Omphalodes 44
Onion, China 59(R)
  Flowering 59(R)
  Ornamental 83(B)
Onoclea 82
Onopordon 44
Onosma 67
Ophiopogon 39(P),
  169(T)
Orache 8
Orange 177
Orange flower,
  Mexican 126
Orchid 27(P), 165(T)
  Algerian 27
Orchid, Ground 171
  Chinese 171
Orchid tree, Hong
  Kong 176
Orchis 27
Oregon grape 144
Origanum 80
Ornithogalum 99
Orobus 38
Osier, Purple 54
Osmanthus 146
Osmanthus, Holly 146
Osmarea 146
Osmunda 82
Osteospermum 44(P),
  167(T)
Oswego tea 43
Oxalis 45(P), 67(R)

Pachysandra 147
Paeonia 45(P), 147(S)
Palm, Bottle 176
  Natal 177
Pansy 58
Pampas grass 27
Pancratium 99
Pandorea 174
Papyrus 72
Parahebe 147
Parrotia 147
Parrot's bill 114
Parsley 80
Parthenocissus 117
Pasque flower 68
Passiflora 118
Passion flower 118
Peacock flower 101
Pearl bush 134
Pearl everlasting 21
Pearlwort 169
Pea, perennial 117
Pea tree 125
Pelargonium 16
Peltiphyllum 75
Pennisetum 46(P),
  167(T)
Penstemon 46(P), 67(R)
Peony 45(P)
  Chinese 45(P)
  Tree 147(S)
Periwinkle 161
Pernettya 147

Perovskia 46
Petroselinum 80
Petunia 17
Phacelia 17
Phaedranthus 173
Phalaris 46
Philadelphus 148
Phillyrea 148
Philodendron 182
Phlomis 47(P), 148(S)
Phlox 17(A), 47(P),
  68(R)
Phlox, Alpine 68
  Annual 17
  Garden 47
  Moss 68
  Summer 47
Phormium 47
Photinia 148
Phygelius 48
Phyllostachys 182
Physalis 48
Physocarpus 148
Physostegia 48
Phytolacca 48
Picea 182
Pickerel weed 75
Pieris 149
Pileostegia 118
Pimpernel 7
Pincushion flower
  18(A), 53(P)
Pine, Barbados 183
  Fern 182
Pink 11(A), 28(P),
  64(R)
  Alpine 64
  Chinese 11
  Garden 28
  Indian 11
  Maiden 64
  Sea 21(P), 61(R)
Pittosporum 149(S),
  182(T)
Platycerium 170
Platycodon 48
Pleione 99
Pleurisy root 22
Plumbago 63(R), 118(C)
Plumbago, Blue 118
  Cape 118
  Perennial 63
Podocarpus 182
Podophyllum 49
Poinciana 101
Poke weed 48
Polemonium 49
Polianthes 100
Polyanthus 50
Polygala 149
Polygonatum 49
Polygonum 49(P),
  68(R), 118(C),
  169(T)
Polystichum 171
Pomegranate 150
Pontaderia 75
Ponytail 176
Poppy 16(A), 41, 45(P)
  Californian 12(A)
  Himalayan blue 41

Poppy, Horned 12(A)
  Iceland 16
  Opium 16
  Oriental 45
  Plume 41
  Shirley see
    Papaver × rhoeas
Portulacaria 183
Potato, Climbing 118
Potato vine 118
Potentilla 50(P), 68(R),
  149(S), 169(T)
Poterium 52
Powder puff 177
Primrose 50(P), 76(W)
  Himalayan 50
Primula 50(P), 76(W)
  Drumstick 50
Privet 143
  California 143
  Japanese 143
Prunella 50
Prunus 150(S), 183(T)
Pukateria 136
Pulmonaria 51
Pulsatilla 67, 68
Punica 150
Purslane tree 183
Pyracantha 150
Pyrethrum 26
Pyrostegia 174

Quamash 86
Queen's tears 164
Queen's wreath 172
Quince, Flowering 126

Ragwort 18
Ramonda 68
Ranunculus 51(P),
  100(B)
Raphiolepis 150
Redbud, American 126
Red hot poker 37
Red ink plant 48
Reseda 17
Rhamnus 151
Rheum 51(P), 76(W)
Rhododendron 151–2
Rhodohypoxis 100
Rhus 129, 153
Rhubarb, Ornamental
  76
Ribes 153
Ribbon grass 46
Rice paper plant 184
Robinia 153
Rocket, Sweet 35
Rock rose 127
Rockspray 129
Rodgersia 76
Romneya 51
Rorippa 80
Roscoea 51
Rosa 104–11
Rosa de Montana 172
"Rosa Mundi" 104
Roses 104–11
  "Apothecary's" 104
  Banksian 109
  Burnet 105

Rose, Cabbage 104
  China 104
  Climbers 109–11
  Damask 104
  Floribundas 108–9
  French 104
  Grandifloras 108–9
  Guelder 160(S)
  Hybrid musks 107–8
  Hybrid perpetuals
    105
  Hybrid teas 106
  Macartney 110
  Miniatures 111
  Memorial 110
  Modern shrubs
    107–8
  Old 104–5
  Provence 104
  Ramanas 105
  Ramblers 109–11
  "Red, of Lancaster"
    104
  Scotch 105
  Species 104–5
  "White, of York"
    104
  "York and
    Lancaster" 104
Rose of Sharon 138
Rose mallow 36
Rosmarinus 80
Rosemary 80
Rubus 153
Rudbeckia 17(A), 29(P),
  52(P)
Rue 80
Rumex 81
Rumhora 171
Ruscus 153
Rush, Corkscrew 73
  Flowering 71
Russian vine 118
Ruta 80

Saffron 78
  Meadow 87
Sage 78(P), 81(H)
  Graham's 154(S)
  Jerusalem 148
  Russian 46(P)
  Scarlet 17(A)
Sagina 169
St Catherine's lace 179
St John's wort 66(R),
  139(S)
St Patrick's cabbage 52
Salal 136
Salix 154
Salpiglossis 17
Salvia 17(A), 52(P),
  81(H), 154(S)
Sambucus 154
Sandwort 60
Sanguinaria 68
Sanguisorba 52
Santolina 154
Saponaria 52(P), 96(R)
Sarcococca 155(S),
  183(T)
Sassafras 155

Satureia 81
Savory 81
Saxifraga 23(P), 52(P),
  69(R)
Saxifrage 52(P), 69(R)
Scabiosa 18(A), 53(P)
Scabious 18(A), 53(P)
  Giant 25
  Tartarian 25
Schizophragma 118
Schizostylis 100
Scilla 94, 100
Scheffilera 183
Scrophularia 53
Seakale 27
Sedge 72
Sedum 53(P), 69(R),
  167(T)
Self heal 50
Sempervivum 69
Senecio 18(A), 39(P),
  155(S)
Senna 177
Shadblow 121
Shadbush 121
Shamrock, Pink 45
Shell flower 15
Shooting star 64
Shrimp plant 180
Sidalcea 53
Silene 69
Silver bells 137
Silver lace vine 118
Silver spreader 168
Sinarundinaria 122
Sinningia 101
Siphonosmathus 146
Sisyrinchium 53(P),
  70(R)
Skimmia 155
Slipper flower see
  Calceolaria
Smoke tree 129
Snakeroot 26
Snapdragon 7(A)
  Trailing 61(R)
Sneezeweed 33
Snowball, Japanese 160
Snowberry 158
Snowdrop 91
Snowdrop tree 137
Snowflake 96
Snow-in-summer 62
Snow on the mountain
  12
Soapwort 52(P), 69(R)
Solandra 175
Solanum 118(C), 175(T)
Soldiers and sailors 51
Solidago 54
Solidaster 54
Sollya 175
Solomon's seal 49
Sorbaria 156
Sorrel 81
  French 81
Southernwood 121
Spanish dagger 161
Sparaxis 101
Sparmannia 156
Spartium 130, 136, 156

Speedwell 57(P), 70(R)
Spearmint 79
Sphaeropteris 171
Spider flower 10
Spider plant 164
Spiderwort 56
Spinach, Red mountain 8
Spindle tree 134
  European 134
Spiraea 156
Spirea, False 156
Spruce, Dwarf Alberta 182
Spurge 12(A), 30(P), 64(R)
Squill 100
  Siberian 100
Stachys 54
Stachyurus 157
Staphylea 157
Star creeper, Blue 168
Starflower 180
  Lavender 180
Star of Bethlehem 99
Star of the Veldt 11
Starwort, Summer 64
Statice 39(P), 166(T)
Stephanandra 157
Sternbergia 101
Stewartia 157
Stock 15
  Brompton 15
  Night-scented 15
Stokesia 54
Stonecrop 69(R), 167(T)
Stranvaesia 157
Strawberry tree 121
Straw flower 13(A), 65(R), 138(S)
Strelitzia 183
Stuartia 157
Stauntonia 116
Styrax 158
Sumac, Staghorn 153
Sunflower 12(A), 33(P)
Sun rose 138
Sweet flag 71
Sweet pea 13(A), 38(P)
Sweet pepper bush 127
Sweet rock see *Hesperis*
Sweet sultan 9
Sweet William 11
Sycopsis 158
Symphoricarpos 158
Symphytum 54(P), 81(H)
Syringa 158
Syzygium 184

Tagetes 18
Tamarisk 159
Tamarix 159
Tanacetum 70
Tarata 149
Tarragon 77
Taxus 159
Tea tree 181
  Australian 181
Tecomaria 184

Tellima 54
Ternstroemia 184
Tetrapanax 184
Teucrium 55(P), 70(R), 159(S)
Thalia 76
Thalictrum 55
Thermopsis 55
Thistle, Common cotton 44
  Globe 44
  Scotch 44
Thorn apple 131
Thrift 21(P), 61(R)
  Giant 21
Thunbergia 119
Thyme 70(R), 81(H)
  Creeping 70
Thymus 70(R), 81(H)
Tiarella 55
Tibouchina 159
Tickseed 10(A), 27(P)
Tiger flower 101
Tigridia 101
Toadflax 14
Tobacco plant 15(A), 44(P)
Toyon 180
Trachelospermum 119
Trachystemon 54
Tradescantia 56
Treasure flower see *Gazania*
Treebine, Kangaroo 172
Tree poppy 51
Tricyrtis 56
Trigonella 81
Trillium 101
Tritelia 85, 94
Tritoma 37
Tritonia 102
Trollius 56(P), 76(W)
Tropaeolum 18(A), 119(C)
Trumpet creeper 113
Trumpet vine 113(C), 173(T)
  Blood red 173
  Violet 173
Tuberose 100
Tulbaghia 102
Tulip 102–3
  Lady 102
  Water lily 103
Tulipa 102–3
Tupidanthus 184
Turtle head 25
Tutsan 139

Ugni 184
Ulex 159
Umbellularia 159
Umbrella grass 72
Umbrella plant 75

Vaccinium 160
Valeriana 56
Valerian 25, 56
  Greek 49
Vallota 103

Veltheimia 103
× *Venidio-arctotis* 56
Venus' fishing rod 90
Veratrum 103
Verbascum 57
Verbena 57
Verbena 18(A), 57(P), 167(T)
  Lemon 79(H)
Veronica 57(P), 70(R), 137, 147(S)
Veronicastrum 57
Viburnum 160
Vinca 161
Viola 58(P), 167(T)
Violet 58(P)
  Australian 167
  Dog's tooth 91(B)
Virginia creeper 117
Virgin's bower 114
Viscaria 58
Vitex 161
Vitis 119

Wake robin 101
Waldsteinia 70
Wallflower 9
Wand flower 90
Watercress 80
Water lily 74, 75
Water plantain 71
Watsonia 103
Wattle 120(S), 175(T)
  Blue leaf 175
  Silver 175
Wax flower 174
Wax plant 174
Weigela 161
Whorl flower 43
Willow 154
  Creeping 154
Windflower 21(P), 84(B)
Wintera 131
Winter creeper 134
Winter's bark 131
Winter sweet 126
Wistaria 119
Witch-hazel 137
Woodbine 117
Woodruff 61
Woodwardia 171
Wormwood 22, 61
  Beach 61

Yarrow 19(P), 168(T)
  Woolly 168
Yaupon 180
Yesterday-today-and-tomorrow 176
Yew 159
Yucca 161

Zantedeschia 76
Zauschneria 58
Zea 18
Zebra grass see *Miscanthus*
Zenobia 161
Zephyranthes 103
Zinnia 18

192